New

A MAGAZINE OF MARXIST POLITICS AND THEORY

NUMBER 10

1994

Contents

EDITOR Mary-Alice Waters

MANAGING EDITOR Steve Clark

CONTRIBUTING EDITORS Jack Barnes, Sigurlaug Gunnlaugsdóttir, Carl-Erik Isacsson, Steve Penner, Ron Poulsen, Jean-Louis Salfati, Samad Sharif, Jonathan Silberman, Mike Tucker, James Mac Warren

New International is edited in collaboration with
Nouvelle Internationale, Michel Prairie, editor, and
Nueva Internacional, Martín Koppel, editor, and
Ny International, Carl-Erik Isacsson, editor.

Many of the articles that appear here in English are also available in French, Spanish, and Swedish. All four publications are available from New International, 410 West St., New York, NY 10014

Cover photograph: Unemployment line in New York City, December 1991. Robert Fox/Impact Visuals

Cover design by Toni Gorton

New International is distributed internationally by Pathfinder Press:
Australia (and Asia and the Pacific):
    Pathfinder, 19 Terry St., Surry Hills, Sydney, N.S.W. 2010
    Postal address: P.O. Box K879, Haymarket, N.S.W. 2000
Britain (and Europe, Africa except South Africa, and Middle East):
    Pathfinder, 47 The Cut, London, SE1 8LL
Canada:
    Pathfinder, 4581 rue St-Denis, Montreal, Quebec, H2J 2L4
Iceland:
    Pathfinder, Klapparstíg 26, 2d floor, 101 Reykjavík
    Postal address: P. Box 233, 121 Reykjavík
New Zealand:
    Pathfinder, La Gonda Arcade, 203 Karangahape Road, Auckland
    Postal address: P.O. Box 8730, Auckland
Sweden:
    Pathfinder, Vikingagatan 10, S-113 42, Stockholm
United States (and Caribbean, Latin America, and South Africa):
    Pathfinder, 410 West Street, New York, NY 10014

IN THIS ISSUE

THIS ISSUE OF *New International* looks at the consequences over the last seven years of the decelerating growth, heightened volatility, and increasing instability that more and more form the pattern of international capitalism—a pattern signaled by the near-meltdown in October 1987 of stock markets from New York and London to Tokyo and Hong Kong. The spreading vulnerability of the market system, sharpening interimperialist conflict, and deepening insecurity in the lives of growing hundreds of millions impose themselves on all of world politics.

Only a few years ago, the authoritative representatives of the world's bourgeois ruling classes were hailing the dawn of a New World Order, built on what they portray as the historic triumph of democratic capitalism over communism. They pledged a future of economic plenty, expanding democratic rights, and growing world peace.

The articles in these pages offer a different point of view. As humanity heads toward the twenty-first century, the future in fact offered by international finance capital is one of deepening economic depression and an accompanying march toward fascism and war.

The political conclusions that best fit this reality—and are thus the best guide to action—are communist conclusions. A cataclysmic outcome of victorious fascist movements and a war of previously unknown dimensions and intensity is not foreordained. Before fascism can triumph and another interimperialist war becomes inevitable, workers will be driven to resist the capitalists' mounting assaults on our living and working conditions, on our democratic rights, and on the very conditions that make possible human solidarity. With revolutionary leadership, forged over time in the workers movement, working people can wrest power from the governments of the ruling families in the United States and other capitalist countries, stop the inexorable march toward a third world war, and open the road to a socialist future of cooperative human labor, truly democratic government, and cultural advancement.

Because of the place of the Cuban revolution in this historic class struggle, we are opening the issue with a report by *New International* editor Mary-Alice Waters on the fight for socialism in Cuba today. The Cuban revolution remains, as it has been for thirty-five years, at the center of the worldwide contest between capitalism and socialism—the contest that has marked world politics since the victory in October 1917 of the Bolshevik-led revolution in Russia.

Today the decisive front in that battle pits U.S. imperialism—the world's most powerful, and final, empire—against a small but unyielding workers and farmers government in Cuba. As Waters explains in this August 1994 report to a convention of the Socialist Workers Party in the United States, Wall Street and Washington from the outset of the revolution have pursued a course aimed at crushing Cuba's toilers and dividing them from their communist leadership. The reason for the U.S. rulers' hostility toward the Cuban revolution is not complicated. Cuban working people in 1959-60 did the one thing imperialism fights most ruthlessly to prevent: they emulated what the toilers of Russia had done some four decades earlier. They overturned the bourgeoisie's monopoly of state power, established a workers and farmers republic, expropriated capitalist property in land and the basic means of production, and set out to support—in both word and deed—those the world over who are fighting to free themselves from imperialist oppression or capitalist exploitation.

Since the crumbling of the Stalinist apparatuses throughout Eastern Europe and the Soviet Union from 1989 to 1991, most voices speaking out about the Cuban revolution—not only its open bourgeois enemies but also many of its liberal and somewhat socialist "friends"—approach it like the last surviving organism of a species that has become extinct. They regard it as a stubborn problem to be gotten out of the way now that all the other regimes that once called themselves communist—from Moscow to Hanoi, from Warsaw to Beijing—are unfurling the banner of capitalism and the market.

"Defending Cuba, Defending Cuba's Socialist Revolution" by Mary-Alice Waters presents a different perspective. The record of three and a half decades offers convincing evidence that what is most decisive about Cuba are not the ways in which it is similar to other states in which capitalist property relations have been abolished but the ways in which it is fundamentally unlike them. The July 26 Movement, the revolutionary organization forged by a team led by Fidel Castro in the 1950s, bypassed the Popular Socialist Party, the Stalinist party in Cuba, in order to lead a successful workers and farmers revolution to bring down the U.S.-backed Batista dictatorship. As the revolution's anticapitalist course deepened, that leadership constructed the first mass communist party to exist since the Stalinist counterrevolution in the 1920s and 1930s.

Today, the revolutionary government in Cuba continues to be distinguished from all the other regimes that have claimed to be communist by two inseparably intertwined features. First, broad layers of the working class in Cuba and its communist vanguard maintain an unbroken will and capacity to fight in defense of the revolution's socialist character. Second, Cuba's workers and farmers government continues to respond to the pressures of the working class and use its power to lead working people in fighting to advance their class aspirations and internationalist commitments.

Waters looks at the current challenges and opportunities before the Cuban revolution today, in face of the defeats of revolutions in Nicaragua and Grenada in the 1980s and the most difficult economic conditions in socialist Cuba's history. As at each prior crossroads in the revolution, but more so than ever before, the way forward today combines defending the state power of the working class at home and maintaining their proletarian internationalist perspectives.

As Waters points out, the setbacks in the Americas and sudden cutoff of heavily subsidized trade with the former Soviet Union have necessitated a retreat by the working class and its leadership in Cuba. But revolutionary-minded working people and youth—in the factories and fields, as well as in mass mobilizations and rallies—continue to show their readiness to defend the socialist revolution in face of these difficulties. The government remains their government. And they remain committed to a course that reaches out to workers, farmers, and youth wherever they are engaged in uncompromising anti-imperialist or anticapitalist struggles.

That's why Washington's course toward Havana is unlike the course it charts toward any other government in the world. The relations between these two governments reflect the most irreconcilable class conflict in world politics today. And that, in turn, is why defending Cuba and defending Cuba's socialist revolution will remain a task of class-conscious workers and revolutionary-minded youth there and around the world until one side or the other has been defeated in that historic battle.

❖

At the World Meeting in Solidarity with Cuba, held in Havana in late November 1994 as this issue was being completed, president Fidel Castro in his closing address pointed to the "billions of human beings who go hungry, who don't have schools, who don't have access to hospitals, who don't have jobs, who don't have a roof over their heads, who can't even count on the most elementary necessities of life." He reviewed the history of bloody military interventions by Washington, London, Paris, and other capitalist powers against sovereign peoples in Latin America, Asia, and Africa.

"And what is the root of all these problems?" he asked. "Can anyone perhaps deny that the root of these problems is neocolonialism, imperialism? Can anyone deny that the root of all these problems is capitalism?" Cuba "will never return to capitalism," Castro told the 3,500 participants in the international gathering. "We'd rather perish than renounce our principles. We'd rather perish than renounce socialism!"

If the future of the world capitalist order were indeed the one its boosters today proclaim, then such a statement would be little more than quixotic bravado in face of insuperable odds. In fact, if such apologetic claims for capitalism have any basis, then communists not only in Cuba but the world over are, at best, a doomed and anomalous minority.

The contents of this issue of *New International* make the opposite case. That is why taking a look at Cuba today provides a good entry point to the other articles, which detail the world conditions in which the prospects for the Cuban revolution rise or fall. Cuba is, and must be understood as, an integral part of the economics and politics of the world of the 1990s.

"What the 1987 Stock Market Crash Foretold" is a resolution discussed and adopted by the Socialist Workers Party of the United States in the wake of the biggest crash of the world's stock markets since 1929. Presented in 1988 to an SWP convention and international conference of communist leagues from around the world, and adopted by the delegates, the resolution looks at the evolution of world politics prior to the crumbling of the Stalinist apparatuses in the USSR and Eastern Europe.

"Imperialism's March toward Fascism and War" is a document based on several talks by SWP national secretary Jack Barnes given in early 1994. It was discussed by members of the Socialist Workers Party in the months leading up to the party's August 1994 convention and adopted by the delegates to that decision-making meeting.

At the close of both the 1988 and 1994 SWP conventions,

delegates charged commissions to prepare the adopted resolutions and reports for publication in light of the convention discussion. The three articles in these pages have been left as edited immediately following those conventions. A number of important subsequent developments have been footnoted, and a number of references have been added by the editors of *New International* to aid the reader.

As the articles explain, the potentially devastating consequences of phenomena such as the worldwide stock market crash of 1987 and the proliferation of highly speculative paper securities such as "derivatives" are not isolated to Wall Street. Today's soaring financial greed and related banking and currency dealings—which have grown to many times the dollar value of world trade over the past decade—are the other side of the deflationary depression conditions world capitalism has sunk into for the first time in half a century.

Capitalists are not plowing the hefty profits they are currently reaping from the exploitation of workers' labor into the expansion of capacity-increasing plant and equipment and a consequent growth of wealth-producing industrial jobs. Instead, cost cutting, "downsizing," computerized speedup, the intensification and atomization of work, and even stock buybacks have become the order of the day for cash-rich finance capital the world over. Despite talk in the business pages about an "investment boom" in the United States since 1991, the biggest expenditures are for computers and telecommunications equipment aimed at squeezing a fatter profit margin out of fewer employees, working in fewer plants, for more hours, with intensified line speed, and for less pay and reduced benefits.

Pointing to this combination of longer workweeks, declining real wages, ongoing layoffs and job insecurity, and conjuncturally rising profits, a front-page article in the November 14 issue of the London-based *Financial Times* proclaimed, "Here is productivity and no mistake. If this is what the peak of the [business] cycle looks like, God help the workers in the next downturn." The article in this leading business daily—hardly known as a champion of workers' rights and living standards—was headlined, "Work harder, or not at all."

The longer-run decline in rates of both industrial profit and capital accumulation described in "What the 1987 Stock Market Crash Foretold," and the consequent slackening in worldwide economic growth, go back a quarter century to the late 1960s and early 1970s. The unfolding of world capitalism since the 1987 crash, however, has registered the fact that increasing layers of the working class in the United States, Europe, and other imperialist countries face rising unemployment, more part-time and temporary jobs, stagnating or declining real wages, and erosion of hard-won components of the social wage, such as social security pensions, workers' compensation, health care, jobless benefits, and public education.

The polarization between wealth and poverty grows worldwide, and economic insecurity mounts. Capitalist horrors that the labor movement and its allies pushed back through decades of struggle—such as homework, the exploitation of child labor, orphanages, and the workhouse—are once again openly advocated by "respectable" bourgeois voices as necessary to restore social discipline and "family values."

IN THE THIRD WORLD, the living and working conditions of hundreds of millions remain wretched or are sharply deteriorating. This is true not just for the toilers of sub-Saharan Africa, or of the least economically developed countries of Asia and the Americas. Class differentiation is also impoverishing broad layers of toilers in the handful of Asian and (even fewer) Latin American countries undergoing the most rapid capitalist industrialization and into whose "emerging" stock and bond markets imperialist capital has been pouring since 1990.

The depression conditions that opened the final decade of the twentieth century will not be reversed by any "automatic corrections" or cyclical action of the capitalist market. Instead, today's deflationary pressures heighten the volatility of capitalism's proliferating paper assets and increase the danger that unanticipated partial crises of whatever origin—political, military, or financial—will precipitate a cascading banking and monetary collapse and breakdown of industrial production and world trade.

Between now and any sustained turnaround in the fortunes of world capitalism, the imperialist rulers will have to confront and win bloody class battles against the workers and their toiling allies. As capitalist disorder increases, growing sections of the employing class, its government, and its political parties will come to recognize the inevitability of these battles. More and more of the exploiters will turn to fascist movements in order to crush the unions and other workers organizations and safeguard bourgeois rule.

The practical implications for class-conscious workers of this difference between a periodic slump in the business cycle, that is, a recession, and a long-term descent in the curve of capitalist development was discussed by the international communist movement in the half decade after the October revolution in Russia. Given the significance of this question to the strategic political issues discussed in this issue, we are reprinting a 1923 article by the Bolshevik leader Leon Trotsky summarizing conclusions that still hold to this day.

If world capitalism today is short on economic certainty, stability, and plenty for the toiling majority, then what about democracy? Is it true, as many spokespersons for world imperialism contend, that the extension of democratic rights goes hand in hand with the expansion of capitalism? In particular, in the wake of the collapse of the Stalinist apparatuses and regimes in Eastern and Central Europe between 1989 and 1991—and assuming capitalism is allowed to flower everywhere—is the world now heading toward states and governments that are more tolerant and democratic than ever before?

Historically, the rise and spread of commodity production and exchange have been accompanied by greater freedom for the producers. Slavery, peonage, feudal bondage, and unfree labor in many forms were driven back as small independent farmers and urban artisans gained control over the tools and the product of their work. At the same time, landed, merchant, and later industrial and finance capital have never stopped trying to keep working people in check in order to monopolize the fruits of our labor.

Contrary to the self-justifying ideology of the capitalist class in the United States, Europe, and elsewhere, their banner is neither "life, liberty, and the pursuit of happiness" nor "liberty, equality, fraternity." Their true values are captured in the mottoes "property, markets, and the pursuit of profit," and the dog-eat-dog individualism of "me, my, and mine." The rebellions by small farmers, urban mechanics, and other plebeian forces to win a Bill of Rights following the American Revolution provide just one example of the irrepressible conflicts between rural and urban toilers, on the one hand, and successive layers of capitalist exploiters and their propertied allies, on the other, that have marked the rise and consolidation of bourgeois states for several hundred years.

All this is true during even the most economically expansive and relatively stable periods of capitalism, when the rulers can afford to use the forms of bourgeois democracy to exercise their rule and grant concessions to layers of working people in response to struggles for political and union rights. From the consolidation of the industrial capitalists' ascent to power in the mid-nineteenth century, however, in times of social and political crisis the rulers have time and again resorted to extralegal goons, death squads, and mass terror against the toilers, throwing off what become the manacles of bourgeois democratic institutions and the political rights they imply.

As explained in "What the 1987 Stock Market Crash Foretold" and "Imperialism's March toward Fascism and War," the onset of depression conditions today is once again setting the stage—for the first time since the years just following World War II—for rightist political figures and incipient fascist movements to gain new ground within bourgeois politics. The social policies of the Democrats, Republicans, and other established bourgeois parties throughout the imperialist world continue to shift to the right, while their appeals to nationalism in face of mounting conflicts feed every variety of antilabor, racist, antiwoman, anti-immigrant, xenophobic, and irrationalist demagogy played on by the ultraright.

SINCE THE OPENING of the 1990s, this tendency has been manifested in presidential politics in the United States by Patrick Buchanan's "culture war" and Ross Perot's demagogy. In Europe we've seen the emergence of substantial ultranationalist and rightist bourgeois parties in Austria, Belgium, Germany, France, and elsewhere, including in Italy where Mussolini's political heirs are today serving in the cabinet. Organized racist and anti-immigrant violence has spread across Europe, from Berlin to Stockholm to London.

What's more, even a relatively cursory knowledge of those parts of the Third World where the bourgeoisie is managing to raise its profit rates—Taiwan, South Korea, Singapore, Malaysia, Indonesia, Chile, Mexico, and a handful of others—is enough to belie the claim that a tangible increase in democratic rights accompanies the advance and enrichment of a capitalist class.

Nor is it true, as a recent issue of the Wall Street magazine *Business Week* asserts, that since 1989 the "West" has "watched warily to see whether the Soviet Union's former satellites would sign on to free-market democracy." Instead of watching warily, the imperialist powers are pressing forcefully for these regimes to sign on to greater capitalist exploitation at home, the better to facilitate the penetration of capital from abroad.

The tendency toward the restoration of capitalism in the former USSR and Eastern Europe (as well as China and Vietnam) is unambiguous. In and of itself, this is nothing new; that has been the tendency in the USSR ever since the triumph and consolidation of the political counterrevolution by a privileged, petty-bourgeois caste in the 1930s. This trajectory was not altered by the establishment of new workers states in Eastern Europe and Asia after World War II, all of which were dominated by Stalinist organizations.

The penetration of capital into these countries has accelerated since the collapse of the hated regimes in the former Soviet Union and Eastern Europe. As pointed out both in "What the 1987 Stock Market Crash Foretold," written in 1988, and in "Imperialism's March toward Fascism and War" six years later, the obstacles to the reimposition of capitalist social relations and the limits to foreign capital investment remain the axis of the class struggle in these countries. At the same time, growing nationalist resistance to Washington-led probes to increase imperialist domination of the region is coming to the center of world politics more and more.

The biggest barrier facing both imperialism and the homegrown wannabe capitalists in these grossly deformed workers states is the working class itself. Every move to reestablish firings, layoffs, and unemployment as the norm, and to dismantle subsidized prices and social benefits, meets working-class resistance, even if still dispersed, politically confused, and without class-conscious leadership. Further steps in this direction bring these societies closer and closer to explosive protests, even social rebellions, by workers and other toilers in city and countryside.

Moreover, rival members of the dominant social castes, officials in government bureaus and managers of former state enterprises (the "nomenklatura"), and nouveau riche middle-class layers are all jockeying to establish themselves as the inheritors of billions of dollars in state-owned plant and production goods and the right to exploit wage labor on a grand scale. At the same time, the members of these layers are competing to attract imperialist capital without being swallowed up by it.

All this is proving, in practice, to deepen more contradictions than it is resolving.

The outcome in these deformed workers states will be decided in struggle, the course of which will depend, in large part, on advances by the working-class movement in capitalist Europe, the rest of the imperialist world, and the semicolonial countries. Meanwhile, the economic and social crisis in the former Soviet Union and Eastern Europe remains sharp, while class tensions and social conflicts are mounting in China and Vietnam.

In face of this instability, the ruling layers in all these countries are reinforcing the repressive institutions and legislation of their states, not expanding democracy and strengthening "civil society." In so doing, as long as they are "opening markets," they have the backing of the ruling classes in the United States and other imperialist "democracies," ritual protestations about "human rights" notwithstanding.

The victory of fascism in Germany, Spain, and elsewhere in Europe in the 1930s was not inevitable. Nor was the second world imperialist slaughter of 1939-45. That war *became* inevitable by 1937-38 only after the political betrayals of the Stalinists and social democrats, whose class-collaborationist course blocked the extension of the socialist revolution in crisis-ridden Europe, above all in France and Spain. Time after time the workers moved toward contending for power; time after time they were betrayed.

In Germany, the mass social democratic and Stalinist-led organizations both placed factional interests ahead of a united fight to block the fascists from crushing the labor movement and political rights for all. Soon panicked by Hitler's rapidly strengthening armed forces, Moscow by the mid-1930s was desperately hoping to hold off an onslaught against the USSR. Stalinist forces worldwide were told to single-mindedly pursue winning the confidence of the "democratic imperialist" governments in Paris, London, and Washington. The degenerated Communist International and its parties diverted worker and peasant struggles toward support for capitalist liberalism of the New Deal genre, and they didn't hesitate stooping to the murder of revolutionists and genuine communists who sought to pursue an anticapitalist course.

This series of defeats for the workers movement culminated at the end of the 1930s in the Second World War. Out of the tumult of that bloody conflict came intensified class struggle and new advances of the world revolution against imperialist oppression and capitalist exploitation.

Washington and Wall Street emerged from World War II the seemingly unchallengeable dominant world imperialist power, both economically and militarily, as the articles in this issue describe. Plans to consolidate an "American Century" included immediate preparations for a third world war. That fact was announced by the Truman administration's decision to drop atomic bombs on Hiroshima and Nagasaki in August 1945 while Tokyo was already suing for peace.

As the lead editorial in the forerunner of *New International* explained in August 1946, "In every branch of government, in every sphere of its activity, a growing body of evidence points to the inescapable conclusion that American imperialism, far from organizing peace, is preparing for a new and more horrible war."[1] The U.S. rulers aimed to consolidate a dominant position not just in their own Latin American backyard but also in the Asian domains in which their Japanese capitalist rivals had been defeated and from which their "allies" in Britain, France, and Holland were being forced to retreat in face of colonial independence struggles.

With the collapse of massive military production in the

---

1. "Review of the Month: 'Hemisphere Defense' and U.S. Preparations for World War III," *Fourth International*, August 1946.

United States at the close of World War II, many in both the working class and bourgeoisie had expected the prewar depression to reemerge. The combination of sluggish growth and bouts of inflation in the immediate postwar years initially suggested such an outcome. Moreover, in the wake of the U.S. labor upsurge of 1945-46, the overturn of capitalist rule in Eastern Europe, and the Chinese revolution of 1949, a bipartisan anticommunist witch-hunt was under way in the United States and was giving a head of steam to the incipient fascist movement whose most well-known propagandist was Wisconsin senator Joseph McCarthy.

H AD U.S. CAPITAL bumped into no major obstacles, it would have pushed toward finishing the job German imperialism had failed at—destruction of the Soviet workers state. But the U.S. war drive foundered on the shoals of the victorious 1949 Chinese revolution and Washington's failure to achieve its goals in the unpopular Korean War of 1950-53. The U.S. rulers were fought to a stalemate in their drive to impose capitalist domination over the whole of the Korean peninsula. Nor were they able to use their invasion force in Korea to drive past the Yalu River and roll back the revolution in China—a revolution Tokyo had failed to stop through its invasion and occupation of large parts of China from 1931 through 1945, and that Washington had been unable to block in the four years thereafter.

By 1953 the Soviet government had broken Washington's monopoly on nuclear weapons. World capitalism had temporarily restabilized, and a depression-fueled social crisis of the kind that would have pushed the U.S. rulers toward ultrarightist solutions and a third world war did not materialize. In late 1953 and early 1954, when McCarthy attempted to extend the witch-hunt into the army officer corps, he was slapped down with bipartisan support. McCarthyism had peaked.

Only when postwar developments had blocked U.S. imperialism's drive toward a renewed hot war against the Soviet Union did the "Cold War" become Washington's fallback option. It was not a strategy of choice for U.S. finance capital; in fact, it was not a strategy at all. It was the registration of a world relationship of forces in which, despite their economic and military strength, the U.S. rulers had run up against the limits of the "American Century" before it had ever really begun.

The articles in these pages explain the shift in the pattern of world politics since the latter 1980s that have once again set the imperialist rulers on a march toward fascism and war. They are part of a package with issue no. 7 of *New International,* published in May 1991, a few months after the U.S. rulers had concluded their weeks-long bombing of Iraq with the massacre of soldiers and civilians on the road to Basra. "Washington's war in the Gulf is not, as the U.S. rulers pretend, the harbinger of a new world order based on peaceful solutions to strife among states," explained Jack Barnes in the lead article in that issue. "Instead, in a world of mounting economic crisis and breakdowns, social instability, political conflicts, and unfulfilled demands for national liberation, it can much more accurately be described as the opening guns of World War III."

Events of the last few years have offered stunning refutation—if any further were needed in a century scarred by the bloodiest wars and holocausts in history—of the notion that capitalism offers a future of growing world peace. In October 1994 the U.S. government mounted another major military buildup in the Gulf and renewed threats of bombardment of Iraq, whose people are starving as the result of a four-year-long imperialist economic embargo. Washington has once again installed an army of occupation in one of its American neighbors, this time in the Caribbean nation of Haiti. In a provocation aimed at the socialist revolution in Cuba and its revolutionary government, U.S. officials are holding some 22,000 Cubans in a virtual concentration camp at the Guantánamo naval station on occupied Cuban territory, and Washington has tightened the unconscionable economic embargo against Cuba.

The slaughter organized by the Serbian regime and its rival

gangs of bureaucrats and aspirant capitalists in the former Yugoslavia is now approaching its fourth year, and British and French troops are on the ground in Bosnia to protect their rival interests the Balkans. Shouldering "the white man's burden" to defend capitalist order in Africa, armies from the United States, France, Belgium, and other imperialist powers have sent occupation forces into Somalia, Rwanda, and Zaire. Civil wars rage between the ins and the outs among the disintegrating Stalinist apparatuses in various republics of the former USSR, with Moscow dispatching troops to back now one, now another faction to reassert Russia's imperial designs from the Black Sea through Central Asia.

All these wars and interventions, in turn, are resulting in sharpening conflicts among the imperialist powers, and between these powers and Moscow.

The decaying capitalist world order described in this issue of *New International* provides convincing proof why the revolutionary road the workers and farmers of Cuba set out on thirty-five years ago offers the only way forward for humanity. The task confronting class-conscious workers and revolutionary-minded youth the world over is to establish workers and farmers governments, expropriate the capitalist exploiters whose pursuit of profits is leading us toward another, devastating world war, and begin the worldwide construction of a new socialist order.

Accomplishing these historic tasks is not possible without building revolutionary workers parties in every country as part of a renewed world communist movement. The crumbling of the Stalinist apparatuses in Eastern Europe and the Soviet Union has removed the biggest obstacle to advancing that effort. Following the political counterrevolution in the Soviet Union at the end of the 1920s, the Stalinists hijacked the banner of the revolutionary workers movement that Marx and Engels had helped initiate in the mid-nineteenth century. For several years following the October 1917 revolution, the Bolshevik leadership had begun transforming that movement into a truly mass worldwide organization, the Communist International.

The parasitic caste that politically expropriated the working class in the Soviet Union had no function in social production, and thus no historic viability. Stalinism nonetheless got a brief extension of its lease on life by claiming credit for the victory of the Soviet workers and peasants in World War II; the revolutions in Yugoslavia, China, Korea, and Vietnam; and the overturn of capitalist property relations in Eastern Europe.

Today, however, for the first time in nearly seven decades, it is no longer a foregone conclusion that the big majority of revolutionary-minded workers, farmers, and youth attracted to a socialist perspective will be won instead to counterrevolutionary organizations falsely presenting themselves as communist. It is above all to the workers and youth who are and will become the cadres of a renewed world communist movement that the perspectives in this issue provide an invaluable guide to political action in the months and years ahead.

Steve Clark
December 10, 1994

CUBA AND THE FIGHT FOR SOCIALISM

The Second Declaration of Havana

FIDEL CASTRO

In 1962, as the example of Cuba's socialist revolution spread throughout the Americas, the workers and farmers of Cuba issued their uncompromising call for a continent-wide revolutionary struggle. Booklet. $4.50

CUBA'S 1962 MANIFESTO OF REVOLUTIONARY STRUGGLE IN THE AMERICAS

The Second Declaration *of* Havana

with The First Declaration of Havana

FIDEL CASTRO

Che Guevara and the Fight for Socialism Today

Cuba Confronts the World Crisis of the '90s

MARY-ALICE WATERS

Socialism can be built only by free men and women working together to lay the foundations for a new society and transforming themselves in the process. That commitment was championed in action by Ernesto Che Guevara in the early years of the Cuban revolution. It remains a living legacy for Cuban working people today. Also available in Spanish, French, and Icelandic. Booklet. $3.50

Che Guevara: Economics and Politics in the Transition to Socialism

CARLOS TABLADA

Quoting extensively from Guevara's writings and speeches on building socialism, explains his views on why "profit" and other capitalist categories cannot be yardsticks measuring progress in the transition to socialism; and the interrelationship of the market, economic planning, material incentives, and voluntary work. Also available in Spanish and French. $17.95

DEFENDING CUBA, DEFENDING
CUBA'S SOCIALIST REVOLUTION

by Mary-Alice Waters

THERE ARE THREE QUESTIONS the delegates to this convention of the Socialist Workers Party need to address and answer today as we discuss the defense of Cuba and its socialist revolution. The answers we collectively arrive at have a great
bearing on what we do as part of an international communist
movement and also as part of the much broader forces working
together in solidarity with Cuba. They tell us a great deal about
the prospects communist workers face worldwide, as well.

The questions we need to pose flow not primarily from our
own internal discussion and debates but are rooted in major
shifts in world politics the last few years and the impact of these
shifts on the vanguard of fighting workers in Cuba. They are

---

*This report, presented on behalf of the National Committee of the Social-
ist Workers Party, was discussed and adopted August 3, 1994, by the
delegates to the 37th Constitutional Convention of the party in Oberlin,
Ohio. Mary-Alice Waters is a member of the SWP National Committee,
editor of* New International, *and the author of numerous articles on
the Cuban revolution. She is the editor of* The Bolivian Diary of Ernesto Che Guevara; U.S. Hands Off the Mideast! Cuba Speaks
Out at the United Nations; *and* To Speak the Truth: Why Washington's 'Cold War' against Cuba Doesn't End, *a collection of
speeches by two of the most authoritative representatives of the Cuban
revolution, Fidel Castro and Ernesto Che Guevara.*

*The report has not been edited to incorporate events that occurred after
August 3. In a few cases, these are dealt with in footnotes.*

the questions being discussed and debated in one way or another by every serious political current among the contending classes in world politics.

We need to look, for a moment, beyond the most immediate battles being waged by those on the front lines of our class in Cuba. We should step back from the pressures of the day-by-day work in defense of the Cuban revolution we are all engaged in on the job, in the unions, on campuses, and in our various cities. We need a longer-term perspective on what is unfolding politically in Cuba and its implications for the working class worldwide.

Let's begin by stating the three decisive questions briefly and answer them. Then we can use the rest of the report to expand on these answers and explain why the evidence before us demonstrates they are correct.

Three questions

The first question is: Does the government of Cuba remain a revolutionary one in the most fundamental sense? Does it—despite enormous difficulties and challenges, and regardless of various political errors, bureaucratic deformities, and Bonapartist balancings—continue to pursue a course on decisive questions that responds to, as opposed to reacts against, pressures from the working class? Is it a government that takes bold initiatives to defend the social and political aspirations of the working class and to preserve its socialist conquests? Or, as some hope, is the government itself leading a headlong rush to scuttle the socialist revolution in Cuba?

The answer to this first question is unequivocal. The government of Cuba continues to be a revolutionary government of the toilers. In fact, the communist leadership in Cuba continues to head the only government in the world that consciously uses state power to defend, respond to, and promote the interests of the working class. It is the only state power that strives to organize working people to advance the fight against imperialism and for socialism. And it is the only one open to helping those abroad who are struggling arms in hand to do the same thing.

Apart from the Bolsheviks under Lenin's leadership in the early years of the Russian revolution, every other governing party that at one time or another has claimed to act in the interests of the working class and in the name of socialism—in the Soviet Union and Eastern Europe, in China and elsewhere in Asia—has in fact carried out a course against the historic interests of the toilers. That is, over an extended period of time, these leaderships implemented policies that destroyed the initiative and fighting capacities of the working class and reinforced social inequalities and stratifications that mimicked some of the worst features of capitalist social relations—with few of capitalism's strengths.

The implications of the answer we give to this question about the Cuban government and its leadership are of no small importance today for the working class worldwide. That is why this report and discussion is the first point on the agenda at this convention of the Socialist Workers Party.

The second question is closely interrelated with the first: Is the proletarian revolution still alive in Cuba? Or, more concretely, is the working class of Cuba—in decisive numbers—still fighting to defend its historic course? Is it still determined to defend new social relations established on the basis of the anti-imperialist and socialist conquests it began making nearly thirty-five years ago, when urban and rural working people mobilized in their millions to expropriate the plantations, factories, warehouses, and hotels owned by Yankee and Cuban capitalists?[1]

---

1. Accurate, firsthand descriptions of how workers and their allies organized to make the Cuban revolution and open the socialist revolution in the Americas can be found in many titles published and distributed by Pathfinder Press. See in particular: *Dynamics of the Cuban Revolution: A Marxist Appreciation* by Joseph Hansen; *To Speak the Truth: Why Washington's 'Cold War' against Cuba Doesn't End,* four speeches by Fidel Castro and Ernesto Che Guevara; *Selected Speeches of Fidel Castro;* "Land Reform and Farm Cooperatives in Cuba" in issue no. 4 (1985) of *New International;* and *Che Guevara and the Cuban Revolution: Writings and Speeches of Ernesto Che Guevara.*

Or as many people believe today, both historic class enemies of the Cuban revolution and—whether they say it openly or not—many who have been supporters, is it really all over in Cuba? More precisely, is it all over for a mass working-class vanguard in Cuba? Are the decisive turning points in the class struggle already behind us? Are we now living through what amounts to nothing more than a protracted death agony of the socialist revolution and its proletarian leadership?

In short: Has the working class in Cuba been defeated? Have the worsening economic conditions and intensified social tensions resulted in the ascendancy of class-collaborationist and aspiring petty-bourgeois currents to such a degree that the mass political vanguard of the working class in the factories and farms has become demoralized, atomized, and has been driven out of politics? Is there no longer a proletarian vanguard capable of asserting leadership of revolutionary forces in Cuba? Has the relationship of class forces within the active, day-to-day leadership of the working class shifted so much that the revolutionary course pursued by millions of Cuban working people for more than three decades can no longer be sustained?

I S THE PROLETARIAN REVOLUTION ALIVE in Cuba? Our answer to that question, too, is an unequivocal yes. The consciousness, capacity, and determination of decisive components of the working class to lead the necessary retreat today—and to continue fighting for the historic class interests of the toilers as it does so—remain at the heart of politics in Cuba.

The answer to this question is central to the international class struggle, to world politics, as well. With the weakening on a world scale of Stalinism, sharply accelerated by the crumbling of the brutal and wealthy apparatuses that nurtured it, there is increased political space in Cuba today, not less, for the working class and its communist vanguard to fight to assert their internationalist class interests.

Saying that the working class in Cuba remains strong and has

more space today to fight for its historic socialist course, however, is not a prediction. It doesn't guarantee that the working
class could not be defeated. We and our brothers and sisters in
Cuba enter the ring as underdogs. But that doesn't bother us.
Cuban workers know something about boxing. We face powerful class forces, both inside and outside Cuba. In face of setbacks in the class struggle in the Americas over the last decade,
and the difficult economic conditions facing Cuba today, middle-class, procapitalist opponents of the revolution's socialist
course are also gaining strength. Communist workers in Cuba,
moreover, continue to pay the price for the legacy of world
Stalinism and the political illusions, errors, demoralization,
and deformations it fostered in Cuba. We have discussed and
written about these factors many times.[2]

More importantly, no matter how determined and clear-
sighted the communist vanguard may be, the future of the
working class and socialist revolution in Cuba will be settled not
just in Cuba but as part of advances or retreats of the international class struggle. Economic instability, crises, social conflict,
and class battles of major proportions are on the agenda worldwide, and they will weigh mightily in the outcome of class battles inside Cuba itself. But these involve forces beyond the immediate control of communists in Cuba, the United States, or
anywhere else.

*What's important for us and for our class today is whether or not we
are still in the fight.* And we say yes—the decisive battles remain
ahead in Cuba. The capacity of the working class to fight has
not been broken, nor is it willing to cede more ground than the
economic necessities of the day compel.

This, then, brings us to the third question we must address at

---

2. See "The Politics of Economics: Che Guevara and Marxist Continuity" by
Steve Clark and Jack Barnes and "Che's Proletarian Legacy and Cuba's Rectification Process" by Mary-Alice Waters in *New International* no. 8 (1991), as
well as *Che Guevara and the Fight for Socialism Today: Cuba Confronts the World Crisis of the '90s* by Mary-Alice Waters (New York: Pathfinder, 1992).

this convention: What do the answers we give to the previous two questions mean for the political course and responsibilities of communists around the world? What does it mean for the Socialist Workers Party as a party of internationalist communist workers here in the United States, the imperialist bastion, where the class struggle and its outcome weigh more heavily than any other single place on the future not only of the Cuban revolution but of all humanity?

We have to answer the first two questions before we can consider this one, of course. If our conclusion were that the decisive battles had already been fought, that the government was no longer revolutionary, and the working class had been defeated in Cuba, then we would be preparing for quite a different world situation at this convention. We would have a responsibility to speak the truth, however bitter. Not all battles are won. Not all strikes end in victories. Revolutions don't always advance. Under the blows of a devastating civil war, imperialist intervention, and defeats of revolutionary struggles in Europe, for example, the Bolshevik-led revolution in Russia succumbed by the latter 1920s to the Stalin-led political counterrevolution. When such defeats or setbacks occur, the communist vanguard of the workers movement must tell the truth and prepare for the consequences and altered tasks. That could be the only basis for ongoing revolutionary work.

But our assessment is that the socialist revolution in Cuba has not been defeated. To the contrary. The fight is still on, and that assessment determines our responsibilities. Communists in the United States—or anywhere else in the world—don't sit on the front porch and watch while our comrades in Cuba are fighting to defend the socialist revolution. *We are part of that fight.* And we bring something important to it, because of our involvement as communist workers in the struggles of our class wherever we live and work and because of our place in the revolutionary political continuity of our class worldwide.

What we have to offer would be important even if our judgment about what is happening in Cuba were different. It would still be important to link up with fighters in Cuba who are politically interested in and identify with the struggles that workers and farmers in the United States are engaged in. It would still be important to meet revolutionary-minded Cuban workers and students who are politically hungry to read *Habla Nelson Mandela*, or to study *The Revolution Betrayed* or *The History of the Russian Revolution* in order to understand the real lessons of working-class struggle in this century and what happened in the Soviet Union and Eastern Europe. We'd still seek out Cubans with an interest in *Notebook of an Agitator* or *Socialism on Trial* by James P. Cannon, or in *The Changing Face of U.S. Politics: Working-Class Politics and the Trade Unions,* because we know they are trying to better understand the class struggle in the United States.

We would still look for opportunities for workers and youth in the United States and Cuba to meet, exchange experiences, and talk politics. We would still learn from these discussions and be changed by them, as part of a process of mutual give-and-take.

O_UR POLITICAL PRIORITIES and use of time and resources would nonetheless be different if the communist leadership in Cuba had been defeated, if the working class had been politically demobilized, if we were able to talk to only a handful of individuals seeking to maintain a revolutionary continuity under such conditions. But our answers to the first two questions tell us that this is not the situation, and, most importantly, that what we do today weighs in the struggle.

That's why we give such importance to the growing opportunities we have to bring together workers and young people —whether in Cuba, in the United States, or elsewhere—who are able to recognize each other as fighters and who draw strength from and reinforce each other's struggles. We strive to bring them together to fight as communists along an internationalist course.

That is why it is so important that the decades-old barriers erected by the Stalinist beheaders of revolutions are crumbling.

They are less of an obstacle than ever before to this process of collaboration, discussion, and common struggle among communists and revolutionary-minded working people and youth in Cuba, the United States, and other countries.

State power
Let's go back and look more fully at the three questions and our answers.

We should start with the question of state power—the most potent instrument the working class has to defend itself and its allies as it advances along its historic line of march. That's the right place to begin, since without a workers and farmers government that leads in a working-class direction, what our class would be facing both inside Cuba and elsewhere would be an entirely different matter.

The Cuban revolution is going through the most difficult economic crisis it has ever faced. We don't need to go into detail here, since delegates to this convention closely follow developments in Cuba. We have discussed the serious economic conditions at numerous national and regional gatherings organized by the Socialist Workers Party or Young Socialists over the past couple of years and reported on them extensively in the pages of the *Militant* and *Perspectiva Mundial*. In fact, a number of the examples we will discuss here today were described more fully in a series of articles run in the *Militant* and *Perspectiva Mundial* this spring and summer, based on reporting trips to Cuba by three international teams over a six-week period from late January through early March.[3]

---

3. See three articles by Argiris Malapanis and Aaron Ruby: "Cuban National Assembly Debates Measures to Deal with Formidable Economic Crisis," "Workers Debate Way Forward for Cuban Revolution," and "Cuban Government Reorganizes State Farms into Cooperatives in Effort to Boost Production." The articles appeared in the April 4, April 11, and April 18, 1994, issues of the *Militant* newsweekly and in the April, May, and June issues of *Perspectiva Mundial*.

On the whole, economic conditions and problems of life are more difficult in Cuba today than they were even a year ago. There continue to be extreme food shortages. Although no one is starving or suffering from serious malnutrition as are hundreds of millions in much of Latin America, Asia, and Africa, average caloric intake in Cuba has declined substantially in the last few years. Cooking oil, soap, and other basic necessities are largely unavailable unless you have dollars. Electrical blackouts lasting for hours remain daily routines, affecting not only residential neighborhoods but further decreasing production already curtailed by diminished ability to purchase raw materials and spare parts. With all petroleum products particularly scarce, bicycles have increasingly replaced buses as transportation for workers and students in the cities, just as oxen have supplemented, and in many cases supplanted, tractors in the countryside. Most people have no choice but to buy the majority of their food and clothing on what is called the black market, since the state distribution and rationing system has proven unable to assure sufficient quantities. More and more the black market functions in dollars, so those with access to hard currency live disproportionately better. Social inequalities are increasing dramatically. The medical and education systems, once the Cuban revolution's greatest pride, are deteriorating sharply.

There's no basis to assert that the worst is over. That remains to be seen. Since 1991, every time I've been to Cuba I've been told—usually by many people—"The worst is behind us now. We've bottomed out." So far, unfortunately, that hasn't been the case.

At some point it will be true, but it's better to be prepared for conditions to get worse and organize the necessary political fight and indicated economic measures.

The reason the economic crisis weighs so heavily in politics in Cuba today is the isolation of the Cuban revolution—flowing from the defeat of the Nicaraguan revolution in the late 1980s and the continuing political retreat of the working-class and revolutionary movements throughout Latin America and the Caribbean. These are not the factors most often pointed to either in Cuba or by other political currents in the workers movement and various Cuba solidarity groups in the United States and internationally. They all point to the collapse of the so-called socialist bloc and its economic consequences for Cuba—exacerbated by the U.S. embargo—as the source of almost every problem.

Beginning in 1989, the abrupt end of the substantial aid and trade at preferential prices with the former Soviet Union and Eastern European countries did trigger the drastic decline in agricultural and industrial production in Cuba the last several years. It is estimated that gross domestic product declined 30 percent between 1989 and 1993, and critical oil supplies dropped more than 50 percent during this same period. Prior to 1990, Cuba had been able to buy and sell at heavily subsidized terms of trade, much more favorable than anything possible on the world capitalist market. Communists and other committed supporters of the Cuban revolution around the world had welcomed that aid ever since it began in 1960, in face of mounting economic assaults and military threats by Washington and Wall Street.

But the Cuban leadership acted as if the Soviet and Eastern European regimes would last forever—and so would the aid. When the collapse occurred, it was as "if they said one day that the sun wouldn't rise," Castro told delegates to the congress of the Union of Writers and Artists of Cuba (UNEAC) in November 1993. "Everyone expects the sun to rise every day in the same way that everybody, revolutionary or not, expected that the socialist camp would continue to exist and that the USSR would continue to exist. But what happened to us was as if one day the sun didn't rise at 6:00 a.m., nor at 7:00 a.m., nor at 10:00 a.m., nor at 12 noon and in the midst of this darkness we have to look for solutions."

As a result of this mistaken political judgment, the Cuban leadership hadn't prepared for the inevitable and wasn't ready when the crisis hit in 1989-1991, as these Stalinist regimes fell one after another. Cuba's workers and farmers government hadn't redeemed the time that had been bought with the aid they received thanks to the October 1917 revolution and its heirs among the toilers. Between the early 1970s and latter part of the 1980s, little had been done to lessen the revolution's economic dependence on Moscow and achieve greater self-sufficiency in the production of food and other basic goods. In fact, the opposite occurred.

TODAY'S PROBLEMS are compounded by the criminal measures such as the trade embargo that the most powerful imperialist force on the earth, the government of the United States, has inflicted on Cuba for nearly thirty-five years. The ruling capitalist families in this country have never lost sight of their central goal—to weaken and eventually crush the revolution. They remain determined to punish the working people of Cuba for having the courage, tenacity, and capacity to declare their independence and make a socialist revolution, virtually on the shores of the United States.

As weighty as these difficulties are for the Cuban revolution, however, none of them is the real problem. If you have any doubt about this, just stop for a moment and imagine how morale in Cuba would change if strikes and peasant land seizures and student demonstrations were sweeping Argentina, or Brazil, or Venezuela, or Haiti, or any other region of the Americas! Or if the class struggle here in the United States were on the rise in a qualitative new way.

The source above all of the difficult times confronting the Cuban revolution is its isolation in the Americas—the fact that there is not a single other workers and farmers government, not another socialist revolution, anywhere in the hemisphere today. The Nicaraguan revolution went down to defeat in the late 1980s, as the Sandinista leadership turned decisively away from its previous anticapitalist course. Half a decade earlier, the workers and farmers government in Grenada had been destroyed from within by a Stalinist-organized counterrevolution.[4]

On top of these defeats—and in part because of them—U.S. imperialism maintained the upper hand in Latin America coming out of the debt crisis of the 1980s. Nowhere on the continent did any government or any official leadership of the unions or mass popular organizations take up the Cuban government's call for a united front of resistance to fight for cancellation of the foreign debt and for radical measures to redress the unequal terms of trade on the world capitalist market.[5] As a result, in country after country across Latin America since the mid-1980s, Wall Street and Washington have succeeded in what they delicately call "restructuring the debt" to the benefit of the imperialist-owned banks versus the national bourgeoisies and better-off layers of the middle class—and to the benefit of all of them versus the working people of the region.

The local capitalist rulers in most Latin American countries are selling off large amounts of state-owned land, natural resources, industries, and other enterprises—to themselves and

---

4. See "The Rise and Fall of the Nicaraguan Revolution," *New International* no. 9 (1994) and "The Second Assassination of Maurice Bishop" in *New International* no. 6 (1987).

5. The Cuban government's political campaign in the mid-1980s for a continental and worldwide campaign to cancel the Third World debt is recounted in speeches and interviews by Fidel Castro printed in *War and Crisis in the Americas: Fidel Castro Speeches, 1984-85* and *Fidel Castro: Nothing Can Stop the Course of History*, a book-length 1985 interview by Jeffrey Elliot and Mervyn Dymally. Both are published by Pathfinder. "Back in those days, we held big conferences on the foreign debt—in 1985—when we warned about many of the things that are now unfolding," Castro remarked at a January 1994 Latin American and Caribbean solidarity conference in Havana. "Our continent lost the best moment then for a great battle [against payment of the debt], when we could have averted many of the calamities we face today." The speech appears in full in the February 16, 1994, issue of *Granma International* and in the March 7, 1994, issue of the *Militant*.

to imperialist interests—for a song. They are busting unions, gutting and increasingly "privatizing" already inadequate state pension funds and other social security programs, and ending subsidies for food, fuel, and other necessities. The mounting human toll this takes can be seen in everything from the epidemics of curable diseases to the millions of children left to live in the streets. And the capitalist rulers have been able to do all this with virtually no resistance organized by the officialdom of the workers movement anywhere in Latin America.

THE OUTBREAK OF PEASANT RESISTANCE in Chiapas province in Mexico and the working-class explosions in Santiago del Estero and other Argentine cities in late 1993 and early 1994 are a sign of the mounting social tensions created by capitalism's "successes," and a premonition of the explosions to come. For the moment, however, they remain the exception.

The Cuban revolution has also been affected by the quiescence, the setbacks, and the retreats in the class struggle in the United States over the last years.

This international picture, taken as a whole, is strikingly different from the ascending revolutionary wave and class struggles that carried the Cuban revolution forward in earlier periods.

In the 1960s, revolutionary-minded workers and youth in Cuba identified with and were buoyed by the mass proletarian struggle for Black rights in the United States; by the Vietnamese revolution and the growing movement in this country and worldwide against Washington's murderous war in Indochina; and by the emergence throughout Latin America of revolutionary organizations that sought to emulate the Cuban victory.

The 1970s saw the triumph of the Vietnamese people over U.S. imperialism and the fall of the Portuguese empire, as well as advances in the revolutionary struggle against colonialism and apartheid in southern Africa. In 1979 a mass upsurge in Iran brought the shah's Peacock Throne crashing to earth, and in Grenada and Nicaragua workers and farmers governments came to power through anticapitalist revolutions. Those victories gave an impulse to revolutionary perspectives throughout the Americas—and to layers of young people elsewhere—that continued well into the 1980s.

These advances in the world fight for national liberation and socialism made it easier for Cuban revolutionists to face economic difficulties, bought time to correct errors and recover from their results, and created breathing space to consolidate the socialist revolution and keep moving forward. Today, however, the absence of similar advancing struggles weighs heavily on social and political life in Cuba.

The U.S. rulers hope the days are over when Cuban revolutionists—using the advantages gained by wielding state power—come to the aid of those struggling against imperialist plunder and capitalist exploitation elsewhere in the world. But what is happening in the Cuban working class, even in face of the current difficult domestic and international situation, is evidence to the contrary. The working people of Cuba would reach out to and politically respond to new revolutionary struggles, especially in the Americas—just as more than 300,000 Cubans volunteers served in internationalist missions in Angola in the 1970s and 1980s, and thousands served as volunteer teachers, doctors, construction workers, and military advisers in Nicaragua and Grenada.[6] Renewed international openings

---

6. Troops of the South African apartheid regime, with the backing of Washington, invaded Angola in 1975, just as it had won its freedom from Portuguese colonial rule. The attempt by imperialist forces and their Angolan rightist allies to overturn the government of the newly independent state was blocked, thanks to the assistance of Cuban volunteer troops. The South African government continued its war against Angola for thirteen years, until its army was decisively defeated in 1988 by Cuban, Angolan, and Namibian forces at Cuito Cuanavale.

Cuban workers and youth also volunteered to carry out a wide range of missions as internationalist volunteers in Nicaragua and Grenada following the 1979 revolutions there, as they had done previously in Algeria, Vietnam, the

would once again bring new advances in the Cuban revolution.

Washington is reminded of this fact every time the Cuban government speaks out—virtually alone—against imperialist military aggression abroad, such as the U.S.-led slaughter in the Persian Gulf, the invasion of Somalia, and U.S. threats to invade Haiti.[7]

Communists in cuba—like virtually the entire population of Cuba—live with the same kinds of grinding *political* pressures communists face here in the United States. They, like ourselves, sometimes need to step back and look at the broader world picture and longer time frame in order to get an accurate compass reading. That's why it's so important when Cuban president Fidel Castro explains in his speeches, as he often does, that so long as capitalism is the predominant economic and social system in the world, the perspective ahead for all of us is one of intensifying social and political struggles. That was at the heart of what he had to say last January, for example, in his closing speech to the 1,200 delegates at the Fourth Latin American and Caribbean Conference for Solidarity, Sovereignty, and Self-Determination, held in Havana.

"On New Year's Day, when we reach the year 2000, we won't be able to greet each other with a 'happy new century,' not in Latin America or many other parts of the world," Castro said. Instead, "the reality that awaits us—which is manifest now before the turn of the century—is one of much effort and struggle." Capitalism "has nothing to offer humanity today," he explained. It is "a sys-

---

Congo, and many other parts of the world.

7. See, for example, *U.S. Hands Off the Mideast! Cuba Speaks Out at the United Nations* (New York: Pathfinder, 1990). The Cuban government was almost the only voice in the United Nations condemning the September 1994 U.S. occupation of Haiti. The October 3, 1994, speech by Cuban foreign minister Roberto Robaina before the UN General Assembly was run in the October 19, 1994, issue of *Granma International* and the October 24 issue of the *Militant*.

tem of injustice, of unequal distribution, of exploitation of man by man." While the economic and social consequences of the capitalist crisis are more acute in the Third World, Castro noted, conditions are deteriorating in the United States, Europe, and Japan as well.

While many people around the world had been disoriented by the collapse of the regimes in Eastern Europe and the Soviet Union, Fidel stated, "today we already see in all parts of the world signs of hope, of struggle."[8]

This realistic, fighting perspective on world politics is what revolutionary-minded workers and youth will respond to, whether in Cuba, the United States, or elsewhere. This is the class truth that must be spoken. Capitalism is in crisis today, not socialism. Time is on *our* side, not the side of the capitalist exploiters.

A necessary retreat

This is the political context in which a retreat is being organized in Cuba today. A retreat is necessary. That's unambiguous; it's hardly debatable. The working class and its revolutionary government must retreat in order to buy time to get production of food, other agricultural products, and industrial goods moving again. Cuba has to reorganize its trade within the world capitalist market in order to make it possible to increase imports of oil and other indispensable commodities and find buyers for its exports. It has to grant concessions large enough to attract foreign capitalists as partners in joint ventures in order to acquire technology, tap mineral resources, develop markets, and bring in capital for economic development.

Without such a retreat the socialist revolution in Cuba could not survive the current crisis. The worker-farmer alliance that sustains the revolutionary government would collapse, and the

---

8. The entire speech appeared in the February 16, 1994, issue of *Granma International* and is reprinted in the March 7, 1994, issue of the *Militant*.

government of the toilers would be replaced by one that represents the class interests of aspiring exploiters. Only if food supplies increase and industrial production begins to recover can a solid basis be laid for a renewed advance in the building of socialism as more favorable conditions—in Cuba, and above all in the class struggle in the Americas and worldwide—open the door to such progress.

"We have had to make concessions, that is undeniable," Castro explained in November 1993 to the congress of artists and writers:

> These changes were inevitable, and we have to make some more which foster individualism, selfishness, make the value of money more important in society, have alienating effects; all of this is a fact. This is not what we wanted to do with our country. We wanted to do what we were doing and what we began to do in the midst of the rectification process[9] when the catastrophe and the

---

9. The rectification process was initiated in 1986 by the Communist Party of Cuba to reverse the mounting negative political consequences of the economic planning and management policies the Cuban leadership had adopted in the early 1970s modeled on those of the Soviet Stalinist regime. By the early 1980s this course had resulted in accelerating political demobilization and demoralization of layers of working people in Cuba. In face of this growing political disorientation, Cuban communists began to reach back toward the course that had been argued for by Ernesto Che Guevara during the early 1960s and that had begun to be implemented in limited ways in those years. Measures adopted during rectification included steps to reduce growing social inequalities and privileged living conditions for those belonging to the upper strata of the government, party, and army bureaucracies; cutbacks in administrative and management personnel; sharp attacks on corruption; increased reliance on volunteer construction brigades to build badly needed hospitals, day-care centers, and schools; and full-time volunteer labor contingents to take on larger construction and civil engineering projects such as roads, factories, and bridges. The shortages and economic dislocation of the past several years have forced the Cuban government and Communist Party to retreat from many of the pro-

collapse [of the Soviet Union] happened. . . . Now we
have to learn how to live, struggle, and win in the midst
of these problems that we have been talking about here.

Any working-class leadership needs to know when and how
to lead a retreat, otherwise its forces will be routed. A leadership has to be able to accurately assess the relationship of class
forces, to know which defensive lines it can fight for and hold
and which it cannot. "In life, war, and revolution there are
times when one has to take steps backwards and times when
one can go forward," Castro explained at the December 1993
meeting of Cuba's elected National Assembly.

But retreats are also more difficult than advances—more
complex, more dangerous to organize and lead. When you are
advancing, your forward momentum can carry you through
and compensate for certain mistakes or weaknesses. When you
are retreating, the working-class movement pays a much higher
political price for every misstep.

Survival of the revolution in Cuba requires not only leading
a retreat, however. Just as important, it demands creating the
conditions to *limit* the retreat: not one step further than necessary to preserve the state power of the toilers. It means continuing to pursue a proletarian course. It means simultaneously
strengthening the class consciousness, combativity, and self-
confidence of the toilers. It means organizing the working class
to use its state power to restrict to the degree possible the growing operations of the capitalist market system, the law of value.
It means preparing the working class for future battles as the
class struggle sharpens—as it will under these conditions.

----

grams and objectives set in motion during the latter half of the 1980s.

See "Cuba's Rectification Process: Two Speeches by Fidel Castro," including
the introduction by Mary-Alice Waters, in *New International* no. 6; Fidel Castro,
*In Defense of Socialism: Four Speeches on the Thirtieth Anniversary of the Cuban Revo-
lution* (New York: Pathfinder, 1989); as well as many of the books and pamphlets cited above.

Greater latitude for the workings of the law of value will increasingly erode the proletarian social relations Cuban workers have conquered in struggle over the last three and a half decades. It will increase class differentiation and inequality and undermine social solidarity. That, in turn, will strengthen the political leverage of the petty-bourgeois administrative and professional layers as well as those whose fortunes are directly tied to the growing weight of foreign capital and the developing market forces. It will increase pressures to look for allies around the world not among the toilers but among wings of the bourgeoisie. Communists must wage a political battle to slow down these inevitable social tendencies and, above all, their political effects.

LOOKING AT THIS CHALLENGE in Cuba, the answer to the first question we posed—Does the government of Cuba remain a revolutionary government?—becomes even clearer. While organizing the necessary retreat, which inevitably strengthens the capitulationist social layers that honeycomb the administrative and professional classes in Cuba, the communist-led government also tries to hold them off and continues to take steps that strengthen the hand of the toilers.

Sectors of the middle-class forces increasingly want one and only one thing: a green light for the headlong pursuit of a course they hope will offer them a personal escape from Cuba's difficulties and greater economic advancement for themselves and their families. They consider this their due, commensurate with their educational degrees and anticipated socioeconomic status in Cuba. They couldn't care less if their individual comfort comes at the expense of the social solidarity of the working class—and the future of humanity. We must have no illusions about the size and social weight of this layer in Cuba today; it is substantial.

Two or three times a year the editors of the *Wall Street Journal* run a feature on Cuba. It's always the same article with updated quotes and anecdotes. They find the manager of some enterprise in Cuba, or an official in some government ministry, and cite this individual (anonymously, of course) on the virtues of the market system. "Resurrection of capitalism in Cuba is inevitable," an economist for a state enterprise is quoted as saying in a typical *Journal* article in February 1993. "We are simply looking for ways to do it while keeping the social cost down."

A year later, in February 1994, *Journal* reporter José de Córdoba built his version of the same story around reports on the Cuban economy prepared by Jacques de Groote, the director of the International Monetary Fund, and by Carlos Solchaga, Spain's former finance minister. "Time is running out for the orderly introduction of a critical mass of market oriented reforms," the IMF report warns, according to the *Journal*.

The articles all end the same way, however, bemoaning the fact that steps in the direction of capitalism just don't seem to be moving very fast. "Hard-line communists" and "incompetent bureaucrats" are usually cited as the obstacle. The most recent article, for example, blames it all on "Mr. Castro," who "vehemently attacked capitalism" at the National Assembly meeting in December 1993, dominating the proceedings, and convincing the delegates not to adopt a package of measures advocated by the government finance ministry. "Some analysts," the *Journal* article wailed, "wonder whether Mr. Castro's deep fear and hatred of capitalism will end up strangling the reforms."

The reporter makes it sound like Fidel has a psychological problem, a phobia, not a scientific world view. What Fidel actually said at last December's National Assembly meeting was: "I believe in socialism and despise capitalism. What I feel is repugnance toward capitalism, not prejudice. I have no prejudice, but repugnance. . . . By its very nature, capitalism harbors hypocrisy, war, competition. I absolutely believe everything we have said about capitalism."

The layer of capitalist-minded managers and bureaucrats the *Journal* loves to quote is a very real one, and it is gaining strength. But that is only one piece of the story. The working class, too, is stronger than it was a half decade ago. There is a sharpening polarization. But it is the working class that holds power and is consciously making concessions, not vice versa.

At a special meeting of the National Assembly in May of this year (the regular, biannual summer session is taking place right now, in August), Fidel explained this very clearly. "We have met here precisely to adopt all those measures that will help save the revolution of the working class," he stated. "Even though we have had to make concessions that are unavoidable in order to survive and to be able to develop ourselves," he said, "we make the conditions."

That's the bottom line: state power remains in the hands of the communist-led government of Cuba's workers and farmers.

M**ANY PEOPLE AROUND THE WORLD**, including those who to one degree or another consider themselves "friends of Cuba," welcome the fact that the revolutionary government is having to make concessions to win capitalist investment. They think it is positive. They are always searching for those in the Cuban leadership who are willing to go further, faster, to be more "reasonable," more "pragmatic."

Some of you probably saw the recent article in Cuba's English-language weekly *Granma International* headlined "U.S. Mayor Visits Havana." The visitor was the mayor of Mobile, Alabama, which has a sister-city project with Havana. *Granma International* reports that the mayor "told the press of his hopes that Cuba and the United States will be able to do business in the future, just as the United States is now doing with Viet Nam."

That statement captures a widely held point of view: the hope that the relationship of class forces in Cuba will shift in the not-too-distant future and the government will begin making the kind of political and economic concessions to capital that are being made by the Stalinist regimes in China and Vietnam. The same course was followed for decades by the governing bureaucratic castes in Eastern Europe and the Soviet Union as well, paving the way for the regimes there today. Under such conditions, of course, the U.S. government would be quite willing to lift the embargo and open trade with Cuba. For example, the Clinton administration earlier this year lifted its economic embargo against Vietnam—cruelly and unconscionably maintained for so many years—just as U.S. trade, investment, and diplomatic relations were opened with Beijing in the 1970s.

Wall Street and Washington, however, maintain their irreconcilable hostility toward the Cuban revolutionary government, and vilify Castro above all, precisely because they know that the course being followed in China and Vietnam is *not* what is happening in Cuba. Despite concessions, when Cuba affirms its sovereignty, independence, and freely chosen socialist course, when it speaks out in solidarity with struggles against imperialist domination around the world, a class divide is posed. The U.S. rulers have no difficulty recognizing that in Cuba there is a different relationship between the working class and its government than exists in Vietnam or China. And that is what they fear. (Their profit hopes for Vietnam and China are far too optimistic as well, but that is their problem, not ours.)

It's useful, in this regard, to take a look at the class questions posed, the real class content of two sets of measures that have been adopted recently in Cuba and that are in the process of being implemented—one having to do with taxes, the other with land and agricultural production.

A heavily progressive income tax
Inflation is one of the most devastating manifestations of the economic crisis in Cuba today. It results from the fact that while an enormous amount of currency is in circulation (since most workers have continued to receive most of their wages, even if they are not working due to shortages of fuel and raw materials and breakdowns of machinery), production has plummeted since 1990 and there are few goods that people can buy with this money. As long as the rationing system held up, Cubans were buffered from the effects of rising prices. But with the

growing shortages of food available through the ration book, the black market became the main source for most Cubans and prices exploded. This is the most debilitating form of taxation, the most *regressive* taxation, working people can face.

To address this inflation, one measure advocated by some government officials is the reintroduction of an income tax structure that includes a tax on wages—for the first time since such income taxes were abolished in the 1960s. The articles in the *Militant* and *Perspectiva Mundial* that I mentioned earlier report on the debate that took place on this question at the December 1993 meeting of the National Assembly in Cuba, as well as the organized debate inside the working class subsequent to that. The articles included firsthand accounts of the discussions that took place in several of the 80,000 *parlamentos obreros,* or workers assemblies, that were organized in the first months of 1994 in Cuban factories, farms, and other workplaces.

At the National Assembly meeting, Finance Minister José Luis Rodríguez said, "We responsibly tell you that we are proposing a tax system for the country. We have already talked about the need to create an awareness among the people, an awareness that we have lost." The need to establish a "tax culture" in the working class in Cuba has been a theme of many government economists and others who are pushing to accelerate capitalist market—oriented measures. The urgent need to impose a tax system has also been among the dire warnings issued by various economic "experts" being sent to Cuba from across the capitalist world—by the government of Spain, the International Monetary Fund, and others.

At the National Assembly meeting, Fidel answered these advisers and experts rather brusquely, saying the working class had never had a "tax consciousness," and rightly so. "No, no, no. We have never had that consciousness," he said. "The other tax system was a bourgeois tax system."

The revolution, he noted, got rid of that system, which was a registration of bourgeois social relations, and instituted a proletarian alternative to it: the ration book. The rationing system enabled the working class to finance the revolution's social gains and economic development programs, Fidel explained, while ensuring an equitable distribution of food, clothing, and other basic necessities. "We built thousands of schools, hundreds and hundreds of hospitals, many things," he said, "and the price of a liter of milk never went up a single cent." Fidel continued:

> Economists frighten me. There is only one thing I know a little about and that is politics. That has been my job, and the most important job I have had. I believe that things must be viewed through politics. The idea presented by the specialists must be analyzed from a political viewpoint. . . . A technocratic approach cannot be used to solve these problems.

The workers in Cuba, Castro said, had not had the chance to discuss a single one of the proposed economic measures that financial specialists had brought to the National Assembly. So despite the dire warnings of the economic "advisers," in the end, all the proposals for a new tax system and other measures were set aside by the December 1993 Assembly meeting, and delegates instead called for a nationwide period of discussion in the working class. Through the 80,000 *parlamentos obreros* the weight of the working class was brought to bear in this debate with the technocrats, the economists, and capitalist forces the world over—all of whom, in their own ways, were seeking to pressure the revolutionary government to adopt a package of measures that would reduce the social wage conquered by the working class in revolutionary struggle and advance capitalist norms of distribution, that is, capitalist social relations, not proletarian ones.

On May Day 1994, the international holiday of the working class, the National Assembly convened a special session to rediscuss the measures. What came out of that discussion and decision-making process codified precisely the two things that, in assembly after assembly, the working class had spoken out on, saying unequivocally, "This we will not accept."

First, as José Luis Rodríguez, the finance minister, acknowledged in his report to the May meeting, "Workers have expressed a clear position in the workers assemblies against the imposition of a tax on wages." Cuban trade union leader Pedro Ross called it "an overwhelming consensus" in his remarks to the National Assembly.

If you saw any accounts of Cuba's May National Assembly meeting in the big-business press in this country—which were few and far between—you would have read that an income tax measure was adopted. The average worker in the United States, of course, would associate this with the big tax hit recorded on his or her pay stub each week. Contrary to the media accounts in the United States, however, what the Assembly adopted was a resolution calling for further study of "the selective introduction of a tax on personal income, *excluding taxes on wages*"!

IN OTHER WORDS, the Assembly voted that no workers' wages should be taxed, and that any new income tax in Cuba should be levied only on the income of the self-employed or other nonwage revenues.

In September 1993, the government legalized self-employment in some 140 types of occupations. By July 1994, 167,000 licenses had already been issued. One complaint that came up over and over again during the workers assemblies is that due to the shortages and excess currency in circulation, some of these self-employed people are now taking home enormous incomes, month after month, and, in addition, often utilize materials stolen from factory warehouses to do so. The *Militant* reported, for example, that—while not the norm for the self-employed—some can make up to 1,000 pesos a day, while most Cuban factory workers make less than 150 pesos a month. So, many workers said, yes, these exceptionally large incomes should be taxed, but wages should not be.

Advocating a steep progressive income tax is nothing new for the working-class movement. In fact, it goes back to the founding programmatic document of the modern communist workers movement, the Communist Manifesto, published in 1848. The Manifesto, which was drafted by Karl Marx and Frederick Engels, says that among the first steps of a government established by "the revolution by the working class" will be "a heavy progressive or graduated income tax."[10] That remains the tax program—the *only* tax program—of the communist movement today.

T HE SECOND MEASURE strongly argued for by workers in their assemblies—and the first decree issued by the Council of State following the National Assembly in May—was aimed at stemming the large-scale corruption and illegal amassing of wealth, mostly through theft from workplaces, warehouses, and farms with managerial personnel and collaborators playing the predominant role. Large quantities of agricultural and industrial goods, and even machinery, are routinely stolen and sold on the black market or used by those who "diverted" them (that's the commonly used term in Cuba) to produce other salable goods.

During the factory assemblies workers spoke out heatedly about this, saying: We know what's going on. We know who's doing it. We see things disappear from beneath our noses from one day to the next.

The *Militant* team reported firsthand on a workers assembly in February at a cigar factory, where workers challenged the managers about the unexplained disappearance last year of nearly 20 percent of the cigars produced. Theft of machinery and other materials was also at the center of discussion during the assembly at a dairy plant outside Havana that I attended. "The government doesn't do anything, the party doesn't do anything, the un-

10. Karl Marx and Frederick Engels, *Collected Works*, vol. 6 (Moscow: Progress Publishers, 1976), p. 504, 505.

ion doesn't do anything," one worker said, "and we know who the people are and where they live." The theft must be dealt with, she said, and if the government will not act, then the workers here should go and take back the stolen goods.

The fact that the working class was demanding action was registered in decree-law 149, issued by the revolutionary government the first week of May authorizing the confiscation of ill-gotten wealth. In the May National Assembly debate, Fidel said the decree "reminds us of the first years of the revolution, when a law was established to confiscate the ill-gotten goods of those who had grown rich" under the Batista dictatorship.

Since May, more than two hundred arrests have been reported for violations of the new law, and legal proceedings have been initiated to confiscate property seized in the raids.

Both these measures, the income tax proposal and the decree on stolen wealth, strengthen—not weaken—the hand of the working class in defending the property relations established by the revolutionary conquests of the workers and farmers more than thirty years ago. They are not the kind of measures that make the IMF and other capitalist advisers jump for joy. That is why we say the government continues to act in a way to hold off those who want a headlong flight toward capitalist social relations.

Many other proposed measures aimed at soaking up excess currency in circulation and reducing inflation were discussed in the workers assemblies, some of which have been implemented in line with the May National Assembly decisions. Prices have been raised on some nonessential items, including sharp increases on cigarettes and rum. Workers don't like these hikes, of course. But most say that at least these prices—if they can be maintained—are lower than on the black market, and that it's better to concentrate subsidies on other, more desperately needed goods.

Electricity rates have been raised, but on a steeply progressive scale that leaves costs unchanged for the first 100 kilowatt hours per month. Air fares, intercity bus fares, and train fares have gone up, but with a 30 percent discount for workers and students who regularly get to work or go to school by train. A relatively small flat charge has been instituted for water and sewage, and postal and telephone rates have been increased.

Cultural and sporting events are no longer all free. There will now be a charge for school lunches, but no student will go without lunch because of an inability to pay. Students enrolled in higher education courses will now receive loans, repayable after graduation, instead of stipends. Those graduating with top grades will be exempt from repayment.

THE CUMULATIVE EFFECT of these measures, and others to come, will be to increase the cost of living, decrease the government deficit, and start to bring down inflation even prior to any increase in production. While families on the lower end of the income scale will be disproportionately affected, for sure, they will benefit the most if the peso begins to recover its buying power. All this is being done while attempting, to the degree possible, to maintain the revolution's essential social programs intact and accessible to all.

The important thing about these measures is, first of all, the relatively high level of support for them in the working class in Cuba as a result of the extensive debate. Secondly, they continue to fundamentally protect the high degree of social equality in Cuba that would be impossible without the collective ownership of productive property—that is, impossible without a socialist revolution.

The most recent of the *Wall Street Journal*'s semiannual articles was published just last week, on July 26, of course.[11] Once again the correspondent—this time the editor of the *Journal*'s

---

11. July 26 is a national holiday in Cuba, the anniversary of the 1953 attack by the young revolutionary forces led by Fidel Castro on the Moncada army garrison in Santiago de Cuba. That uprising marked the beginning of the revolutionary struggle to topple the Batista tyranny.

Americas column—interviewed an unnamed procapitalist official. "We need private enterprise," the official explains. And, he
is reported as saying, we have to figure out the point beyond
which we can no longer protect "the revolutionary gains that
conflict with private property."

The *Journal*'s reporter then comments that "those 'gains' are
represented by education, health and social services." According to another Cuban official, those programs account for
"only 30 percent of the [government] budget deficit" in Cuba.
The rest of the deficit, the reporter says, comes from subsidies
to inefficient state enterprises. "So why not eliminate subsidies," he writes, "and allow private enterprise to fund the revolutionary accomplishments?"

That's the *Wall Street Journal*'s tongue-in-cheek answer. Of
course, it echoes things said in Cuba as well. But those of us
who know capitalism from the inside can write our own op-ed
piece on how well private enterprise does at funding education,
health care, and other basic social services for the working
class.

The remark by the anonymous official and the *Journal*'s commentary on it points to one of the political problems in Cuba
today. On recent reporting trips there, we've discovered it's
very common to find Cubans who equate "the gains of the revolution" with health care and public education. Then they will
say, But look what's happening to those social gains. We don't
have any textbooks for the children anymore. We don't have
light bulbs or notebooks or pencils in the schools.

They point to the sharp deterioration of the health-care system under current conditions because of the lack of medicines,
equipment, and other resources, they point to the declining
morale among workers in the hospitals and clinics (morale is
declining among a broad layer of these workers, who are not
being led politically). And then these Cubans ask, So what are
we defending, what does socialism have to offer any more?

The same question is being asked, openly or not, by many of
those in the United States and around the world who have

been longtime supporters of the Cuban revolution. If, over the years, you have tried to convince people that Cuba should be defended against U.S. government policy primarily by pointing to the health and education advances achieved, then your case is weaker today.

But the gains of the revolution can't be reduced to health care and education—as important as these conquests are, and as powerful and inspiring the example is that they set for toilers the world over. The fact that the workers and farmers established their own government, overturned capitalist property relations, and began building a society on new economic foundations is infinitely weightier than the gains made in health care and education.

That is why the communist course identified with Ernesto Che Guevara is so essential. In making, defending, and advancing the socialist revolution in Cuba over the past thirty-five years, millions of working people have transformed themselves and their own consciousness. They have developed a deeply ingrained sense of social solidarity, internationalism, new attitudes toward work, self-respect, and confidence in the face of capitalist pressures. They are committed to something bigger than their own personal advancement and the betterment of their families and friends. In short, new social relations, based on new property relations, have begun to develop, and the braiding of one generation with the next in Cuba along a proletarian line of march is the most secure and important gain of the socialist revolution.

Whatever adversities lie ahead—and we should have no illusions: Cuban revolutionists will have to retreat farther than they have done so far—so long as the working class is able to maintain political power, it can fight along a proletarian course to address these difficulties and be in the best position to renew its advance as victories in the world class struggle open up some space. That—and only that—is what the fight is all about. Communists in Cuba may not always explain it as we do, or say it as clearly as Lenin did in the early years of the Russian revolution.

But the working class in its majority in Cuba today is not confused on this fundamental question. Nor is imperialism. Both sides know what the stakes are.

The most politically conscious workers and youth recognize that the class struggle will continue for some time along these lines. But they also gain confidence, as we do, from the fact that the working class in Cuba is holding its own in the rounds it has fought so far.

Land, state farms, and cooperatives

The other measure implemented in the last year that we should look at is the reorganization of agricultural labor and production in Cuba. The change was initiated by the responsible government ministries in September 1993 and was ratified by the meeting of the National Assembly in December. The big majority of Cuba's state farms, which at the time comprised some 80 percent of land under cultivation in Cuba, have been subdivided into smaller farms and transformed into cooperatives—Basic Units of Cooperative Production, or UBPCs, as they are called there.

The process began with the big sugarcane enterprises, the large majority of which were rapidly transformed into UBPCs by the beginning of 1994. State farms producing citrus, tobacco, vegetables and other food crops, and some livestock and dairy farms are also being reorganized as cooperatives. By the middle of 1994 some 1,600 sugarcane-growing co-ops and some 1,100 others had been established. The workforce in each co-op averages 100 workers. One of the articles in the *Militant* describes this development in some detail and reviews the history of the agrarian reform and debates over the organization of farm labor since the earliest years of the revolution.

Unlike state farms, the cooperatives own their harvest and sell it to the state at prices established by the government. The co-op owns the machinery (bought from the former state farms with long-term low-interest loans), and it purchases needed supplies out of its revenues, which depend on its overall output. The income of co-op members, the workers who belong to it, is linked to their individual jobs as well as their collective productivity. In addition to producing crops for consumption in Cuba and for export, the UBPCs are expected to be largely self-sufficient in food, and to build housing for member families.

The land remains nationalized and cannot be sold, rented, inherited, mortgaged, or used as collateral for other liens.

Most members of the new co-ops are former workers on the state farms who have voluntarily signed up. Given the urgency of increased food output and declining opportunities for productive employment in industry and other urban workplaces, however, others are also joining. This is especially true of workers who have been part of the voluntary agricultural work contingents that have played a vanguard role in food production the last couple of years.

THIS IS UNDOUBTEDLY the single biggest change in the organization of agricultural labor and production since the second agrarian reform in 1963. The evolution of the workers and farmers government's political course on the land and the reasons for its agrarian policies is a subject that deserves to be studied on its own. Whatever errors and mistakes, and there have been plenty, the Cuban agrarian reform and subsequent measures have been a model of communist policy aimed always at forging, maintaining, and strengthening the worker-farmer alliance. Major elements of this policy and its evolution are explained in several documents of the Communist Party of Cuba and speeches by Fidel Castro that are available in English translation and are distributed by Pathfinder.[12]

---

12. See *Marxism and the Working Farmer* (New York: Pathfinder, 1979), which includes a 1962 and a 1967 speech by Castro; as well as the feature on "Land Reform and Farm Cooperatives in Cuba" in *New International* no. 4, which includes the Communist Party of Cuba's 1975 "Theses on the Agrarian Question and Relations with the Peasantry," along with a 1982 and a 1984 speech by Castro, and an introduction by Mary-Alice Waters.

In one of those speeches, presented to a congress of delegates of sugarcane cooperatives in 1962, Castro explained the proposal by leaders of the revolutionary government to transform the original co-ops established following the first agrarian reform in 1959 into state farms. Because of how the expropriated capitalist landowners had organized production for decades, he explained, the big majority of rural toilers in Cuba were wageworkers. This was unlike most of Latin America and other Third World countries at a comparable stage of economic development, where the majority of the rural population are exploited peasants, often working and living under semifeudal conditions.

The agricultural workers were one of the backbones of the Cuban revolution, Fidel said. "Traditionally, the group with the best fighting spirit, the most revolutionary of the agricultural proletariat, was the cane worker, the worker of the cane latifundios," the cane plantations.

At the moment when the proletariat began to guide the destiny of the country," however, with the victory of the revolution and its growing socialist direction, "a great proletarian and exploited group of yesterday ceased being proletarian," Fidel said. Co-ops were established on farms expropriated from the capitalist landowners, and many workers were in fact being turned into small owners, and, sometimes, into exploiters of other rural toilers who they hired to meet seasonal labor needs. While the co-ops were an advance over capitalist ownership, he said, from the standpoint of the working class "the cooperative was a backward step."

Actually, they weren't so much a step backward as a contradictory step, one that registered both the rapid advances of the working class and the limitations to what they were yet ready and able to do in the first years of the revolution.

With the reorganization of the co-ops into state farms, Castro said in the 1962 report, "the agricultural proletariat begins to advance, becomes the most numerous sector of the working class in our country . . . a great and formidable force for the revolution."

In light of these considerations, the question is posed: Was the Cuban government's decision last year to dismantle the state farms and reorganize them into cooperatives a retreat whose political price was too high? Does it undermine nationalization of the land and fatally set back the organization of agricultural production along socialist lines based on cooperative labor?

The answer—given the growing weight over the years in Cuba of the nonproductive bureaucratic layers associated with agriculture and the corresponding decline in political consciousness, self-confidence, and combativity of the workers on the state farms—is that, to the contrary, this reorganization opens up space for the agricultural proletariat to take greater control over the production of food and export crops in Cuba. It *opens up space* for them to play a weightier, more conscious vanguard role. Whether the proletariat proves strong enough to take advantage of that space and use it is another question. As with everything else we're discussing here, that will be decided in struggle. There are no guarantees.

The sharp drop in the sugar harvests and food production in the last several years is not just the result of very real problems caused by chronic shortages of fertilizers, pesticides, fuel, and other inputs, as well as several storm-related disasters. It is not just a product of the collapse of Cuba's preferential trade with the Soviet Union and Eastern Europe and the ongoing effects of the U.S. embargo.

The necessity for a retreat in the organization of farm production stems above all from the social and political consequences of the economic planning and management policies copied from the Stalinist bureaucratic caste of the Soviet Union. These policies fostered the growth in Cuba of a massive, nonproductive administrative bureaucracy in agriculture, as elsewhere. We were told by many different people, and reports published in the trade union newspaper *Trabajadores* confirm, that more than 50 percent of those employed on some state farms are administrative personnel who contribute nothing directly to production.

Instead of organizing and leading the agricultural working class to take growing control over their conditions of work and production, as Che sought to do, this "most revolutionary of the agricultural proletariat," as Fidel called them, played less and less of a role. The fact that agricultural labor is generally the lowest paid work in Cuba tells you a great deal about the social and political structure.

POLITICAL DEMORALIZATION of growing layers of agricultural workers, registered in extremely low levels of productivity, (four- or five-hour days were reported as common) led to the collapse first in food production and then in the sugar harvests. These problems were compounded by the absence of fertilizers, fuel, pesticides, and storm damage.

"The fact is that the same thing happened to the state farms as happened to . . . many factories and many industries," Castro said in a November 7, 1993, speech to the Havana provincial assembly of the Communist Party. "The same thing happened to all of them: oversized staffs, a tendency toward excess personnel, paternalism, a less demanding attitude. . . . Let's be frank; these problems were created by the revolution."

Of course, Fidel is right that what happened in the countryside reflected broader communist leadership failures in the management of factories in the cities as well. In the modern world, what happens in the countryside is determined first and foremost by what happens in the city, not vice versa. Despite the progress that had begun to be made during the rectification process in the late 1980s—when agricultural wages were demonstratively raised and plans were laid to dramatically increase food production and improve rural living conditions—Cuban communists had barely begun to tackle the challenge of reversing the disastrous course of organizing state farms and factories along political and economic lines modeled on the policies imposed in the USSR and Eastern Europe. In those countries, such policies were consciously designed to *prevent* workers from taking initiatives and increasing their control over all administrative and management tasks, not to encourage and organize workers to do so.

THE CURRENT REORGANIZATION *can* open the door to progress by agricultural workers in knocking the dead hand of bureaucracy off their backs. A genuine political struggle and class orientation is involved here. There will be resistance and even sabotage from some of those in danger of being displaced from administrative positions. The last thing many—probably most—of them are inclined to is to work the fields as co-op members. They have been miseducated, in the Stalinist tradition, to think of themselves not as workers but as agronomists or engineers or technicians who deserve a higher social status, registered by a substantially higher wage. But these smaller cooperative units—which elect their managers and leadership committees, vote on their own work norms, and share the fruits of their labor—at least have a better opportunity to begin to address some of the long accumulating problems.

Any progress along these lines in the countryside would also give impetus to workers in urban factories and other workplaces to begin addressing similar obstacles to the organization of production. One of the things we heard workers in a number of enterprises comment on positively was the fact that the new co-ops elect their managers, who must receive 70 percent of the votes cast to be elected.

The decision to retreat to the UBPCs also registers the failure of efforts by Cuban revolutionists to meet the growing food shortages by the mobilization of voluntary agricultural work brigades from the cities from 1991 to 1993. Each year hundreds of thousands of workers, students, and professionals were mobilized to work on the state farms to cultivate and harvest food crops, usually for two-week stints. These mobilizations initially built on the momentum from the voluntary minibrigades that had constructed thousands of apartments, schools, clinics, day

care centers, and other projects during the years of the rectification process between 1986 and 1991.

At the start this revolutionary response to the food crisis did
increase the output of fruits and vegetables somewhat. But by
1993, support for the mobilizations had largely dissipated, because they hadn't been led effectively over time, either politically or organizationally.

Volunteer work brigades such as Che fought for—real schools
for communist consciousness and leadership—are controversial
in Cuba. If they are led politically, as an adjunct and spur to other
proletarian measures, they are a way to raise the self-confidence
and cohesion of the producers, to develop working-class consciousness. They start to limit the operation of the law of value,
and begin transforming labor power from a commodity into conscious activity through which we realize our humanity. As Che
put it in his magnificent notes on *Socialism and Man in Cuba,*
"man truly reaches his full human condition when he produces
without being compelled by human necessity to sell himself as a
commodity."[13]

As Fidel has noted many times in recent years, however,
economists and technocrats and administrators trained in the
Moscow tradition fear and detest volunteer work brigades. The
manager-types, the social engineers, who really don't think the
working class is or should be the ruling class, do everything in
their power to kill the brigades, to deaden initiative, to push
the working class out of political life.

The organization of volunteer labor by administrators on
state farms who don't like volunteer brigades, and didn't want
them anyway, was often slipshod and wasteful; the distribution
of the products being grown and harvested by the brigades was
a disaster. As a result, what began as a revolutionary social
movement to meet the food crisis rapidly turned into its oppo-

---

13. Ernesto Che Guevara, Fidel Castro, *Socialism and Man in Cuba* (New York:
Pathfinder, 1989) p. 9.

site. The disorganization and lack of proletarian leadership had demoralizing consequences.

I've spoken with many friends and comrades both from Cuba and from the United States and other countries who have participated over the past year or two in the volunteer work brigades in the countryside. They all have similar stories—how they sat for most of a day next to a field of cabbage they had harvested waiting for a wagon to come pick up the produce, but no transportation ever materialized. And no one organized them to do anything productive instead.

Such examples of "hurry up and wait," of bureaucratic contempt for the importance of other human beings' time and energies, were repeated over and over, on a grand scale—with the inevitable demoralizing results. So the volunteer brigades have declined, as they were bound to unless they had become part of a broader revolutionary movement to transform the leadership of the state farms, with the workers themselves coming forward to take production in hand.

Cuba is not the first workers and farmers government whose revolutionary leadership has turned to the organization of co-operatives in order to revive agricultural production and strengthen the alliance of working people in city and country-side. This was an important part of what Lenin advocated during the period of the New Economic Policy in the Soviet workers and peasants republic more than seventy years ago.

At the time, the Soviet Union was still emerging from several years of civil war and imperialist military intervention that had decimated and exhausted the urban working class and devastated industrial and agricultural production. The vast majority of rural toilers—and this is different from Cuba today, of course—were peasants who tilled small family plots. In this situation, Lenin argued, encouraging peasants to form cooperatives was the road toward organizing them under the leadership of the working class to advance the building of socialism.

It's useful to go back to what Lenin had to say in "On Cooperation."[14] These articles—written in January 1923, less than two months prior to the stroke that finally debilitated him— were part of the political battle Lenin was leading against a rising petty-bourgeois layer within the bureaucracy of the state, the Communist Party, and various economic enterprises. He wrote:

> It seems to me that not enough attention is being paid to the co-operative movement in our country. . . .
> By adopting NEP we made a concession to the peasant as a trader, to the principle of private trade; it is precisely for this reason (contrary to what some people think) that the co-operative movement is of such immense importance. All we actually need under NEP is to organise the population of Russia in co-operative societies on a sufficiently large scale, for we have now found that degree of combination of private interest, of private commercial interest, with state supervision and control of this interest, that degree of its subordination to the common interests which was formerly the stumbling-block for very many socialists.
>
> Indeed, the power of the state over all large-scale means of production, political power in the hands of the proletariat, the alliance of this proletariat with the many millions of small and very small peasants, the assured proletarian leadership of the peasantry, etc.—is this not all that is necessary to build a complete socialist society out of co-operatives, out of co-operatives alone . . . under NEP? Is this not all that is necessary to build a complete socialist society? It is still not the building of socialist society, but it is all that is necessary and sufficient for it.

---

14. V.I. Lenin, *Collected Works*, vol. 33 (Moscow: Progress Publishers, 1966), pp. 467-71.

The dismantling of the state farms and their breakup into cooperatives is a retreat. But when economic conditions have deteriorated to the point where it is no longer possible to plan production in the countryside, then the working class has to retreat. Workers can't pretend to have conquered the conditions for advancing the collectivization and mechanization of agriculture on huge state farms when they are faced with the necessity of using oxen instead of tractors and other machinery. The large fields simply can't be tended under such conditions. And the top-heavy bureaucratic structure and management of the old state farms were a further barrier to the workers themselves taking this new situation in hand and seeking solutions.

It is too early to draw a balance sheet on the UBPCs. The indications are that the sugar crop this year may be even lower than the 4.2 million tons harvested in 1993.[15] There has been no substantial change in the supply of fruits, vegetables, or root crops coming into the cities. Some signs of improvement have been reported on several fronts, however. Food consumption by UBPC families has increased, and the construction of housing for agricultural workers, much of it organized on a volunteer basis, has reportedly gone up over the past year as well. Many of these new homes are what Cubans today call *"bajo consumo"*—low consumption—houses, which they have learned to build using substitutes for cement and other hard-to-get supplies. Further retreats will be necessary, however, before the production and distribution of food and other crops first stabilizes and then begins to substantially increase.

As with other measures being undertaken today, the dynamics

---

15. The 1994 crop fell to a reported 4 million tons, due in part to heavy rains and flooding that prevented some fields from being harvested and crippling shortages of everything from fuel to boots.

and consequences of the UBPCs will be determined by the outcome of much bigger political struggles between contending
class forces both inside Cuba and internationally. There has
been very little public discussion in Cuba about the formation of
the UBPCs, despite the sweeping character of the move. In many
ways, this is one of the most negative things we can point to. It
was simply announced last September, and implementation began immediately. There was nothing comparable to the *parlamentos obreros* to involve the entire working class in discussing the
problems and finding solutions. It is evident, however, that there
are various opinions concerning the formation of the co-ops.

The chairman of the Commission on Economic Reform of
the National Assembly, Osvaldo Martínez, recently told *Cuba
Business* magazine, published in Great Britain, that "one of the
problems at the moment is that the cooperative members
themselves"—that is, the workers from the previous state farms
—"have still to become aware that they themselves are the owners. . . ." In other words, the problem is that the workers still
think like workers, and Martínez considers this negative. "It's
not easy to change a style of work, of thinking that's developed
over thirty years," he added, which is true. The obstacle, however, is not the workers but the weight of the bureaucracy that
has not yet been displaced.

To cite another example, this one from the United States,
Harvard professor Jorge Domínguez—a Cuban-American who
is no supporter of the revolution—told the *Miami Herald* that
he hopes the UBPCs are "the first step toward privatization of
state agriculture" in Cuba. "If you can't own the land, if you
can't subdivide it, if you must sell to the state, the changes are
not going to be really radical."

These comments by Martínez and Domínguez go right to the
heart of the class struggle unfolding in Cuba today. The UBPC
members are *not* owners of the land. They are owners of the
product of their labor. The land remains nationalized in Cuba.
And members of the cooperatives have not suddenly become a
class of "owners" as opposed to workers.

Although a retreat, the formation of the UBPCs is not in contradiction to the socialist direction of the revolution in Cuba. Under the circumstances, in fact, it offers a chance for the working class in the countryside to begin taking greater control of agricultural production and to join with the working class in the cities in tackling the problem of distribution. The interviews the *Militant* conducted with members of some of the new UBPCs confirmed the complaints of people like Martínez: the UBPC members indeed acted and talked and reacted like workers. They liked the change because they thought they could organize their resources and labor to be more productive. They wanted to stop carrying the deadweight of so many administrators and "advisers." They hoped to make their cooperatives more democratic and effective instruments of production than the previous, bureaucratized state farms.

The working class in Cuba

Let's turn now to take a look at the second question: Is the proletarian revolution still alive in Cuba? Does a decisive layer of the working class still have the consciousness, determination, and capacity to fight to defend its historic course? We've already dealt with aspects of this in answering the first question, of course. The two are inseparable.

If your only source of information about what's happening in Cuba were the weekly *Granma International,* which many of you read, I don't think you would answer this question in the affirmative. Over the past couple years, *Granma*'s pages have been increasingly taken up by articles about the newest Spanish hotel on Varadero beach, or Mexican debt-swap deal, or British trade delegation visit, or some other investment opportunity in Cuba. To the degree there is much of anything about the working class, it usually consists of articles presumably addressed to potential capitalist investors about how wonderful "our workers" are—how well-educated, how stable, how disciplined they are.

If you read *Trabajadores,* the newspaper of the CTC, the Central Organization of Cuban Workers, however, you begin to see a more accurate view of the working class in Cuba, I believe. And you see a different class perspective expressed in commentaries and on the editorial page.

You can't figure out what is happening in the working class in Cuba by following the major bourgeois media in the United States or elsewhere either. That is not just because the reporters, newscasters, and editors consciously distort the truth, which they often do. They start with an editorial line, report whatever seems to confirm their position, and ignore what doesn't. But there is something even deeper: there is a class bias that blinds them. Their own conditions of life often prevent them from even knowing what questions to ask. They are always somewhat off balance, because they don't understand what is important to working people in Cuba and what is not.

Fundamentally, it's related to the same question we face in the United States. How many articles do you read that tell you anything about what is going on inside the working class in the United States, or Sweden, or New Zealand? With rare exceptions, they don't have a clue.

A newspaper like the *Miami Herald*, for example, despite its hostility toward the revolution, covers Cuba consistently and provides useful facts about particular political developments. But the paper is absolutely useless when it comes to trying to understand social and class dynamics in Cuba.

It is only from *inside* the factories and inside the industrial unions, the basic defense organizations of our class, that an accurate picture is possible of what's happening politically in the working class. Being there doesn't mean your answers will be correct; but without being there you don't even have a starting point. That's why the communist movement has an advantage. When class-conscious workers visit Cuba, we go to factories and farms, as well as hospitals, child-care centers, and universities. We talk as workers to workers, as fighters to fighters. And we speak the same political language.

More than anything else, the confidence with which we answer the question—Has the working class in Cuba been defeated? Has the consciousness and will to fight for a socialist course been broken?—is based on our own experiences there in the factories and in the fields. The international team of some dozen worker correspondents for the *Militant* and *PM* who altogether spent nearly six weeks in Cuba earlier this year were, above all, trying to answer this question to our own satisfaction. We knew we could rely on no one else. And we tried to convey the answers we came to in the articles we wrote.

We went to numerous meetings of the workers assemblies. We visited several of the newly established UBPCs. We interviewed dozens of workers. And more than anything else, we listened.

We heard workers get up in assemblies and confront the management over the theft of tobacco, the theft of meat, the theft of fish, the theft of sugar from the factories, saying, You are responsible; the problem is up there where you are sitting.

We listened to them demand that their government confiscate and return property that had been stolen from the workplaces, saying, either you do it, or we will.

We listened to them vehemently reject any steps toward taxation of wages. We heard them demand that price increases or rate hikes that might be necessary—such as charging more for lunches in factory cafeterias, or charging for school uniforms—be done in such as way as to protect the lowest-paid workers.

The *Militant* reported the confident response by workers at a Havana dairy plant to criticisms by supervisors that they had been breaking too many milk bottles. Workers replied that the conveyor belts were set up badly and that their proposals for changes that would have prevented such breakage had been ignored. They insisted that they be allowed to correct the problem without further delay.

Over and over, workers in the assemblies demanded that they be allowed to reorganize the work force in the factories so that everyone could work productively. One example of this, reported by the *Militant*, came from another worker at the same

Havana dairy plant. This worker was concerned about the growing problem of excess labor in the plant due to the sharp drop in domestic milk production and disappearance of dried milk supplies that used to come primarily from East Germany.

Of particular interest was the way he explained his proposal. "I don't want to be laid off," he said. "I hate to think about what I would do if I had no job and couldn't afford to buy food for my family." But, he noted, coming to the factory every day when there is no work to do is demoralizing as well. "Let's take some of the land surrounding the factory and organize ourselves to farm it and produce badly needed food. Why can't we do that immediately?" he asked.

WE LISTENED. We asked questions. We talked to workers there about what workers in the United States and other capitalist countries face. We exchanged experiences. And we knew we were not talking to workers whose spirit had been broken. The attitude of workers setting the pace in factory after factory was, "We can do it." We felt comfortable among workers who were ready to fight, to change things, to produce, to lead. After participating in a few workers assemblies, you understand why Wall Street doesn't think investment perspectives are particularly bright in Cuba today. Reestablishing capitalist relations of production there would not be easy. In fact it would be impossible, short of inflicting a crushing defeat on a strong, cohesive, and confident proletariat in Cuba, a working class that thinks socially and acts politically. And that's not the direction in which history is moving.

This is why *Granma International* and others in Cuba really aren't very convincing when they point out how well-educated and disciplined the working class is, in order to convince capitalists why they should invest in Cuba. As we know from our own experience, a working class that is well-educated, organized, and self-confident is not exactly what capitalists are on the lookout for. They are more interested in workers who believe they are lucky to be hired to work long hours, for low wages, under brutal speedup conditions—and who have no historical memory as a class, no effective organization, and no battle-tested leadership. The capitalists are not looking for young workers who are more internationalist than workers anywhere else in the world; who are less divided by racism than any other working class; who consider it their right that women in Cuba have made more gains in three and a half decades than anywhere else on earth during any comparable time span. The employing class worldwide takes a look at such a working class and isn't really convinced it's a hot prospect for extended capitalist exploitation.

Thirty-five years of fighting for socialism in Cuba, despite errors and setbacks and real weaknesses, have resulted in a working class that is more cultured in the broadest human sense. They are more citizens of the world, more citizens of time.

IN EVERYTHING THAT LEADERS of the Socialist Workers Party have written and said in public talks over the past few years, we've emphasized that the working class in Cuba—despite the enormous difficulties and challenges it faces—is stronger today. It is a working class that was politically strengthened by the rectification process, even though that proletarian renewal was abruptly cut short by the economic crisis that unfolded from 1990 on. Without the rectification process that began in earnest in 1986, odds are high that as the bureaucratic regimes in Eastern Europe and the Soviet Union came tumbling down there would have been major social tremors in Cuba too.

In fact, the prospects for the working class in Cuba have been strengthened, not weakened, by the crumbling of these Stalinist regimes. The working class is less weighed down today than ever before by the burden of Stalinist political miseducation. They carry less political baggage from the counterrevolutionary counterfeit that passed for communism for so many years. They are less isolated from the class struggle around the world.

All this is especially true of the new, younger generation who are taking on more and more of the leadership challenge today in Cuba. The communists in this generation have less of a stake in defending past policies if they become convinced they were erroneous. They are looking for working-class continuity and a way forward. And the communist leadership in Cuba has taken steps in recent years to draw more cadres from this generation into political responsibility in the government and the party.

Finding that continuity and the way forward, of course, also means going back. For many comrades in Cuba it means going back to reread and restudy the basic works of Marxism in light of the events of the last half decade and to reevaluate what they had been taught. It means recovering the real history and political lessons from the experiences of the modern working-class movement—from Marx and Engels, to Lenin and the Bolshevik-led workers and peasants government in the Soviet Union, to the practical political consequences of the Stalinist degeneration following Lenin's death. It means learning the real history of the Spanish revolution of the 1930s and why it was defeated, the real record of the German Communist Party and the rise of fascism in the Third Reich—the price the working class internationally paid for the betrayals of Stalinism. It means going back to Che Guevara and the political and economic course he fought for in Cuba. It means combining study with action, learning through practice. It means earning the right to be called communists, leaders of men and women fighting to lead a class along its historic line of march.

There is more openness and discussion on these kinds of questions among young people today than at any time since the generation that led the working people of Cuba to power in the early 1960s.

There are also more young people who openly proclaim they are sick of hearing terms like socialism and communism and never want to listen to another political speech in their lives. They feel helpless and hopeless. That's part of the real leadership challenge.

The changes taking place in Cuba today, the political ferment, is only possible because—unlike what eventually happened in the Soviet Union—communist continuity in Cuba has never been broken. This is true despite the political deformations we've been discussing, resulting from the influence of Stalinism that came via Moscow for so many years.

A broad communist vanguard of the working class, spanning several generations, lives and fights in Cuba—from the fields and factories, to the universities, to the highest levels of the government and Communist Party. The Marxist legacy of Che is still part of the revolution, something that can be fought for, recovered, and conquered by the new generation seeking to defend the revolution's socialist foundations under today's difficult conditions in order to continue moving forward.

A<small>T THE SAME TIME</small>, the class divide is deeper in Cuba today than anytime since the early years of the revolution. The world of the professionals, the technicians, the intellectuals, the administrative personnel is light-years away from the world of the fields and factory production lines. I'm not referring primarily to those middle-class layers—and they are substantial—that are looking out for number one and make no bones about it. I'm not talking about the hotel managers at Varadero beach with their gold chains and expensive watches. I'm talking about something far more important. There is a divide between communists who are workers and communists working jobs not related to production.

This is very striking. It's not a categorical, schematic divide, of course. Yet all of us who have spent time in Cuba have had similar experiences—discussions with members of the party, defenders of the revolution, working in all kinds of professions, where you realize after five or ten minutes that you are talking to someone who is politically demoralized. The difficulties of daily life—food, transportation, electricity, water, clothing, keeping clean, whatever—grind people down. They project a sense of despair, sometimes near hysteria, about the future.

I don't think this is hard to understand. Because of their social position, their class position, they often don't have any confidence that they can affect what is happening, that what they do matters. They don't have the calm confidence expressed by layers of the working class that *we* are the producers, that *we*, through our capacity to labor, can create the means necessary to get out of the crisis. As one worker put it so directly, "Now is not the time for weeping and wailing. We have the courage to get ourselves out of the hole we're in."

Some Cuban comrades joke that the class composition in the country is actually improving every day under these pressures. A disproportionate number of those who take off in search of more comfortable conditions in the United States or Europe, of course, are from the relatively better-off layers. Many of these middle-class Cubans are able to travel abroad for one or another reason and simply don't return. The director of Cuba's famous film festival recently turned up in Miami, for example, complaining about the difficulties of organizing a film festival when there are daily electrical blackouts!

But the working class really doesn't need people like that to find a way forward. Nor do they need the discouraged friends and neighbors who jump on inner tubes lashed together hoping to survive the Florida Straits and strike it rich in Miami. The number of Cubans leaving the island by this means has reached record levels already this year and will grow, especially now in the summer months with relatively calm seas. Many individuals from the middle-class layers, especially those who are young, are among these rafters too. Most Cubans wish them well and then go back to work, convinced that by pulling together, the society they have built with sweat and blood over the last three decades will not only survive but come out stronger. The test of the past five years—the fact that through their own collective effort, and with no economic aid from the former Soviet bloc, they have survived, despite dire predictions by class enemies and fainthearts alike—has, in fact, reinforced the political confidence of a broad vanguard of workers in Cuba.

There is one image I like that captures the proletarian spirit in Cuba today, the continued vitality of the revolution and will to impose broader working-class justice in face of petty-bourgeois, bureaucratic resistance, corruption, and sabotage. That is the image of *los amarillos*. They are special traffic inspectors, called the "ones in yellow" because of the color of their uniforms. Their task is to stop cars with state license plates and fill them up with passengers who need a ride in the direction the driver is going. *Los amarillos* are among the heroes of the working class in Cuba today.

It is these experiences, and many more like them, that help us affirm with confidence that the working class is still fighting for its historic course in Cuba, that the fight for the communist heart and soul of the Cuban revolution is still on. Nothing has been settled.

Defense of Cuba's socialist revolution
The answers to our first two questions are the starting point for answering the third: What are our tasks and responsibilities as a communist workers party in defending the Cuban revolution?

We don't have a separate approach to this work. In defending Cuba, we don't do something different from what we do in other political activities. To the contrary. We do the same kinds of work and look to the same class forces whether here in the United States, or in Cuba, or in New Zealand, or in South Africa, or France, or anywhere else in the world.

We sell books, newspapers, and magazines that help knit the communist continuity of our class and increase the odds that out of our struggles our class will forge a leadership capable of meeting the challenges we face. We talk about socialism and the lessons of a century and a half of class battles. We bring fighting workers, farmers, and young people together to share their experiences, to learn from each other, to identify with each other, to reinforce each other, as they seek a communist road forward for our class and all humanity. We work together with whoever we can to organize public actions around concrete demands in defense of the Cuban revolution, and in the process attract new forces toward the working class and its line of march.

One of the conclusions that has been driven home time and again by our political work over the past few years is that the literature tables we put up during a Caterpillar strike solidarity rally in Peoria, Illinois, are the same as those we put up at the University of Matanzas in Cuba or an ANC congress in South Africa. The discussions we have are the same; the issues that workers and youth want to discuss are the same.

This is the heart of everything: the response of fellow workers, of fellow fighters to each other. The borders, the language differences don't matter. They have no difficulty recognizing and responding to the integrity and combativity of others like themselves.

That's why Mark Curtis gets such a response in Cuba, for example.[16] When you show the video on the frame-up of Mark Curtis to a group of workers in Cuba, they immediately identify with Mark and his battle for justice. They understand what he is fighting for. They don't need an explanation of why the cops and other government officials would want to frame up a revolutionary worker like Mark and go to such lengths to keep him in prison. They see the video, they read some of the literature, they learn the facts, and they say, Yes, Mark is our kind of person.

It's also why Cuban youth leader Pável Díaz got a standing ovation from locked-out workers at the A.E. Staley corn-pro-

---

16. Mark Curtis, a socialist and union packinghouse worker, was framed up and sentenced to twenty-five years in prison in 1988 on charges of rape and burglary. A leader of the Socialist Workers Party, Curtis has repeatedly been denied parole by Iowa prison authorities, despite an international defense campaign demanding his release. Information on the case, including two videos and many pieces of literature in English, Spanish, and French, are distributed by the Mark Curtis Defense Committee in Des Moines, Iowa. Also see the Pathfinder pamphlet *The Frame-Up of Mark Curtis: A Packinghouse Worker's Fight for Justice* by Margaret Jayko.

cessing plant, in Decatur, Illinois, when he was on tour here in the United States this year.[17] As Pável described what they are fighting for in Cuba, many of the Staley workers identified with him as a fellow warrior up against many of the same powerful forces they are confronting.

When Mark Curtis's story is told in Cuba, when Pável Díaz speaks to fighting workers in the United States, we find we are speaking the same language.

A concrete picture of what's happening in the class struggle in the United States, explained by working people who know this reality from the inside out, has a real impact in Cuba. We've experienced this many times over in the last years. The most recent example was just a month or so ago, in June, when two communist workers from the United States—Laura Garza and Aaron Ruby—took part in the Sixth Cuba-U.S. Conference on Philosophy and Social Science at the University of Havana and reported on that gathering for the *Militant* and *Perspectiva Mundial.* Laura's remarks made an impact, and she was featured in the article on the conference in the newspaper *Juventud Rebelde.*

Identifying her as "a worker at an aluminum door and window factory in Miami," the paper, published by the Union of Young Communists, cited Laura as saying that given the stepped-up employers' assault on working people in the United States, including on the growing numbers of immigrants from Latin America, now "is a good time to work with those forces to try and make them understand the need to eliminate the coercive measures against Cuba" by the U.S. government. The "hope and enor-

---

17. In March and April 1994, Pável Díaz conducted an eight-week speaking tour of forty cities in fifteen states in the United States. In Illinois, he spoke to some 250 locked-out union workers at the A.E. Staley plant and met officers of the United Auto Workers local at the Caterpillar plant in the same town. In other parts of the United States, Díaz met with airlines workers, with striking Teamsters and steelworkers, and with packinghouse workers, farmworkers, and farmers. He spoke at fifty-three university and three high school meetings as well.

mous dignity" she found among working people in Cuba, Laura told the paper, renewed her conviction in their capacity to solve the problems facing the revolution.

ONLY BY LOOKING AT OUR WORK in defense of the Cuban revolution in the broad political context we are discussing at this convention can we appreciate why what we do here in the United States genuinely weighs in the balance of the outcome in Cuba— not in the material sense of substantively easing the current shortages, but in a political sense. Because the fight for the future of the socialist revolution in Cuba is a fight above all for communist workers to link up with other communists around the world, reinforce each other in struggle, and reknit our common political heritage. Our movement brings a necessary and irreplaceable piece into that battle, because the fight we have waged for some seventy years to maintain communist continuity and build a proletarian party on that foundation is unique.

Armed with that class axis as we work to defend Cuba, and given the long-term priorities and goals flowing from that work, we participate, along with others, in building and helping to lead activities that reach out as broadly as possible to new forces. In this context, the political and tactical problems we confront at any particular moment, and the liberal and Stalinist perspectives of various political currents that take part in and sometimes dominate Cuba solidarity groups, take on their proper place, weight, and proportion.

The consistency of our communist line in defense of the Cuban revolution extends from the visit in 1960 by Socialist Workers Party presidential candidate Farrell Dobbs and *Militant* editor Joseph Hansen, to the trip in 1992 by SWP presidential candidate James Warren and *Militant* reporter Selva Nebbia. It extends from the active participation by members of the SWP and Young Socialist Alliance in the First Latin American Youth Congress in the summer of 1960, through the initiation of the Venceremos Brigade in 1969, to the work brigades and tours in

the United States and Cuba that young socialists will be organizing coming out of this convention. It's all part of the same
communist line of march.

This political framework enables us to respond in a timely
way to every real opening to work with others to organize educational activities to tell the truth about the socialist revolution
in Cuba and take to the streets to protest Washington's economic blockade, travel ban, occupation of Guantánamo Bay,
and other unceasing efforts to weaken and destroy the revolutionary government. This class approach equips us to fight effectively to prevent race-baiting, agent-baiting, red-baiting, and
anticommunism from gaining ground among Cuba solidarity
forces and in the broader workers movement. That kind of political poison, promoted by Stalinist and other class-collaborationist or ultraleft currents in the workers movement, serves
only to debilitate the capacity of the working class to fight.

The challenge to communist workers, as in all the political
work we carry out, is to turn toward every opportunity for united
action, never abstaining or adapting politically to the liberal capi-
talist-oriented forces that often predominate. What we are always
looking for is the same thing: opportunities and initiatives to
bring greater numbers of workers, working farmers, and fighting
youth together in struggle along this proletarian line of march.

These are the questions we should address, discuss, and decide today as the delegates to this convention.

SUMMARY OF DISCUSSION

[After more than three hours of discussion by convention delegates on the report, Waters presented the following summary
prior to the vote.]

First of all, there's a small item of business. After the report
this morning, a conference participant gave me a copy of a pro-
motional mailing that recently came her way. It seems that the

V.C. Acquisition Limited Partnership, based in the Cayman Islands, is offering to buy up any outstanding shares of the Vertientes-Camaguey Sugar Company. They're evidently betting they can buy cheap from those who held stock before the revolution, and sell them a bit dearer to people taken in by the talk about the impending collapse of the revolutionary government in Cuba.

The president of the Vertientes-Camaguey Sugar Company himself informs recipients of the mailing that "the Company is required to advise its shareholders of its position with respect to the offer. Given the history of the Company, the claims established against the Cuban Government for payment or return of the expropriated properties, and the political situation in Cuba, your Board of Directors feels it cannot express an opinion, and must, therefore, remain neutral as to the offer."

Capitalists never give up hope of redeeming their past property holdings, one way or the other!

Youth and the working-class perspective

Let me start with the important point raised at the beginning of the discussion, and addressed by a couple of delegates, concerning youth in Cuba and the leadership questions posed.

It's important to recognize that young people in Cuba don't have a political perspective on the revolution that's different from that of other Cubans. There are conflicting class pressures and responses among youth in Cuba just as there are among all generations, and just as there are among young people in the United States or anywhere else.

What you do find, of course, is that young people in Cuba, like young people the world over, are often more impatient for solutions, more open to new proposals, and quicker to consider ideas that are taboo to a larger number of their elders. They have less of a stake in defending past policies that were erroneous, and they often have more energy and will to blaze new trails.

The real communist leadership challenge, as one delegate

pointed out, is not to win young people in Cuba to the Union of Young Communists, the UJC—that needs to be done, of course—but above all to win them to the side of the working class. Those who are despairing what the future will bring, those who think that socialism has proven itself a failure, those who never want to hear the word spoken again, will be won—or won back—to the revolution only if the working class seems to offer a clear alternative that its leaders explain and fight for. A new generation will become revolutionaries—communists— only if they see a powerful class force that is leading the way forward and they become part of it.

Isn't that how you became a communist? How could it be any different in Cuba?

T HE PROBLEM IS NOT that the way forward may first demand a large-scale retreat. Every fighter is ready to maneuver. But you have to know where you're headed and have confidence in yourself, your comrades-in-arms, and your commanders. The biggest problem in Cuba today is that this longer-term class perspective is not clearly presented.

As the report explained and tried to concretize, class divisions are deepening in Cuba, and decisive layers of the working class, as well as important forces among the youth, are not broken or demoralized. They are fighting to limit the retreat, to cede no more territory than necessary. But this is difficult to see except from inside the working class, and even there experience and consciousness are not generalized. One of the delegates who has been in Cuba recently made the correct observation in the discussion today that the lack of a clear political perspective is among the things that weighs most heavily on people in Cuba, including on cadres who are revolutionists and communists—"Where is this all going? I may or may not agree with any particular measure, but where are we headed? There is no clear battle plan."

The political disorientation, as we've been discussing, is greatest outside the working class. The middle-class professionals, intellectuals, administrative personnel, and government functionaries—and their families and others they influence —comprise a large nonproletarian social layer. And the social distinctions among them and between them and the working class have been sharpened, not lessened, by the influence of the highly tracked and stratified education system adopted from Stalinism. Out of Cuba's eleven million people, we're talking a million or more, not a few hundred thousand, let alone thousands. We're talking about substantial numbers within the membership and leadership of the Communist Party and Union of Young Communists as well.

The Communist Party of Cuba is a mass party. It has 700,000 members, and the UJC has more than 600,000. The members of these organizations come from all layers of society in Cuba, and a majority are not currently workers in the factories or fields. So disorientation and confusion, as well as the struggle for perspectives, take place among members of the party and youth organization as well as around them.

That being said, we should reiterate two points above all.

First, despite all the pressures and difficulties they are confronting, despite various political errors and social deformations, a decisive component of the Communist Party—which certainly does not mean every member—continues to chart a course to defend the socialist conquests of the working class, continues to organize and lead the toilers to bring their weight to bear in determining policy. They do this at the same time they make necessary concessions to the capitalist market in order to try to secure investment and trade.

Second, the class consciousness and capacity of the working class in Cuba to fight for its historic interests has not been broken. Restorationist social forces are gaining ground in Cuba today, but the working class too is strong, stronger than most observers come close to grasping.

We must be conscious, however, that these issues, which are so important to the defense of the socialist revolution in Cuba, and which we are trying to clarify for ourselves, are rarely posed in clear class terms in Cuba.

New Economic Policy

In this respect it's politically misleading to draw an analogy between the retreat under way in Cuba today and the New Economic Policy carried out under Bolshevik leadership in the Soviet workers and peasants republic in the early 1920s, following the devastation of several years of civil war and imperialist intervention. Several delegates made references to the NEP in the course of the discussion. The difference, above all, is the question of leadership and political clarity. Lenin and other central Bolshevik leaders repeatedly explained to the working class the reasons for the necessary retreat; the proletarian foundations of the revolution that made the retreat possible; and the limits that needed to be placed on the retreat in face of the inevitable strengthening of capitalist and capitalist-minded layers. In an October 1921 report, for example, Lenin said:

> In substance, our New Economic Policy signifies that, having sustained severe defeat [on the economic front], we have started a strategical retreat. We said in effect: "Before we are completely routed, let us retreat and reorganise everything, but on a firmer basis." If Communists deliberately examine the question of the New Economic Policy there cannot be the slightest doubt in their minds that we have sustained a very severe defeat on the economic front. In the circumstances it is inevitable, of course, for some people to become very despondent, almost panic-stricken, and because of the retreat, these people will begin to give way to panic. . . .
>
> From the point of view of strategy the root question is: who will take advantage of the new situation first? The whole question is—whom will the peasantry follow? The proletariat, which wants to build socialist society? Or the capitalist, who says, "Let us turn back; it is safer that way;

we don't know anything about this socialism they have invented?"[18]

A few months later, at the eleventh congress of the Communist Party in March 1922, Lenin reaffirmed the necessity of the NEP but emphasized the need to "call a halt" to aspects of the retreat that were no longer necessary and were endangering the worker-peasant alliance that was the foundation of the proletarian state power:

> Retreat is a difficult matter, especially for revolutionaries who are accustomed to advance; especially when they have been accustomed to advance with enormous success for several years; especially if they are surrounded by revolutionaries in other countries who are longing for the time when they can launch an offensive. Seeing that we were retreating, several of them burst into tears in a disgraceful and childish manner, as was the case at the last extended Plenary Meeting of the Executive Committee of the Communist International. . . .
>
> Perhaps it is now difficult for me to understand this West-European mentality, although I lived for quite a number of years in those marvelous democratic countries as an exile. Perhaps from their point of view this is such a difficult matter to understand that it is enough to make one weep. We, at any rate, have no time for sentiment. It was clear to us that because we advanced so successfully for many years and had achieved so many extraordinary victories (and all this in a country that was in an appalling state of ruin and lacked material resources!), to consolidate that advance, since we had gained so much, it was absolutely essential for us to retreat. We could not hold all the positions we had

---

18. "The New Economic Policy and the Tasks of the Political Education Departments," in Lenin, *Collected Works*, vol. 33, pp. 63-65.

captured in the first onslaught. . . .

When an army is in retreat a hundred times more discipline is required than when it is advancing, because during an advance everybody presses forward. If everybody started rushing back now, it would spell immediate and inevitable disaster. The most important thing at such a moment is to retreat in good order, to fix the precise limits of the retreat, and not to give way to panic.

In that 1922 report, Lenin pointed to the growing bourgeois-minded layers in the state and party apparatus who had previously opposed the workers and peasants government but now said, "I am in favour of supporting Soviet power because it has taken the road that will lead it to the ordinary bourgeois state." He continued:

[These individuals] express the sentiments of thousands and tens of thousands of bourgeois, or of Soviet employees whose function it is to operate our New Economic Policy. This is the real and main danger. And that is why attention must be concentrated mainly on the question: "Who will win?" I have spoken about competition. No direct onslaught is being made on us now; nobody is clutching us by the throat. True, we have yet to see what will happen tomorrow; but today we are not being subjected to armed attack. Nevertheless, the fight against capitalist society has become a hundred times more fierce and perilous, because we are not always able to tell enemies from friends.[19]

Fight for communist perspective
Unfortunately, we can't quote from any similarly clear, communist

19. "Eleventh Congress of the Communist Party of Russia (Bolsheviks)," in Lenin, *Collected Works*, vol. 33, pp. 280-82, 286-87.

explanation being put forward in Cuba today. Aspects of such a working-class perspective are laid out in some speeches by Fidel, along the lines quoted a couple of times in the report this morning. But the explanations are partial, and too rarely presented by others in the central party leadership. Read *Granma International* every week and imagine how confused—how demoralized—you would be if that were your only source of information about what's happening in Cuba, to say nothing of the rest of the world. *Trabajadores* and *Juventud Rebelde* are politically stronger than *Granma*. And the daily *Granma* in Cuba is better than the international weekly edition. But *Granma International* is not an aberration.

This is another reason why the things we write and publish, and the political work we do, are important. We explain politics to friends and comrades in Cuba the same way we do here at our convention, the same way we do in the factories or on campus. We always put what's happening in Cuba in the context of the class struggle in the world—starting with the genuine crisis of capitalism, the growing conflicts among the imperialist powers, the polarization and explosive pressures that are building. We explain, concretely, what's happening in the United States, what's happening in South Africa, what's happening in Eastern Europe and China, what's happening to our fellow workers in the Americas. We put forward a world political perspective, a communist world outlook, that workers and revolutionary-minded youth in Cuba are eager to hear and discuss.

Despite the confusion and absence of a clear, longer-range political perspective, however, the strength of the working class in Cuba, as they confront the challenges they face, is what keeps coming through. "We know the future does not lie with capitalism. That's the past, even if not the past I personally lived through. There's got to be a way to get out of this hole and go forward"—that's the response by the majority of working people in Cuba. They think the social relations they have begun to establish are superior to those of the capitalist jungle. They look to the revolutionary government as *their* government, a state power that is fighting with them not against them, and that is ultimately answerable to them.

The majority of people in Cuba today have never lived under capitalism. Grandparents and sometimes parents tell them what capitalism was like, but that's a minority. Yet many among the younger generations do have some personal knowledge of the capitalist world. Hundreds of thousands went to Angola as internationalist volunteers, or to Nicaragua, Grenada, Ethiopia, or elsewhere. They have seen capitalism at work. It's not all out of a textbook; it's not all stories from their parents and grandparents.

So, many young Cubans will tell you, with feeling: "We know what capitalism is. We know that what is the past for us remains the present for most of the world, and we don't want that to be the future."

To prevent that willingness to fight from being dissipated, however, revolutionary-minded workers and youth in Cuba need the same political tools you do, the same that are needed by communist workers anywhere in the world. How confident would you be without the arsenal of political weapons you have available? Without your communist political continuity? Without drawing on the accumulated lessons of struggles by our class for 150 years?

Only the scientific historical perspective gained in this way enables us to say with confidence—as Marx and Engels did—what the class struggle is leading toward. Not in a prophetic sense— when and where the next revolutionary struggles will occur, and whether or not they will result in victories. Nobody can predict that. But we know that the economic, social, and political contradictions inherent in capitalist social relations will multiply; that the class struggle between the exploiting classes and the workers and their allies will continue to erupt; and that our class has the capacity and the will to forge a proletarian leadership that can organize the toilers to make a revolution and win.

We know our class will get its chance to lead human society out of the abyss. We know that this perspective is not some utopian notion pulled out of the hat of an idealist dreamer in the nine-teenth century. It is a scientific world outlook that makes the laws of the class struggle understandable, that makes all recorded his-tory comprehensible. Without this unbroken communist conti-nuity right back to the foundations of the modern workers move-ment, we'd be as rudderless as most of those who consider themselves part of the "left" today the world over. But this clear historical perspective is what communists inside Cuba are trying to find their way to, as well.

UBPCs, taxes

In the absence of clear, *class* explanations from the leadership, there is a lot of confusion in Cuba about many measures taken by the government to address the economic crisis.

Take the new farm cooperatives, the UBPCs, for example. Are they a necessary retreat, the goal of which is to better prepare workers in countryside and city to advance toward food self-sufficiency, increase their control over production, and reduce the size and weight of the separate administrative layer? Or are they a first step toward restoring capitalist social relations on the land? Few people are willing to discuss what is involved because officially no explanation has been given.

Virtually all that's said about the UBPCs is that they've been established in order to try to increase efficiency in the produc-tion of food and export crops such as sugar. Most Cubans ex-press no opinion about the move. They simply hope it will work. They know that the state farm system is in total crisis and the situation is desperate. Why the crisis is so deep, and what lessons should be drawn, is rarely discussed.

In the two provinces surrounding Havana, almost 50 percent of all vegetables and food crops to feed some 3 million people are now being produced by special units of the Revolutionary Armed Forces called the Youth Army of Labor, the EJT. The EJT members are doing military service, but, as a recent article in *Granma* put it, "soldiers and officers leave their military status at the entrance to the farms." These units work "alongside civilians, and contribute the lion's share of the workforce," the article says. There are only around a hundred of these army-run farms, comprising less than 4 percent of agricultural land in Cuba. But the ones surrounding Havana—which is potentially the biggest food-producing area in the country—have for the moment become vital to producing enough to feed Havana.

Nobody in Cuba disputes that something had to be done to boost food crops and restore sugar production. But why is no political perspective for the UBPCs being given? I believe part of the answer is that there is no consensus.

Many in the Communist Party leadership in Cuba today approach the UBPC decision in much the way we've discussed it here, as a necessary retreat. They stand on the positions from the opening years of the revolution that I cited in the report. They are committed to defending the nationalization of the land, and also to organizing production on the UBPCs not along the lines of competition among an emerging layer of property owners but as cooperative labor by class-conscious rural workers. Doing so, they are convinced, will lay the foundation for the revolution to move forward again when conditions allow.

But others, including in the leadership of the Communist Party of Cuba, have a completely different view. They don't see the new cooperative farms as a retreat in any way, shape, or form. They see the UBPCs as the first of many steps leading as rapidly as possible to the privatization of land ownership and expanding capitalist relations of production in agriculture. They see this as a long-overdue step forward, not a retreat.

Such conflicting positions are not explained and debated openly, however, so confusion and demoralization are the inevitable result. Will this prove to be a first step toward reestablishing capitalist property relations on the land? Or will it prepare space to be used to strengthen the working class? There is no right or wrong answer in the abstract. That will be decided in struggle. It will depend on how the cooperatives are led; whether the weight of the working class is brought to bear in the organization and management of labor and production; whether the workers themselves more and more take over the administrative tasks, reducing the size and weight of a separate management caste, much as the volunteer contingents began to do at the height of the rectification process.

It is important to understand that the former state farms are not some special case. Similar questions are posed and the same struggle will break through to the surface more and more in every factory in Cuba. Production has collapsed in many of them too. In face of resistance by bloated administrative layers, workers are trying to assert greater control over production and management and to combat the growing theft and resale on the black market of the tools and the products of their labor. We saw and heard it clearly in the *parlamentos obreros* as the workers told management: shape up or ship out. If you can't do the job, get out of our way because we *can* do it.

Is the working class strong enough, confident enough to take the leadership more and more? We don't know. The class struggle carries no guarantees. All we can offer is the certainty of struggle and the chance to be part of the fight.

Tax policy also is a class question, of course. Wage differences in Cuba today range from a little over 100 pesos a month for the lowest-paid workers to about 450 pesos a month for the most highly paid physicians, engineers, and so on. With a few important modifications, the spread has been substantially the same since the early 1970s. No other country in the world has ever narrowed wage inequality to that degree.

But just as class differentiation is accelerating under today's pressures in Cuba, so is the spread in *income* levels, as opposed simply to wage rates. That's why workers are more than willing to consider the imposition of some kind of income tax. As we discussed in the report, for the lowest-paid workers in particular, inflation and the breakdown of the rationing system are already imposing the most regressive tax conceivable. The working class sees its purchasing power erode from one week to the next. It's quite a different story, however, for the growing layers who have access to dollars, or who traffic in stolen goods on the black market, or some of the self-employed, or those with an additional income flow or privileged access to goods. Under these conditions, a government that defends the interests of the workers must institute an income tax. And a policy guideline to that effect was what the National Assembly adopted in May.

Discussion continues, however, on exactly how that tax will be implemented. Who will pay, and how much? As the report explained, the working class won the first round in the fight. Workers in factory after factory, workplace after workplace, made clear their demand that no taxes be imposed on workers' wages, and the National Assembly meeting in May concurred.

A bureaucrat or a technocrat can try to explain that tax policy is "class neutral." Working people may pay a disproportionate share of their income in taxes, so the story goes, but they get back a disproportionate share in government services and subsidies. But few workers fall for such demagogy. They know that who pays taxes and for what is a political question, a class question—100 percent. It brings class conflict sharply into focus.

In Cuba you often hear complaints that government policy is "paternalistic"—meaning workers get all kinds of services and benefits for which they pay no direct fee. But indirectly workers pay for everything, of course. Their labor makes possible the schools, hospitals, factories, and all else, *all else*. The ration book, as Fidel pointed out, was the revolution's alternative to the former bourgeois tax system—a proletarian as opposed to bourgeois system of distribution.

A steeply progressive income tax, one that exempts the wages of working people, will meet stiff resistance from the expanding capitalist-minded layers in Cuba. The international capitalist "advisers" of the IMF and Spanish variety will demand, as a condition for investment credits, that a bourgeois tax structure and mode of distribution be imposed. The working class will fight tax measures that erode the proletarian norms they have conquered, and demand steeply progressive taxes on nonwage income from all sources. Workers have a very deep—and deepening—class hatred for the *macetas,* the "flower pots," who sit in the sun and just grow, becoming wealthy trafficking in property stolen from the working class.

Once again, however, the fight for a tax policy in the interests of the toiling majority demands that the issues be explained in clear class terms.

The National Assembly is actually meeting to discuss how to concretize different proposals on tax policy tomorrow. So we'll see what they decide.[20]

---

20. At the August 1994 National Assembly meeting delegates discussed, modified, and adopted a new tax law. Despite the accord reached at the May meeting, the draft law presented to the delegates in August contained a provision authorizing taxes on all personal income, including workers' wages. Opposition to this provision was led by delegates representing the labor movement. At the end of nearly twelve hours of debate, a contradictory compromise resolution proposed by Cuban president Fidel Castro was adopted. It established that "as a general principle all income, wages included, is taxable in proportion to amount."

At the same time, with firm support from the central leadership, the Assembly rejected the proposal to tax wages now. "Once the principle has been established," Castro said, "there is no need to establish—either today, tomorrow, or hopefully ever—any income tax [on wages]. I hope circumstances will never compel us to do that."

The income tax adopted applied only to the self-employed. A 5 percent tax on income of private farmers has existed for some years.

A second provision of the new tax law dealing with contributions by workers to the social security fund was also agreed to in principle, though adoption of a specific law implementing it was postponed. In 1967 social security taxes were eliminated along with an 11.9 percent tax on wages. Since then, retirement and sick-leave benefits in Cuba have been funded by a contribution paid by each enterprise equal to 12 percent of its payroll, with the deficit made up out of the state budget.

Given the current large and growing deficit in the social security fund, start-

The disintegrative pressures on the alliance of the working class and small farmers in Cuba have been sharply intensified by precipitous declines in production and the burgeoning black market in food.[21] The number of small farmers who are either refusing to plant, letting the land lie fallow, or are diverting crops from the state distribution network to the black market is significant enough that the phenomenon has become a topic of commentary in the press in Cuba. The ministry of agriculture has announced that measures are under consideration to tax idle land and institute legal proceedings to confiscate fields from farmers who divert crops.

How could things be otherwise? As one of the delegates here pointed out, if a farmer can sell a pig on the black market for ten, twenty, or a even a hundred times the price offered by the state distribution agency, he's going to do so, unless he has working-class consciousness and a communist world outlook. And, yes, under such conditions the alliance of the working class and peasantry will rapidly be frayed.

It was exactly such an accelerating breakdown of social solidarity that convinced the communist leadership in Cuba to

---

ing January 1, 1995, workers will be asked to contribute directly to the fund out of their wages. The exact percentage and how the levy will be organized is still being discussed.

21. In addition to the workers on the remaining state farms and members of the newly formed UBPCs, there are two other groups of toilers in the countryside in Cuba today. There are some 1,200 agricultural and livestock production cooperatives (CPAs) made up of small farmers who have voluntarily pooled their land and work it jointly. Most of these have been established since the late 1970s. In addition, there are more than 100,000 remaining small family farmers who produce individually but participate in more limited credit and service cooperatives. Between them, the members of the CPAs and the small farmers till about 20 percent of the arable land in Cuba and account for more than a third of agricultural output. They produce a majority, in some cases a large majority, of such basic food crops as garlic, tomatoes, onions, sweet potatoes, and carrots, as well as a large percentage of a few export crops such as coffee, tobacco, and cacao.

shut down the six-year-old free farmers market in 1986 at the beginning of the rectification process. The bureaucratic bungling of the state food production and distribution system in Cuba opened the door to profiteering that jacked up food prices and spawned layers of parasitic middlemen who reaped huge profits from the price-gouging. Co-ops began diverting crops from state agencies to the street stalls, and some started setting up sideline business operations to produce brooms and other consumer items in short supply. The theft of raw materials, equipment, and crops on state farms became a growing problem.

UNDER TODAY'S ECONOMIC CONDITIONS, however, we should not be surprised if the Cuban government decides to reestablish some form of agricultural market. Given the advanced disintegration of the state distribution mechanism and rationing system, it's impossible to imagine that this step won't prove necessary to provide incentives to get production going in the countryside again. Doing so will exert its own corrosive pressures on the worker-farmer alliance, as the last experience proved. But it can help limit the extent and slow the advance of the current rupture, and start to increase food supplies to the cities, which is a vital necessity. Only after basic food production begins to meet demand again can a stable proletarian distribution system be reinstituted.[22]

---

22. Agricultural markets began operation in all provinces and cities on October 1, 1994. The markets, unlike those in the 1980s, are supplied not only by small family farmers but by cooperatives and state farms as well, including those run by the armed forces. After fulfilling deliveries to state distribution agencies at fixed prices, farms may sell surplus produce at unregulated market prices through the new outlets. They are licensed by the municipalities, and revenues from these sales are taxed.

In December a similar network of markets selling handicrafts and industrial goods was opened. These retail stands sell goods made by licensed self-employed individuals, as well as excess inventory of state enterprises and items

Big social forces are contending in Cuba today around the resolution of the contradictions inherent in all these questions— the UBPCs, the tax question, agricultural markets, and many others. Up till now it has been rare for these conflicts to take clear political forms for all to see and judge. But that can't last for long. We shouldn't be surprised when they break into the open, even into the streets. The truth is that only as the polarization becomes more open will the workers, as well as the youth who are determined to defend the revolution, be able to judge their own strength and gain confidence in their ability to lead. [23]

---

made by them using by-products from their primary productive activity. Licensed individuals or cooperatives are permitted to rent out their vehicles to transport agricultural goods to market. State enterprises are also authorized to rent underutilized vehicles for this purpose.

23. On August 5, 1994, a group of some twenty Cubans tried to hijack a boat in Havana harbor in order to leave the country and go to Florida. There had been four other boat hijackings over the previous month, including one a day earlier in which the hijackers killed a young police officer who tried to stop them.

The August 5 hijacking was repelled by dockworkers and the police in Havana. Later that day a crowd of several hundred people gathered along the Malecón, Havana's ocean-front boulevard, throwing rocks and bottles at police, hotels, and other targets. Several thousand workers and youth, supporters of the revolution, poured into the streets to respond to the provocation, effectively quelling the riot. Two days later, on August 7, a half million Cubans paid their last respects to the slain police officer and demonstrated their support for the revolution in the streets of Havana.

In interviews with reporters for the *Militant* newsweekly, young Cubans who mobilized in response to the August 5 antigovernment riot stated with pride, "This was our Moncada," referring to the 1953 attack on the Moncada army barracks in Santiago de Cuba that marked the beginning of the revolutionary struggle that brought down the hated Batista dictatorship in January 1959. They said this was their first chance to defend the revolution in the streets.

Following these events, the Cuban government ended its coastal patrol aimed at preventing Cubans from launching rafts headed for Florida, and over the next several weeks thousands set out to sea. The mass exodus was triggered not only by the extremely harsh economic conditions in Cuba, but also by U.S. government policy. While refusing to abide by its 1984 agreement

Imperialist rulers hate Cuban revolution

The U.S. ruling class sees all the pressures and polarization building up too. That is why they are not about to back off and give the workers and farmers of Cuba a little breathing space. From the point of view of their class interests, now is not the time to ease the economic embargo, the travel ban, or aggressive threats. Just the opposite. They will continue to ratchet up the pressure, in hopes of strengthening the hand of those in Cuba most open to accommodation with imperialism. Only to the degree the U.S. rulers are convinced they are making progress along that road—or that they cannot make such progress, because of a new rise in revolutionary struggle—will they make further tactical shifts in their policies.

I'm glad that one of the fraternal delegates from Canada made the point that it's not just the U.S. capitalist rulers who are determined to weaken and ultimately destroy the socialist revolution in Cuba. The imperialist bourgeoisie in Canada— just like its brethren in Britain and Spain and elsewhere—has no more love

---

to grant 20,000 visas a year to Cubans to enter the United States legally, Cubans who made it across the Florida straits were welcomed and given immediate asylum, including those who had committed murders, hijackings, or other crimes in the process of leaving.

As the exodus of rafters continued in August, Washington stepped up its aggressive moves against Cuba. Reversing its long-standing policy of granting residency to any Cuban who reached U.S. shores, Coast Guard and naval ships were stationed off Cuba's shores to intercept Cubans at sea. More than 30,000 were picked up and transferred to virtual concentration camps at the U.S. naval base at Guantánamo, located on occupied Cuban territory, where they joined more than 14,000 Haitians already interned there. Washington tightened the nearly thirty-five-year-old economic embargo against Cuba. New regulations barred sending dollars to relatives and friends in Cuba and further tightened restrictions on travel to Cuba by family members, journalists, and academic personnel.

In September, as the numbers of Cubans held at Guantánamo mounted, posing growing political difficulties for Washington, U.S. officials signed an accord with the Cuban government to admit a minimum of 20,000 Cubans a year to the United States.

for the Cuban revolution than the bourgeoisie that presides over Washington and Wall Street. The employing classes support doing whatever is necessary and possible to prevent the working class from exercising state power and expropriating capitalist property *anywhere* in the world—and they ceaselessly work to roll it back whenever we succeed in doing so.

No other capitalist class, however, has the same strategic military power, and thus the same stake in and responsibilities for policing the world capitalist order, as does U.S. imperialism. Nor did any other imperialist ruling class have anything close to the same amount of property expropriated by the revolutionary action of the working class in Cuba. Like the good folks who used to own the Vertientes-Camaguey Sugar Company, they never forget. Cuba was "theirs," only a ninety-mile ferry ride away from Key West.

As a result, the bourgeoisies in some of the other imperialist countries have a bit of a freebie with regard to trade and investment in Cuba right now (although the amounts involved are a tiny percentage of their overall foreign commercial dealings). Businesses in Canada, Spain, as well as Mexico and other semicolonial capitalist powers are happy to get an edge on their U.S. competitors while they can. They have nothing to lose.

The U.S. rulers, for their part, are not really worried about the competition in Cuba. If and when the day comes that they succeed in bringing the Cuban workers and farmers to their knees, they are confident they will have no problem rapidly regaining dominance and shoving aside their rivals from Canada, Spain, Mexico, Britain, or anywhere else. Until then, the price they pay in a few lost markets for commodities and capital is chump change. They're in for bigger stakes.

One problem, as several delegates recounted from their own direct experience, is that some people in Cuba have really bought into the argument that it's in the interests of the imperialist ruling classes for the U.S. to lift its embargo. They explain this to groups from the United States and elsewhere who visit Cuba. Especially with the demise of the Cold War, they say,

Washington's policy toward Cuba is obsolete and if the U.S. rulers were acting rationally they would drop it immediately. This hopeful view gets a broad echo in Cuba solidarity groups in the United States and elsewhere.

THE PROBLEM WITH ALL THIS—just as Fidel and Che explain in *To Speak the Truth*—is that U.S. policy toward Cuba *never* had its roots in the Cold War standoff with Moscow. The Cuban revolution has never been a threat to the U.S. rulers' "national security." The problem has never been Moscow; it has always been the living example of Cuba's working people and their revolutionary government, their unspeakable audacity. And that is precisely what has not changed. As we discussed in the report, the U.S. rulers *would* lift the embargo next week if the Cuban government were committed to an anti-working-class course like that of Hanoi or Beijing—or if they thought that easing the policy could help tip the balance decisively in that direction. But the job of class-conscious supporters of the socialist revolution in Cuba is not to second-guess the imperialists on how best to achieve their goals.

We're convinced that the *stronger* the Cuban revolution is —the more advances are made in the class struggle in the United States and worldwide—the more the pressure will mount on a weakened U.S. ruling class to lift the embargo and retreat from other hostile actions against Cuba. That's why the closest we've been to that goal since the opening of the revolution was in the 1980s, when the revolution was still on the march in the Caribbean and Central America and Washington's initial military efforts to intimidate the Cuban leadership and defeat the Nicaraguan workers and peasants government had come a cropper.

There are individuals in Cuba, of course, who *do* identify their interests with the interests of the imperialists. However consciously—and some are very conscious—they share the conviction that capitalism must be restored in Cuba. In a similar vein, some in the leadership of Cuba solidarity groups in the United States and elsewhere think of Washington (or Toronto or London) as "our" government, and seek to pressure them to correct their "misguided" policies in "our" national interest. They genuinely believe it when they argue that the policies toward Cuba of every U.S. administration since 1959 have been against the interests of "our country." But for the working class, Washington is not "our" government.

What disorients workers in Cuba and elsewhere are not false arguments made by various liberals and petty-bourgeois layers in the United States or elsewhere. The political disorientation comes when these same arguments about "outmoded" government policies, and how capitalists are "missing investment opportunities," are used by leaders of the government and Communist Party in Cuba—who have many times in the past explained extremely well why Washington, as well as Toronto, London, and Madrid fear the working people of Cuba. A "clever" diplomatic argument becomes too clever by half. It underestimates the class instincts of capitalist diplomats and politicians. More importantly, it politically disarms workers and revolutionary-minded young people in Cuba and elsewhere who genuinely begin to wonder why the economic war against Cuba continues.

It shouldn't surprise us that among the solidarity forces here in the United States, there is a broad range of views, and much confusion, about what's happening in Cuba. It shouldn't surprise us that the working-class perspective we bring into the committees and united actions is often a minority view. Some of those we work with in building various activities are genuinely shocked when we defend the socialist revolution in Cuba. They openly argue that they oppose U.S. government policy because, in their opinion, it is an obstacle to the Cuban people's desire to be finished with socialism.

None of this should surprise the cadres of a communist workers party. It should neither lead us to abstain from united activities that advance defense of the Cuban revolution, nor to accommodate politically to anyone as we do so. The political health and welfare of the solidarity forces in the United States or in any other country will never rise above the health and welfare of the political leadership of the broader working-class movement of which it is a part. When the class struggle begins to accelerate, then a new relationship of class forces will start asserting itself in many related political arenas as well. We'll know when that begins to happen. We shouldn't worry. We won't miss it.

Meanwhile, we will work with whoever we can around concrete protest actions, public teach-ins, and other activities in defense of the Cuban revolution.

Working-class solidarity
Given the political situation and balance of class forces that does exist, our challenge right now is to be clear and consistent about our perspectives and our proposed course of action and to fight for them effectively. If we are capable of doing that, then we can play an important role in a broad range of united front activities and win new forces to a proletarian political understanding. For all the reasons we've been discussing today, and will be discussing under other agenda points at this convention, those who are going to be most open to what we have to say will come primarily from the working class and layers of revolutionary-minded youth.

As working people enter into struggle and their conflicts with the employing class and its political representatives in Washington deepen, the most combative and politically class-conscious workers will increasingly identify with embattled workers in other countries. They will understand the stakes in standing shoulder to shoulder with the working class in Cuba, which is fighting in similar trenches against a common class enemy—the most powerful and bloody exploiting class in the history of humanity.

What working people in Cuba are fighting to defend and advance is in the historic interests of the workers of the world and of humanity as a whole. It's what revolutionary workers the world over are fighting for.

That's why "socialism or death!"—which communists in Cuba have added to their banners in face of the crisis conditions of recent years—is not just a slogan, or a romantic idea, or a suicide pact, as reactionary opponents of the revolution joke. That *is* the perspective for the Cuban revolution. There is no future for the working class in Cuba without fighting along a socialist course, the proletarian internationalist course, that they opened in the Americas thirty-five years ago and have maintained against powerful odds ever since.

Either we'll triumph in that fight—*all of us,* working people in Cuba, as well as those around the world who understand the importance of defending the Cuban revolution—or our class will sustain a terrible defeat on a world scale.

But the question of victory or defeat is not settled. Not by a long shot. That depends on what happens in the world class struggle in coming years, and on what communists do in Cuba, in the United States, and elsewhere to prepare to give effective leadership to our class as big battles are posed and fought. That's the perspective—to fight along these lines, understanding that what we do to build a communist movement in the working class here in the United States is a vital front in the political battle going on in Cuba.

This is not a time for the fainthearts, as our comrades in Cuba call those who break under the pressures and corrupt enticements of the capitalist world. There will be no quick fixes. The tension won't go away. It's going to keep ratcheting up more and more, as the crisis of the disintegrating capitalist order deepens worldwide. That's what's coming for all of us.

But if you're a fighter, a communist, then that's not a fearful prospect. It's a future we keenly anticipate, a future of struggle. Because we know that out of these coming battles, the toiling majority of humanity will have its chance to emulate the workers and farmers of Cuba by overthrowing the political rule of the landlords and capitalists, expropriating the land and factories they monopolize for the benefit of a handful, and opening the road to a socialist world that will put an end once and for all to class exploitation and oppression.

FROM PATHFINDER

February 1965: The Final Speeches

MALCOLM X

Speeches from the last three weeks of Malcolm X's life, presenting the accelerating evolution of his political views. $17.95

The Eastern Airlines Strike

Accomplishments of the Rank-and-File Machinists

ERNIE MAILHOT, JUDY STRANAHAN, AND JACK BARNES

The story of the 1989-1991 strike in which rank-and-file resistance by Machinists prevented Eastern's antiunion onslaught from becoming the road to a profitable nonunion airline. $9.95

To See the Dawn

Baku, 1920—First Congress of the Peoples of the East

How can peasants and workers in the colonial world achieve freedom from imperialist exploitation? By what means can working people overcome divisions incited by their national ruling classes and act together for their common class interests? These questions were addressed by 2,000 delegates to the 1920 Congress of the Peoples of the East. $19.95

Basic works of Marxism

■ COLLECTED WORKS
Karl Marx and Frederick Engels

The writings, in 50 volumes, of the founders of the modern revolutionary working-class movement. 43 volumes available now. Still to be published are vols. 35-37 (Capital) and vols. 47-50 (Engels's final correspondence, 1883-95). $1,075 for 43-vol. set, $25 per volume.

■ CAPITAL
Karl Marx

Marx explains the workings of the capitalist system and how it produces the insoluble contradictions that breed class struggle. He demonstrates the inevitability of the revolutionary transformation of society into one ruled for the first time by the producing majority: the working class. Volume 1, $13.95

■ WHAT IS TO BE DONE?
V.I. Lenin

Explains the historic stakes in creating a disciplined, militant organization of proletarian revolutionaries capable of responding "simultaneously to the same political questions, incidents, and events that agitate the whole of Russia." Written in 1902, one of the basic works that guided the vanguard workers who led the October 1917 revolution in Russia. $6.95

■ THE HISTORY OF THE RUSSIAN REVOLUTION
Leon Trotsky

The social, economic, and political dynamics of the first socialist revolution. The story is told by one of the revolution's principal leaders writing from exile in 1929, with these historic events still fresh in his mind. Unabridged edition, 3 vols. in one. 1,358 pp. $35.95

Available from Pathfinder. See front of magazine for addresses.

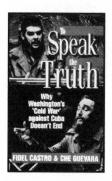

WHAT THE 1987 STOCK MARKET CRASH FORETOLD

I. THE OCTOBER 19, 1987, STOCK MARKET CRASH AND WHAT IT SIGNALS

THE OCTOBER 19, 1987, crash on the New York Stock Exchange was the steepest plunge in stock prices in this century, a larger and faster drop than the 1929 crash that signaled the coming Great Depression. Between Wall Street's opening and closing bells October 19 there was a 23 percent plummet in average stock prices, resulting in roughly $500 billion in losses. The Chicago futures market fell even more sharply, diving 36 percent in 10 hours over two days. The crash culminated a stock market slide that had begun in late August; overall, share prices fell by more than one-third over that period. This came on top of a collapse in the bond market, with prices of U.S. government securities falling 26 percent between late March and October 19.

Unlike the 1929 crash, the dive on Wall Street did not pause at the U.S. borders. With explosive computerized rapidity, over

---

The following resolution was discussed and adopted by the August 1988 convention of the Socialist Workers Party. The resolution and the report on it by SWP national secretary Jack Barnes were referred by the delegates to a commission for final editing in light of the convention discussion. The resolution is published here without revisions to take account of events since 1988. Footnotes have been added by the editors of New International *to aid the reader by pointing to related published materials or, in some cases, by providing more recent information.*

the next twenty-four hours it spread to every other stock market around the world. Hundreds of billions more dollars in paper values were destroyed. This reflected the tightening interlinkages, especially since World War II, of the U.S.-dominated imperialist world system of capitalist monetary relations, credit, production, and trade. Rather than buffering the shocks from the crash in New York, stock markets from London to Hong Kong, from Tokyo to Toronto, from Sydney to Mexico City helped drag each other down.

The most devastating decline hit the exchanges in semicolonial countries. The Hong Kong stock market ended trading altogether for a week. Shares on the Mexico City exchange dropped 75 percent in October, setting off a loss of nearly one-third of the peso's value and a capital flight of more than $2 billion from Mexico over the next two months.

The October 19 crash verged on what business-page commentators, borrowing from the vocabulary of nuclear catastrophe, termed a "meltdown" of the capitalist world's stock exchanges. More importantly, given the degree to which trading on the stock, bond, commodities, and futures markets depends on massive and continuous infusions of borrowed funds, this meltdown threatened capitalism's international banking network as well. Major securities firms, suffering staggering losses as the day went on, borrowed frantically to buy up stocks in hopes of halting the free-fall of share prices and thus the cash value of their own assets. When this effort failed, the big Wall Street houses were left deeply in debt, with piles of devalued stocks. Major banks, suddenly finding themselves with mounting bad debts, began turning down requests for further credit. To head off disaster, the U.S. government directly intervened. The Federal Reserve Board flooded the banking system with money on October 20 and credit lines were prevented from squeezing shut. A complete collapse was narrowly averted.

Nonetheless, many small stockholders were wiped out. A shakeout of even the largest traders left most with big losses and some—such as E.F. Hutton and L.F. Rothschild—on the ropes. While a few Wall Street houses made a killing in October, overall losses of securities dealers for the final quarter of 1987 were twenty-two times larger than their previous record loss, and their 1987 profits fell 80 percent from their 1986 level. Capitalists' confidence in the stability of the stock market has still not recovered, as shown by the decline in the average daily volume of shares traded on the New York exchange ever since. Repeated and unpredictable sharp one-day declines over the months since October keep reminding the masters of finance capital that it is not within their powers to prevent a sudden recurrence of an even more devastating crash.

At the same time, however, the exploiters' ceaseless quest for the highest returns will eventually force them to pour money capital back into stocks, sending volumes and prices soaring once again. Under capitalism, the blind laws of the market are ultimately more powerful than the mightiest state in matters of values and prices. And in a world where almost everything is a commodity, that is powerful indeed.

T HE NEAR MELTDOWN on October 19 also further exposed the vulnerability of the capitalist world to the towering pile of government and private debt whose buildup worldwide has accelerated since the early 1970s. The indebtedness of the oppressed countries of Latin America, Africa, Asia, and the Pacific increased at a dizzying pace in the 1980s as these nations suffered the combined blows of exploding interest rates at the opening of the decade; the deep 1981-82 recessions that rolled through the United States and several other capitalist countries; and the sharp drop in the prices of most raw materials and other commodities sold by Third World countries on the world market.

The total debt owed by the capitalists and governments of these countries to the wealthy families that own the major imperialist banks reached the almost unimaginable figure of $1.2 trillion by the end of 1987, more than twelve times its level in

1973. Much as bankers in the United States goaded farmers into bigger and bigger debt loads throughout the 1970s, the massive borrowing that resulted in today's Third World debt was initiated, pushed, and sustained by finance capital, which stood to profit mightily off the interest payments.

Mounting international debt slavery has not only meant economic and social devastation for hundreds of millions of peasants and workers; it has also increased the instability of the entire imperialist banking system. The so-called Third World debt crisis is in fact a dance of death between the capitalists in the imperialist countries and those in the semicolonial world, in which the primary victims of an international monetary calamity will be the working people of both the oppressed and oppressor countries.

Fictitious capital and imperialist economies

Over the past century trade in stocks, bonds, and other commercial paper—the devices that Karl Marx called "fictitious capital"[1]—have become integral to the very functioning of the world capitalist system: its interrelated banking and monetary operations, government finance, domestic and foreign trade, industrial production, mining, and agriculture. Capitalism does not operate on the basis of a "real economy" in which the ups and downs of production determine the conditions of both capitalists and working people, and a "paper economy" whose price gyrations affect only speculators and middle-class professionals who play the markets. The trading in stocks and bonds, together with intertwined credit and monetary flows, are part and parcel of the capitalist mode of production. They are inseparable from the production and circulation of commodities,

---

1. Fictitious capital—in the form of stocks, bonds, and other securities issued by businesses or the government—is a paper title to claims on money capital. Karl Marx, *Capital* (New York: Penguin, 1981) vol. 3, p. 641. See also pp. 595-601 and 625. This edition of *Capital* is identical to the one printed for several years under the Vintage imprint.

including the sale and purchase of human labor power. Debt and paper values are not *things*. Like the commodity itself, they are part of the production and reproduction of capitalist *social* relations.

The growing instability on Wall Street is a symptom of the profound crisis of capital accumulation infecting the entire body of the world imperialist system. Another crash cannot be prevented by new regulations aimed at altering the habits of operators on the stock, bond, and options markets: bans on computer-assisted "program" trading, measures to shut down markets if fluctuations become too stormy, stricter credit regulations, or the myriad other "reforms" much-discussed in the big-business press in the wake of October 19. Nor can the banking system be sealed off from the blows it will receive.

The explosive expansion, internationalization, and accelerating transaction speed in the securities markets have become necessary to the circulation of money capital and its interpenetration with industrial, mining, and agricultural production and trade. In order for the surplus value created by the labor of working people to be transformed into profits, the capitalists must compete among themselves to sell the commodities produced in the fields, mines, mills, and factories. They must compete to maximize further gains from their accumulated profits, whether by plowing this money capital back into production or finding other sources of investment or speculation that they believe will yield a larger return.

The circulation of money capital, Marx observed, is the "most striking and characteristic form of appearance of the circuit of industrial capital, in which its aim and driving motive— . . . money-making and accumulation—appears in a form that leaps to the eye (buying in order to sell dearer)." Under capitalism, he pointed out, "The production process appears simply as an unavoidable middle term, a necessary evil for the purpose of money-making." Frederick Engels, in preparing a second edition of volume two of *Capital* a decade after Marx's death in 1883, added in light of further experience: "This explains why all nations characterized by the capitalist mode of production are periodically seized by fits of giddiness in which they try to accomplish the money-making without the mediation of the production process."[2] Today the world capitalist system has evolved to the point that just such a fit of giddiness has become unavoidable. Its duration and volatility remain to be seen.

STOCK, BOND, and other markets for paper securities did not occupy this central place in the process of production, circulation, and expanded reproduction and accumulation of capital during the emergence of industrial capitalism in the latter part of the eighteenth and throughout much of the nineteenth centuries. While editing the third volume of *Capital* for publication in 1895, Engels wrote a brief outline for a supplement on the evolution of the stock exchange.[3] Almost thirty years earlier when Marx had drafted the manuscript, Engels explained, "the stock exchange was still a *secondary* element in the capitalist system." There was trading in government bonds, he wrote, but "even these were still relatively small in amount. . . . At that time, then, the stock exchange was still just a place where the capitalists plundered one another of their accumulated capitals, and it concerned the workers only as a new piece of evidence of the demoralizing general effect of the capitalist economy. . . ."

In the intervening years, however, the accumulation of capital "has proceeded at an ever growing pace, and in such a way moreover that in no industrial country, least of all England, can the extension of production keep step with that of accumulation, or the accumulation of the individual capitalist be fully employed in the expansion of his own business," Engels noted. The stock and bond markets thus had taken on growing importance as channels for capitalists to redeploy money capital

---

2. *Capital,* vol. 2, pp. 140, 137.

3. *Capital,* "The Stock Exchange," vol. 3, pp. 1045-47.

where they could reap the biggest interest or profits. This was not just a question for a small or degenerate layer of speculators. To keep a business going and revenues coming in, few capitalists could avoid becoming involved in the buying and selling of paper. As a result, Engels continued, the stock exchange "has the tendency to concentrate the whole of production, industrial as well as agricultural, together with the whole of commerce—means of communication as well as the exchange function—in the hands of stock-exchange speculators, so that the stock exchange becomes the most pre-eminent representative of capitalist production as such."

These markets in paper, Engels pointed out, had become necessary with the maturation of capitalism "in order to aid the investment of the mass of money capital . . . afloat." Engels was writing only at the very beginning of this development, when limited-liability, joint-stock corporations themselves were just becoming the dominant form of capitalist enterprise. But his initial assessment of this tendency under capitalism is confirmed by and illuminates the proliferation of types and varieties of fictitious capital over the subsequent century, a trend that has accelerated during the past fifteen years. Stocks, corporate and government bonds, and commodities futures contracts have been joined by an array of financial paper featured daily in the business sections of the press: so-called put and call options, stock futures, "junk" bonds, and new semigovernment securities whose profiteering aim and destabilizing potential are cloaked behind cute names such as "Farmer Macs," "Ginnie Maes," and "Fanny Maes."[4]

---

4. "Farmer Macs" are farm-loan securities issued by the Federal Agricultural Credit Corp. "Ginnie Maes" are home-mortgage securities issued by the Government National Mortgage Association. "Fannie Maes" are mortgage securities issued by the Federal National Mortgage Association. All three institutions are privately owned; the securities they issue, however, are in part indirectly subsidized by the federal government. The impression that they are "guaranteed" in some way by the government is illusory.

This expansion of the forms of fictitious capital helps explain why all large

Already in 1895 Engels took note of the growing role of the stock exchange in financing exploitation abroad and promoting colonial expansion and oppression. Colonial policy, he wrote, "is a pure appendage of the stock exchange, in whose interest the European powers divided up Africa a few years ago."

Today, while the regulation of stock markets themselves —like the issuance of currency—remains the prerogative of *national* state institutions, the *international* character of trading in stocks, bonds, and currencies is greater than ever before in history. It is only through unceasing exchanges of money capital denominated in dollars for marks, yen for dollars, today's dollars for tomorrow's lira, today's pesos for tomorrow's dollars that world trade, domestic trade, international and domestic debt creation, and thus the hiring of workers and their production of goods take place.

Massive amounts of money capital are transferred electronically all day and night from the bond market in London or Tokyo, to an investment bank on Wall Street, into shares on the New York Stock Exchange, into government securities held by a major bank in Bonn or Stockholm, into the stock market in Zurich, into currency speculation in Singapore, into a loan to the government of Brazil or Zambia, into interest on a previous loan

---

capitalist enterprises are sinking billions of dollars today into so-called hedge funds and derivatives, despite the big losses taken by several of them in 1994 (e.g., Procter & Gamble, $150 million; Sears, $237 million; Kodak, $220 million, Gibson Greetings, $20 million). Under a system driven by the competition of capitals, and in a world market with many currencies of rival national capitalist classes, the financial departments of larger corporations will inevitably seek ways to protect the money value of their capitals from erosion and unanticipated fluctuations. This leads to more—and more complex—forms of paper securities designed to hedge bets, offset currency devaluations, and reap enormous windfalls to boot. All these new "financial products," however, are also the stuff of speculation on a scale never before possible in history, creating the potential for shifts that can not only bring down individual capitalists but also, under today's increasingly unstable conditions, trigger a collapse of the entire world banking and monetary system as well.

that ends up in a U.S. or French bank, into mortgages on Canadian or New Zealand farmland, and so on. The prices of sugar, tin, cotton, copper, and other primary commodities on which the oppressed countries with semicolonial economies are dependent for export earnings are subject to destabilizing fluctuations due to what happens on the futures market at the Chicago Board of Trade or other commodities exchanges. Debts on which Third World capitalists and governments are required to pay massively compounding interest to the modern-day usurers are resold to these same wealthy coupon clippers on the international bond market at current prices from as low as five cents on the dollar (Peru) to around fifty cents on the dollar (Brazil).

The coming social crisis

The October 1987 international stock market crash was a product of explosive pressures that have been built up by the evolution of the imperialist-dominated world economy since the deceleration of capital accumulation in the late 1960s and early 1970s. These pressures have become much more volatile following the sharp 1981-82 recession in the United States.

The stock market crash was a warning that the creeping social crisis during the "Reagan boom" of the 1980s—which has devastated layers of working people and geographical regions in the United States, as well as hundreds of millions of toilers in the semicolonial countries—will become the reality for the vast majority of workers and farmers throughout the world. Whatever the exact course and tempo, coming partial crises— whether a sharp downturn in the business cycle, an inflationary outburst, another stock market crash, a major crop failure, a banking or debt disaster—instead of being buffered and absorbed by a robust and expanding international capitalist economy, will more and more threaten to trigger a credit collapse and a worldwide depression of industrial production and employment. This will result in a world social crisis whose inevitable product will be mass political battles and polarization that will tie together as never before in human history the prospects of working people in city and countryside across the globe.

Hundreds of millions will be thrown out of work throughout the capitalist world. Massive unemployment will deepen not only in the Third World, but will reach levels in the imperialist countries not experienced since the 1930s. More farmers will be driven off the land. Millions more dispossessed peasants—a major element in capitalism's increased production today of what Marx described as a "relative surplus population"[5]—will join the ranks of unemployed and underemployed workers in the miserable slums that already ring and thread cities throughout the semicolonial world. Waves of ruination will sweep small businesses.

Homelessness, malnutrition, and outright starvation will increase. The capitalists' destruction of the environment will accelerate, as will the breakdown of roads, bridges, and mass transportation used by working people. Employers will attempt to impose conditions in the plants, mines, and mills that are more and more intolerable. Disease from the decline of public health measures will mount, and infant mortality rates will rise for the working classes. Educational opportunities will decrease for the producers and their families. All these economic and social blows will fall with special intensity on those layers of working people who are already the most oppressed and exploited due to racist discrimination and national chauvinism: workers whose skin is black, brown, or yellow, and workers who are foreign-born. Working-class women and youth will suffer disproportionately.

Wars and the threat of war will become more frequent in an imperialist system in deepening crisis. As working people organize to fight back against the mounting assault on their living and working conditions, attacks on democratic rights will increase. The capitalists will back more and more violent methods, legal and extralegal, in order to maintain their rule. Reac-

5. See "The Progressive Production of a Relative Surplus Population or Industrial Reserve Army," in *Capital*, vol. 1, pp. 781- 94.

tionary political movements will begin to grow, seeking to take on and crush the increasing struggles by labor and its allies. The brutal face of capitalist rule will become clearer to see. Longtime, stable institutions will be shoved aside, as political parties and trade unions are shattered and routine politics is transformed by mounting class struggles.

The growing social and political crisis in the Soviet Union and Eastern European workers states will sharpen, as these countries feel the effects of economic and political convulsions throughout the capitalist world. Especially hard hit by the consequences of a world depression will be those workers states that inherited a semicolonial economic structure imposed by decades of imperialist domination and aggression.

This is the future whose imminent arrival was announced by the October 1987 stock market crash.

Growing premonition of depression and social crisis

Throughout the history of capitalism, every major economic and social crisis has been signaled in the most volatile and vulnerable spot in the capitalist economy: the arena of credit and monetary relations. With the emergence of the stock market's centralizing role in capitalist finance, production, and exchange, Wall Street has registered the early tremors of each sharp economic downturn. The most notable example is the crash of October 1929, which signaled the Great Depression that began before the following year was over.

The failures of the then-existing workers leaderships to respond to the stunning, brutal blows of the capitalist social crisis of the 1930s, and then to the revolutionary opportunities presented by the growing fightback of workers and farmers, resulted in the victory of reaction in country after country. This historic defeat culminated at the end of the decade in the global slaughter of the second world imperialist war.

The October 1987 crash affected the thinking and expectations of working people around the world, most strikingly in the United States and other imperialist countries. For the first time since the end of the 1920s, there is a growing premonition among millions of workers and farmers that the question of a coming depression and social crisis is "when," not "if." This premonition is compounded by the recognition among growing numbers of working people that the debt crisis currently wracking the Third World is an integral part of an exploding international debt structure and that it threatens a worldwide catastrophe that would shatter their own lives as well as those of the peoples of Asia, the Pacific, Africa, and the Americas.

This anticipation will not make the actual onset of a world depression and social crisis any less stunning a jolt to the working class. There is no way for the masses of working people to prepare for it. But the increasing realization of the inevitability of a depression is becoming a weightier political factor to a growing number of working people as they consider proposals to organize to defend their living conditions and right to a job. It makes a vanguard of them more ready to emulate those who take considered and determined initiatives, and on the basis of new experiences to listen objectively and with decreasing prejudice to political answers they had previously discounted. It broadens the recognition that homelessness, long-term unemployment, and deteriorating health conditions that have already struck layers of workers and farmers, as well as working people in particular industries and regions, offer a foretaste of every worker's tomorrow. They have become a matter of more pressing interest—and action—to all.

A generalized social crisis will not sweep the earth like a Great Leveller, reducing the conditions of all workers to those of the most exploited, and those of working people in the imperialist countries to those of the masses in the semicolonial world. It will devastate the world's toilers as a whole, hitting with particular force those already worst off and intensifying competition among workers. At the same time, however, a world social crisis will also push working people closer together both in their conditions and consciousness. A different world view will begin to be forged by the workers themselves. The conditions facing hundreds of millions of working people in the United States and other imperialist countries will lead more of them to begin seeing the jobless, the homeless, the dispossessed farmers and peasants, and the masses of the Third World not as pariahs—not as the "underclass," the "marginalized," the "poor," the "illegals," the "drunk and disorderly"—but as fellow workers with shared interests, goals, and the same class enemy.

Working people worldwide will discover in themselves a worth that can be realized through common class-struggle action. In the process, millions will be won to building an international communist leadership capable of leading these struggles to victory.

Rebuilding a world communist leadership

While the working class as a whole cannot prepare for the coming crisis, the political vanguard of the working class *must* prepare or it will fail to meet its challenge. The coming depression and world social crisis have practical political, organizational, and strategic consequences for communists today precisely because we can anticipate what lies ahead.

Unions and political parties in the working-class movement will be shaken to their foundations. The labor officialdom and Stalinist organizations will be thrown into deeper crisis. Lacking a proletarian composition and orientation, the "radical movement" will be atomized, some layers demoralized, and others thrown far to the left or far to the right. The truth of Fidel Castro's observation that in today's world "being a revolutionary means and will increasingly mean being a communist" will become more evident to growing numbers of revolutionary-minded fighters.[6] The opportunity and responsibility will grow for vanguard workers to rebuild an international communist leadership of the working class.

---

6. Fidel Castro, speech at Fifth Congress of the Union of Young Communists, April 5, 1987, reprinted in the *Militant,* May 29, 1987.

Communists must do more than anticipate what is coming; they must understand it, explain it, and prepare for it. This requires deepening the turn to the industrial unions and the proletarianization of communist organizations.[7] It changes what can and must be explained and proposed by communists to other vanguard workers. It shapes what communists must focus on in their newspapers, books, pamphlets, and political campaigns, as they fight alongside fellow working people who are looking for a way forward in union battles and social and political struggles.

Only the intensified class battles and deepening class political polarization that will inevitably accompany a coming depression can create the conditions under which truly mass communist workers parties can be built in the imperialist countries. The illusions in capitalism held by the labor aristocracy will ring more and more hollow, undermining the base of the bureaucratized misleadership of the labor movement. The assumption that capitalism and democracy go hand in hand will be shaken. Hundreds of millions of lives will be changed. Only these conditions can lead to revolutionary situations that pose the struggle for power by the workers and farmers in the imperialist countries.

The weakening of the imperialist system of oppression and exploitation will accelerate the disintegration of the political stranglehold of the consolidated bureaucratic castes in the Soviet and Eastern European workers states. This will create more fertile conditions for a world communist movement to develop communist organizations in these countries as well.

The growing realization that a world social crisis is on the agenda raises the stakes in understanding that a communist leadership can only be rebuilt if it is truly international. What is decisive is the construction in each country of organized

---

7. For a discussion of the Socialist Workers Party's political orientation to the industrial trade unions, see Jack Barnes, *The Changing Face of U.S. Politics: Working-Class Politics and the Trade Unions* (New York: Pathfinder, 1994).

and tested communist nuclei that are an integral part of an increasingly homogeneous world movement of communist organizations. The prior existence of independent proletarian organizations of these seasoned cadres will be a condition for meeting the coming opportunities to build mass communist parties in the very heat of titanic battles, parties capable of leading the workers and farmers to the conquest of their own governments.

II. FALLING AVERAGE RATE OF PROFIT AND THE COMING WORLD DEPRESSION

THE FALLING AVERAGE RATE of industrial profit accruing to the ruling capitalist families in the imperialist countries lies behind the evolution of the economic factors that make the initiation of a worldwide depression inevitable in the coming years. As a result of this fall, starting as early as the mid-1960s in Britain and as late as the mid-1970s in Japan, a crisis of decelerating capital accumulation has been deepening throughout the major world capitalist economies.

The postwar high point in the average profit rate of the industrial capitalists in the United States came within a half decade of the end of World War II. At that time, the U.S. employing class was still riding the crest of a war-driven rise in capital accumulation initially fueled by massive military production and by the rulers' success, with the union officialdom's jingoistic collaboration, in sharply increasing the exploitation of labor.

U.S. industrial production doubled by 1943 from its immediate prewar level in 1940. Meanwhile, the union bureaucracy's willingness to police government-imposed wage controls, rollbacks of labor legislation, and a no-strike pledge led to a leap in the average workweek to forty-five hours by 1943-44 from just over thirty-eight hours in 1940, and held the rise in real wages in manufacturing over the entire course of the war to 20 percent. Meanwhile, total after-tax corporate profits more than tripled in the United States between 1940 and 1948, while the capitalists' average rate of profit nearly doubled.

Evolution of capitalist world's economies since World War II

The average profit rate in U.S. industry peaked by 1950. For the subsequent two decades, however, a slow descent in the rate of profit was more than offset for the owners of industrial capital by a huge growth in their mass of profits. Buoyed by this cash flow and consequent further profit expectations, the employers invested capital in replacing worn-out plant and equipment from the war and prewar periods with new factories, heavy equipment, and rolling stock that greatly expanded the capacity for industrial production and transportation. The capitalists invested in the mechanization and automation of new branches of manufacturing. There was a massive growth of the automobile, consumer durables (refrigerators, washing machines, clothes dryers, televisions, etc.), and related industries.

A QUARTER CENTURY of overall expansion of U.S. capitalism was further powered by investment in, and loans extended for, the rebuilding of war-shattered Western Europe and Japan; the subsequent rise in world trade; and the intensified superexploitation of regions of the semicolonial world where Washington's imperialist rivals had been displaced during the war. All the imperialist ruling classes profited handsomely from the postwar surge of capital accumulation, whether its start dated from 1941, as in the case of the United States, Canada, Australia, and New Zealand, or the end of the 1940s in the case of Western Europe and Japan.

By the late 1960s this prolonged expansion—which spanned four business cycles in the ups and downs of capitalist production and trade—began to give way to a crisis of decelerating capital accumulation. Not only did average profit rates begin to drop more rapidly, but the growth in the mass of profits raked in by the capitalists also began to stagnate. In the United States, after-tax profit rates on investment in factories and machinery dropped from an average of 8 percent in the mid-1960s to just over 4 percent today.

Halting growth, intensifying interimperialist price competition, and increasing inflation and instability were hallmarks of this new stage in the evolution of the world's major capitalist economies. Stable exchange rates between the dollar and the currencies of the other imperialist powers had formed the bedrock of the international capitalist monetary system and trade relations ever since late 1944. This arrangement had been based on the U.S. industrial monopoly coming out of the war.

Before the end of the 1960s, however, this monopoly had been broken. At the same time, Washington found itself running larger and larger budget deficits to finance the Vietnam war. Superimposed on government economic policies aimed at countering the beginning of decelerated capital accumulation and growing price competition, these deficits fueled inflationary pressures throughout the world's capitalist economies. As growing numbers of the U.S. rulers' competitors sought to cash in their depreciating dollar reserves for gold from the U.S. Treasury, the Nixon administration in August 1971 halted the convertibility of the dollar for gold. This action brought an end to the fixed exchange rate for the dollar on international currency markets that had been put in place a quarter century earlier, following the U.S. victory in World War II.

By 1973, oil and meat shortages swept the United States and inflation rates reached double-digit levels. This was followed in 1974-75 by the first world recession since 1937-38, hitting all the major capitalist economies simultaneously. This combination of exploding prices, shortages, and an international recession began to undermine confidence among millions of working people in the rulers' post–World War II claims that the capitalist system had entered a new and irreversible stage of economic growth, stability, and increasing well-being for all sections of the population.

The 1976-80 upturn in the capitalist business cycle was at the same time shallow and marked by inflation. Growth rates that had averaged 5 percent throughout the imperialist countries during the 1960s and early 1970s dropped to just over 3 percent during the recovery. Official unemployment in the United States and other imperialist countries hovered at rates well above those over the previous quarter century. The rate of inflation initially slowed under the impact of the 1974-75 recession but, like unemployment rates, remained at levels higher than average for the postwar years.

By 1979-80 the U.S. dollar had been dropping against the currencies of its main imperialist competitors for nearly half a decade, and price rises in the United States had hit double-digit rates again. Inflation averaged more than 11 percent in 1979 and more than 13 percent in 1980. In face of this inflationary burst, the U.S. rulers moved to shore up the dollar and slow down price increases during the last two years of the Carter administration. The Federal Reserve Board sharply constricted the money supply, nearly doubling interest rates over a two-year period. By 1981 prime interest rates in the United States had shot up to almost 20 percent, the highest level since the U.S. Civil War, with disastrous consequences for debt-ridden working farmers, Third World countries, and working people trying to pay off a loan on a car or house. As capitalists in Japan, Germany, Britain, and other imperialist countries poured capital into the United States to profit from these soaring interest rates, the price of the dollar was bid up on world currency markets in a giddy rise against the yen, mark, and pound.

The abrupt moves by the U.S. rulers to halt an inflationary erosion of their profits undermined the shallow upturn in the capitalist business cycle that had begun in 1976. In the United States a brief slump in 1980 was quickly followed by the deep 1981-82 recession. Sky-high interests rates had caused already-sagging investment in new plant and equipment to collapse. This was rapidly followed by a wave of shutdowns and layoffs. Bank and business failures began to rise sharply. Land values collapsed just as farmers' indebtedness was rising at a record pace, leading to the greatest surge of foreclosures since the 1930s.

The mounting debt of the Third World countries accelerated to its current unpayable, unsustainable, and intolerable proportions. World trade growth decelerated and interimperialist competition intensified. Unemployment shot over 10 percent in the United States for the first time since the end of the 1930s. Real wages of workers in the United States, already eroding in the late 1970s, slid downward at a faster pace. The gap began to widen between the average conditions in the working class, and those of workers who are victims of discrimination because of their skin color or national origin.

THE EFFECTS OF THIS BRUTAL RECESSION would have cut qualitatively deeper had the downturn hit all the major imperialist countries simultaneously as in 1974-75. Japan and several Western European countries did not slip into a recession, however, and this cushioned to a degree the slide in the United States, Canada, Britain, and West Germany. Nonetheless, the consequences of 1981-82, and what they revealed about the worsening crisis of capital accumulation, placed their stamp on the rest of the decade.

Average annual economic growth in the imperialist countries slipped to about 2.5 percent in the 1980s from more than 3 percent in the 1970s and 5 percent in the 1960s. Annual growth in industrial production has fallen sharply, along with the rate of expansion of world trade.

In the United States, the steep 1981-82 downturn coincided with a sharp acceleration of the employers' assault on labor, announced by the crushing of the air traffic controllers union (PATCO) in 1981. The utter collapse of the union officialdom in the face of an onslaught by the bosses and their government precipitated a rout of the industrial working class and industrial unions over the subsequent half decade.

For the semicolonial countries the consequences have been far worse. Many of these countries have never pulled out of the

1981-82 recession, experiencing little or no economic growth in this decade. For Latin America as a whole, real per capita gross national product in 1987 was 5.5 percent below 1980, and for nine countries (Bolivia, Guatemala, Venezuela, Nicaragua, Argentina, El Salvador, Haiti, Honduras, and Mexico) the decline ranged from 10 to 27 percent. This sagging growth has magnified the debt crisis throughout the Third World.

Cumulative consequences of falling average rate of profit

The imperialists' crisis of capital accumulation will soon enter its third decade. Like the preceding period of capitalist expansion, it has stretched across several business cycles of recession and upturn. Its consequences have been and continue to be far reaching:

1. Intensified interimperialist competition

The downward pressure on profit rates intensified price competition among capitalists, including on an international level. This broke down the de facto industrial monopoly held by the U.S. capitalists coming out of World War II.

When the U.S. rulers entered the war they were producing about one-third of the world's manufactures; they emerged less than four years later with that figure having leapt to one-half. That edge in their share of the world market encouraged U.S. capitalists to defer major costly postwar investment in modernization of plant and equipment in industries such as steel and auto. It enabled them to maintain price levels on the world market well above actual production costs, collecting monopoly rents in the form of superprofits.

By the end of the 1960s, however, the monopoly position of the U.S. capitalists had been challenged in one industry after another: steel, auto, farm equipment, electronics, aerospace, computer-related technology, garment, and textile. Initially the U.S. rulers faced increasing competition in the world market primarily from their Japanese, West German, and other imperialist allies. By the 1970s price competition was even growing with industrial capitalists in a handful of semicolonial countries such as South Korea, Hong Kong, Singapore, and Taiwan. Competition for markets in cereal grains and other farm commodities has come not only from imperialist rivals, but also—as a result of the "green revolution" and a reorientation of agriculture toward the world market—from capitalists in some semicolonial countries. Stiffer competition has forced U.S. and other capitalists to bring prices down on both manufactured and agricultural commodities, reinforcing the squeeze on profit rates.

Marx's observation that "it is the fall in the profit rate that provokes the competitive struggle between capitals, not the reverse" has been confirmed once again by the events of the past twenty-five years.[8]

2. Overproduction and excess capacity

This interimperialist competition is sharpening in a world capitalist market plagued by overproduction of commodities and excess industrial capacity.

The big-business media has stressed that manufacturing in the United States, after falling to a low of 68 percent utilization of plant and equipment during the 1982 recession, was functioning on average at about 83 percent of capacity in May 1988. What is rarely noted is that this "high" is actually the lowest level of capacity utilization at the peak of an upturn in the business cycle in the United States since the mid-1960s. By contrast, capacity utilization in 1966 went above 91 percent; in 1973, to nearly 88 percent; and in 1979, to 85 percent.[9]

---

8. *Capital,* vol. 3, p. 365. For how these trends have played out since 1988, see the article, "Imperialism's March toward Fascism and War."

9. In October 1994 the U.S. government capacity utilization figure reached 84.9 percent. Although the official consumer price increase index remained at among the lowest levels since the early 1960s, the rising capacity figures in 1994 were among the factors cited by Federal Reserve Bank board members as they made their sixth hike in interbank interest rates for the year, announced in mid-November. They conjured up the specter of overstretched

The capitalists continue to have too much industrial capacity. They are plagued by overproduction of commodities: that is, by more output than they can sell at a high enough profit to justify expanding their productive plant and equipment. The employers have made working people pay the price through mounting work reorganization, speedup, plant shutdowns, and layoffs as they drive along the only road open to them: increasing absolute surplus value (lengthening the workday) and relative surplus value (intensifying labor through speedup and adding so-called labor-saving machinery) as much as the relationship of class forces will permit.

In the auto industry alone Ford has closed fifteen plants since 1979 and eliminated 30 percent of its employees; General Motors has announced plans to shut down at least 15 percent of its existing plant capacity and eliminate some 100,000 workers in the next few years. Seventy-five meatpacking plants were shut down between 1980 and 1985, with speedup and retooling in the remaining packinghouses resulting in increased output with a quarter million fewer workers. The workforce in steel has been cut in half with the shutdown of many mills in Pittsburgh, Birmingham, Baltimore, Gary, Chicago, and elsewhere.

The overproduction and excess capacity affecting the ruling classes in the imperialist countries is reflected not only in mounting plant shutdowns and layoffs, but also in the stagna-

---

production lines, sudden shortages, and consequent spikes in prices.

The truth about these capacity utilization figures, however, is that over time they reveal less, not more, about the actual functioning of capitalist production. First, these figures do not include factories, mines, and equipment that have been shut down by capitalists for now but can be brought back into production as profit needs dictate. Second, the official figures do not account for increased production achieved through longer hours (absolute surplus value) and increased productivity (relative surplus value), as described in this section. Finally, the figures are limited to mines, mills, and factories located in the United States, failing to take account of the growing share of parts and supplies turned out in U.S.-owned plants abroad for use in domestic production.

tion of trade on the world market. World trade has fallen from a yearly growth rate of nearly 9 percent between 1963 and 1973 to less than half that over the subsequent fifteen years.

Overproduction, excess capacity, plant closings, unemployment, intensification of labor, and decelerating world trade, however, have nothing to do with what billions of the world's working people need and can use. Workers and farmers are in need of food, clothing, housing, means of transportation, books, medicine, and many other goods that advances in labor productivity make less and less time-consuming to produce but that the producers themselves are less and less able to afford.

As Marx observed about the history of capitalism: "Since capital's purpose is not the satisfaction of needs but the production of profit . . . there must be a constant tension between the restricted dimensions of consumption on the capitalist basis, and production that is constantly striving to overcome these immanent barriers. Moreover, capital consists of commodities, and hence overproduction of capital involves overproduction of commodities. . . .

"It is not that too many means of subsistence are produced in relation to the existing population. On the contrary. Too little is produced to satisfy the mass of the population in an adequate and humane way. Nor are too many means of production produced to employ the potential working population. On the contrary. . . . Periodically, however, too much is produced in the way of means of labour and means of subsistence, too much to function as means for exploiting the workers at a given rate of profit."[10]

3. Declining capital investment in capacity-increasing plant and equipment
Over the past decade there has been a sharp decline in the rate of new investment by U.S. capitalists in capacity-increasing

10. *Capital*, vol. 3, pp. 365-67.

plant and equipment. Factory closings and layoffs have registered the competitive pressures on the rulers to shed less-pro-
ductive capacity. Large amounts of value have been destroyed
in the process. But stagnating profits continue to make it less
worthwhile for the capitalists to invest in building new factories
and purchasing major new industrial technologies that would
expand productive capacity. There has been no extensive
preparation by finance capital to draw new labor power in substantial amounts into expanded and modernized sectors of industrial production.

When the 1974-75 recession began, investment in construction of new factories was 172 percent higher in the United
States than it had been thirteen years earlier. Over the thirteen
subsequent years, however, the rate of growth in new factory
construction has been cut more than half. And since the sharp
1981-82 recession, annual investment in new plant has actually
fallen by nearly 25 percent, from $17 billion in 1981 to $13 billion in 1987. Adjusted for inflation over those six years, the
drop in real terms has been much steeper.

Instead of expanding productive capacity, manufacturing investment during the post-1982 upturn in the business cycle has
focused on upgrading and retooling a part of existing plants
and equipment.[11] This investment in "labor-saving" technology
has resulted, as intended, in brutally labor-intensifying reorganization of work, from meatpacking to paper production.
This speedup takes a devastating toll on health and safety,

---

11. Spending in 1993 on what the U.S. Commerce Department itself defines
as "expansion"—new factories and buildings that require more workers—ran
at little more than half the pace as that during periods of capitalist expansion
in the 1960s. Once outlays on cost-cutting computer and information processing equipment are subtracted from equipment expenditures (for the period
from the March 1991 upturn in the U.S. capitalist business cycle through
June 1994), then investment for that period in new, capacity-expanding
equipment actually declined 5 percent and spending on the construction or
expansion of factory buildings declined more than 25 percent.

means longer hours for workers who remain on the job, and leads to permanent layoffs for many other workers. While Washington boasts that the U.S. economy has created 15 million new jobs since the upturn at the end of 1982, there has been a decline of nearly 1.5 million jobs in mining and manufacturing over that same period. And the average length of the workweek in industry has risen from thirty-nine to forty-one hours, with many factory workers putting in fifty, sixty, or more each week.

The most important revelation from the October 1987 crash was not what was happening on the world's stock and bond markets, but the destabilizing worldwide impact of what was *not* happening in the expansion of capital investment in capacity-increasing industrial plant and equipment.

4. Speculative binge and debt explosion

The post-1982 recovery has been fueled by an enormous expansion of fictitious capital. The owners of U.S. corporations have been issuing "junk" bonds to finance an orgy of mergers and takeovers and sinking their capital in a burgeoning variety of paper securities.

Business debt has tripled over the past decade to $3 trillion, and many corporations are spending 50 percent of their earnings on interest payments to banks and bondholders. In 1986, commercial banks—which unlike so-called investment banks are supposed to make their money from interest on loans that are backed up by collateral in real productive assets such as land and factories—instead collected one-quarter of their profits from capital gains (i.e., rising prices) on the securities markets. The U.S. government debt has shot up from $1 trillion to $2.5 trillions in six years, with about 20 percent of the federal budget now going to siphon revenues directly to wealthy bondholders. (Including these interest payments, well over half the budget goes to pay for past or present imperialist wars and to prepare for future ones.) There has been massive borrowing of capital on international securities markets, with purchases abroad of U.S. stocks and bonds leaping thirteenfold from $7 billion in 1980 to nearly $90 billion in mid-1987. Billions of dollars in interest payments squeezed from the sweat and blood of Third World toilers have poured into the banks. Consumer and mortgage debt has increased more than twelvefold since 1980 to its current level of $2.9 trillion.

While overall employment increased 15 percent between late 1982 and September 1987, jobs in brokerage houses and investment banks jumped by more than 60 percent; in credit agencies by more than 50 percent; in real estate–related employment by more than 30 percent; and in insurance companies by nearly 20 percent.

Each additional six months that a downturn in the capitalist business cycle is pushed off by these means will be paid for by an even more wrenching shakeout when the next recession hits. Moreover, at this late stage in the capitalists' falling average rate and stagnating mass of profit, any partial crisis—a recession, another Wall Street crash, major crop failures, Third World debt disaster, or bank failure—could initiate a chain of events that would wipe out today's mountain of paper values overnight, bringing a collapse of the markets to buy and sell them. No degree of lowered interest rates by the U.S. Federal Reserve Board or flood of dollars from the Treasury could stem such a plunge. No matter how easy the money comes, capitalists will only put it to use if it can be converted into capital and invested at a sufficient profit.

The capitalists' search for higher returns in the face of a falling average rate of industrial profit led to the run-up in stock prices that came crashing down in late 1987. Wall Street's pre-October "bull market," however, obscured the fact that the underlying stagnation of profits since the late 1960s has been accompanied by a steep decline in real, inflation-adjusted stock prices. Marx explained that stock and bond prices are to a degree "independent of the movement in the value of the real capital that they represent," but at the same time "fluctuate with the level and security of the receipts to which they give a

legal title"[12]—that is, with the anticipated profits of the capitalists who issue these pieces of paper. A sustained crisis of capital
accumulation must in the long run result in a drop in the stock
market. Today's fluctuations of the Dow Jones index of industrial stocks around 2,100 points, down from more than 2,700 in
August 1987, would have to leap to almost 3,500 in real,
inflation-adjusted terms in order to return to the level registered at the high point of the stock market index in 1966.[13]

5. U.S. bank and business failures

Another consequence of the U.S. capitalists' declining profit
rate has been registered in the greatest wave of bank and business failures since the Great Depression of the 1930s.

Between 1947 and 1978 an average of 3 banks failed in the
United States each year. That jumped sharply to 10 per year between 1979 and 1981; another sharp jump to nearly 50 failures
during the 1982 recession and the year after; to 80 in 1984; and
120 in 1986. Last year nearly 200 banks went under (about 1.5
percent of U.S. banks). Twenty-five failed in Texas alone during
the first quarter of 1988. Registering the instability of the world
financial system under the lengthening shadow of government,
corporate, consumer, and Third World debt, nearly 1,600 banks
are now on Washington's "problem list," up nearly 800 percent
since 1980.

In addition, about one-third of the 3,120 U.S. savings and loan
institutions accumulated losses totaling $13.4 billion in 1987,

---

12. *Capital*, vol. 3, pp. 598-99.
13. Six years later, as of November 1994, the inflation-adjusted Dow Jones Industrial Average is still below the 1966 level. Wall Street stock markets
dropped sharply in the first months of 1994, as described in the final article
in this issue. Although the Dow Jones index turned back up for several
months in June, the volatility of the market was once again shown as these
footnotes were being completed just before Thanksgiving. Following a decline of nearly 150 points since late October, the index fell steeply by 140
points during the three days prior to the late-November U.S. holiday.

with almost $4 billion more in losses during the first three months of 1988. More than 500 failed over the past year, and up to 500 others are close to being insolvent. The true situation of these institutions is even worse than reported figures reveal, since their owners and managers use accounting tricks to maintain outstanding loans and the interest due on them as assets long after these debts have obviously become uncollectible.

The so-called government bailouts of failing banks and savings and loans institutions are not aimed at protecting the small checking or savings accounts of working people and small business owners. Nor are they intended to prevent foreclosure on the land, buildings, livestock, and equipment of exploited farmers in debt to these loan sharks. The aim is to bail out the wealthy shareholders and bondholders who stand to lose billions of dollars of money capital when these financial institutions collapse.

The current surge in bank and savings and loan failures is exposing the myth promoted by the capitalists that the earnings deposited by working people in these institutions are eternally "guaranteed" by the government. Total "insured" bank and savings and loan deposits today amount to $1.6 trillion. Yet the Federal Deposit Insurance Corporation (FDIC), which "stands behind" bank deposits, currently has only $18 billion in its account, and it is estimated that up to one-sixth of this will go to bail out a single major Texas bank before the end of 1988. The Federal Savings and Loan Insurance Corporation (FSLIC) was $13.7 billion in the red by March 1988, even after Congress lent it $10.8 billion the previous year. The FSLIC announced in June 1988 that it was spending more than 40 percent of its cash on hand to liquidate two small California savings and loan institutions. These facts give a taste of what is in store for millions of workers and farmers in the more and more likely event of a large-scale banking collapse in the United States.[14]

---

14. The U.S. government will have spent in the range of $250 billion by the

Business failures, which hit the smallest proprietors especially hard, in 1985 reached their highest rate since the opening years of the Great Depression. The rate of failures rose still further in 1986 before leveling off at that high plateau in 1987.

6. Devastation of semicolonial countries

The toilers of the oppressed countries of Africa, Asia, the Pacific, and the Americas have been dealt the heaviest blows by the sharpening of the imperialists' accumulation crisis over the past decade. These countries, which have inherited economies distorted by centuries of colonial and semicolonial domination, are being devastated by an accelerating transfer of values produced there into the hands of the imperialist ruling classes.

Marx pointed out that interest-bearing capital is always "the mother of every insane form." Thus "debts, for example, can appear as commodities in the mind of the banker."[15]

So it has been with the imperialists' debt offensive against the Third World. Lacking sufficiently profitable ways to invest money capital in expansion of industrial capacity, the capitalist rulers from New York to Tokyo and from London to Sydney have foisted gigantic loans onto governments and groups of capitalists in the semicolonial countries. To the imperialist bankers, these mounting debts appear on the balance sheet as massive assets—a "right" to suck in billions of dollars in interest payments each year from the wealth produced by the labor of workers, peasants, and artisans across the world.

---

latter part of the 1990s to bail out the owners of failed savings and loan institutions. The final article in this issue describes how U.S. banks pulled back from lending money—their long-established function in capitalist society—and spruced up their balance sheets by buying and selling various forms of paper at a profit. The rise in both long- and short-term interest rates in 1994, and the narrowing gap between them, is for the first time since the late 1980s squeezing the banks' capacity to make a fast buck by borrowing money at cheap rates to buy government bonds that pay high rates.

15. *Capital*, vol. 3, p. 596.

These debts, which take the form of pieces of paper, are actually the registration of a social relationship of forces between the exploiting families of finance capital and their states, and the capitalists and governments of the oppressed countries. The compounding interest quickly outstrips the principal, and the whirlpool of indebtedness drains ever more wealth produced by the toilers in the semicolonial countries. As the interest due mounts, the imperialists bring their enormous power to bear on governments in the semicolonial countries, pressing them to squeeze out funds for payments by imposing more and more severe austerity measures on the workers and peasants: currency devaluations, abolition of price subsidies on food and other necessities, wage cuts, longer hours, speedup, and sharp cutbacks in spending for health, education, and housing.

In exchange for rescheduling payments on interest and principal, governments in the Third World are being forced to turn over ownership of entire factories, mines, or tracts of farm and forestland to imperialist interests, or to hand over a set percentage of earnings from the sales of commodities on the world market. The government of Argentina has announced plans to transfer 40 percent ownership of the state telephone company and airline to foreign capital in return for funds to pay off a small piece of the debt. A "debt repayment" project in Brazil will deforest an area the size of Britain by the mid-1990s, while another endangers an area the combined size of France and Britain. On the basis of such "renegotiation deals," the imperialist bankers make further loans and collect interest on these new debts as well.

In recent years, however, the size of the Third World debt load has become so staggering that sections of finance capital have begun to worry about sudden defaults that could trigger a cascading disintegration of the international banking system. Total debts owed to the imperialist ruling families by the semicolonial countries now stand at $1.2 trillion. Between 1982 and 1987 these countries were robbed of $140 billion by means of interest paid to the banks.

The combined $228 billion debt load of the African countries is equivalent to half the continent's annual gross national product; for seventeen sub-Saharan countries the debt amounts to more than 100 percent of their yearly GNP, and for five countries more than 200 percent. Interest payments on Africa's debt eat up some 40 percent of the continent's annual export earnings. Yet the debt continues to mount year by year.

For Latin America, payments to the imperialist banks on its $410 billion debt absorb an average of one-third of export revenues of the continent's propertied classes, while the overall debt rose another 4.5 percent in 1987. Mexico alone was drained of $50 billion in interest payments between 1982 and 1987. Of the Latin American countries with the largest foreign debt, Argentina devoted more than half its export earnings to interest payments last year; Mexico spent 40 percent; and Brazil 28 percent.

WHILE THE DEBT BURDEN on the semicolonial countries was already reaching crisis dimensions in the 1970s, it did not explode to its current mountainous proportions until the opening years of the 1980s. In 1973 the entire Third World debt stood at under $100 billion, and Latin America's at $42 billion. By 1979 total indebtedness of the semicolonial countries had reached $300 billion, still only 75 percent of the current debt of the Latin American countries alone. In less than a decade, however, the debt load quadrupled. The loan weapon used by the imperialist banks to plunder the Third World had itself become a source of increasing crisis, uncertainty, and instability throughout the world capitalist system.

The explosion of interest rates in the United States and sharp rise of the dollar in 1979 rapidly inflated the outstanding debts, sending the governments of semicolonial countries back to the banks in a race for further loans to keep up payments. Then the 1981-82 recession reduced the market in the imperialist countries for agricultural and raw materials exports from the semicolonial countries, sending the prices for these commodities into a nosedive. Falling export earnings, in turn, deprived these countries of the dollars, yen, pounds, and marks they needed both to cover rising interest payments and to buy necessary imported food and manufactured goods from the imperialist countries. The sharp fall in raw materials prices accelerated a more long-term decline caused by such factors as the development of cheaper manufactured substitutes like synthetic rubber, textiles, sweeteners, and new metal alloys. According to a World Bank report, after adjusting for inflation the 1986 prices of raw materials (excluding oil) on the world market were at their lowest level since the late 1930s. The modest upturn in some commodity prices in the first half of 1988 will not mark a reversal of this long-term downward drift.

Meanwhile, world market prices for manufactured goods imported by the semicolonial countries, which skyrocketed between 1979 and 1982, have continued to run ahead of the declining export earnings of these countries. Under this one-two punch, the buying power of Africa's export earnings has plummeted by more than 30 percent since 1980; Latin America's by one-quarter; and Asia's (not including Japan) by close to 10 percent. This evolution has worsened the unequal trade relations between the imperialist ruling families and the capitalists in the Third World.

Even under the best monetary and market conditions for the ruling families in the semicolonial countries, unequal terms of trade are built into the higher average productivity of labor in the industrialized capitalist countries due to their generally greater economic and technological development. A commodity produced with an hour of labor in an imperialist country is usually exchanged for one produced with many hours of labor in a semicolonial country, siphoning surplus value created by workers and peasants in the Third World into the pockets of international finance capital.

Capitalists in the imperialist countries also compete with semicolonial producers for buyers of many raw materials and agricultural commodities. Nearly 70 percent of raw materials exports come from North America, Western Europe, Australia, and other imperialist countries. Over the past decade the imperialist ruling classes have increasingly resorted to quotas, tariffs, or other restrictive measures against Third World imports to boost their own sales and profits at the expense of the semicolonial producers. One-half of the exports from these African, Asian, and Latin American countries are estimated to face such trade restrictions.

The U.S. government, for example, has sought to protect the capitalist families that own the giant sugar monopolies by annually lowering the quota for sugar imports into the United States. The 1988 quota was decreased by 25 percent to the lowest quantity of imported sugar in more than 100 years. In 1988 the United States will import only 685,000 tons of sugar, nearly 14 times less than the five million tons imported in 1981. Combined with increased dumping of noncane sugar and substitute sweeteners on the world market by U.S. and European capitalists, the U.S. quota has drastically reduced export earnings of many Caribbean and Latin American countries, the Philippines, and other sugar-producing countries. Caribbean sugar and other exports to the United States have dropped by more than 30 percent since the opening of the 1980s.

FINANCE CAPITAL also reaps vast profits from ownership and control of the giant monopoly distributors, transportation networks, and insurance companies that capitalists in the semicolonial world depend on for access to the world market.

The decline of the dollar against other major imperialist currencies between late 1985 and early 1988 has not improved the debt situation for the Third World. Most commodities sold by the semicolonial countries on the world market are denominated in dollars, so their net export income sank in tandem with the U.S. currency. But since only one-third of the outstanding Third World foreign debt is denominated in dollars, the total amount has been inflated by the strengthening of the yen, mark, and other imperialist currencies. Moreover, since the currencies of most Third World countries have been depreciating against the dollar, the dollar-denominated portion of their debt has grown more burdensome as well.

As the threat of default on the Third World debt has mounted in recent years, imperialist banks have slowed down the pace of new lending. At the same time, they have increased the use of muscle to collect as much as possible on the uncollected interest and to gain compliance with onerous conditions from Third World governments for any concessions in rescheduling payments and floating new loans.

In both 1986 and 1987, Third World countries sent out some $30 billion more in debt payments than they received in new loans. According to the World Bank, the Third World countries have suffered a net drain of $85 billion since 1982 from a combination of interest payments and capital flight by domestic and foreign exploiters. The International Monetary Fund and World Bank—the latter set up supposedly to provide inexpensive "development loans" to semicolonial countries—have themselves been central to this transfer of capital from Asia, Africa, and Latin America into the coffers of the ruling families of North America, Western Europe, Japan, Australia, and New Zealand.

While it is the bourgeoisies and middle-class technocrats in the semicolonial world who sit down with the representatives of imperialist finance capital to renegotiate ever-deeper indebtedness, it is the workers, peasants, and small producers of these oppressed countries who pay the toll for this rip-off. According to the World Bank, since 1980 the debt burden has reduced real income by 25 percent in the poorest semicolonial countries, mostly in Africa, and by nearly 15 percent in relatively better-off countries in Latin America and East Asia.

7. Farm crisis in imperialist countries

A front-page *New York Times* article in May 1988 made the grotesque claim that "the world's farmers produce vastly more food and other goods than the world can use." In a world where some 10 million people face starvation, hundreds of millions suffer from malnutrition, and hundreds of millions more are ill-housed and ill-clothed, nothing could be farther from the truth. But neither could anything underline so pointedly the consequences both for farmers and all humanity of the intensifying price competition among the capitalists of the major imperialist powers in processing, packaging, transporting, and marketing agricultural commodities.

The living standards of exploited farmers in the United States were already under pressure in the 1970s, as rising prices of machinery, seed, fertilizer, fuel, and other inputs outpaced any increase in prices farmers received for the commodities they produced. With rising land prices pushing up the collateral value of farms, and with the exploiters seeking ways to turn around the declining profitability of their capital, interest-hungry federal and private banks pressured farmers to go more and more heavily into debt to buy new equipment and to expand acreage and production of crops and livestock.

Real income of working farmers had already begun falling in the closing years of the 1970s. But the calamity came with the six-year collapse in land prices sparked by the 1981-82 recession. By 1986 average land prices in five Midwest states had plunged 58 percent since 1980, and in Iowa by 63 percent. For the United States as a whole, agricultural land prices fell by 35 percent over this period, for a total drop of some $300 billion.

For farmers who had seen their indebtedness shoot up like a geyser with rising interest rates between 1979 and 1982, this collapse in the value of collateral they could use to maintain outstanding loans and obtain future ones spelled disaster. The continuing decline of agricultural prices throughout this period exacerbated farmers' plight.

Working farmers have already been hit by depression conditions. The annual income of more and more of them has been driven below a living wage. Growing numbers have been forced to look for a factory job or other full-time employment to support themselves and their families. And hundreds of thousands have been driven off the land altogether.

Of the 2.43 million farms in the United States in mid-1981, some 260,000—11 percent—were no longer operating by mid-1987. At the end of that year the acreage of foreclosed land held by the owners of big banks, insurance companies, and government agencies was roughly comparable in area to one-third of all the farmland in Iowa.

As the result of foreclosure on tens of thousands of indebted farmers, together with declining interest rates since 1982, the total farm debt in the United States has fallen from more than $200 billion earlier in the 1980s to under $150 billion today. As a Federal Reserve Board economist put it, the farm picture has "improved because the weak people have been bankrupted."

But the scourge of farm foreclosures is far from over. In May 1988 the federal Farm Home Administration (FmHA), a semi-government agency purportedly set up to help the worst-off farmers, announced that as many as 65,000 of these producers would have to liquidate their assets or be forced into foreclosure. Thousands of other farmers in debt to private banks or other government agencies are still being driven off the land as well. It is estimated that more than 15 percent of farmers today are so deeply in debt that they face losing their land, buildings, livestock, and equipment even before a recession begins.

Tens of thousands of farmers in the United States are being pushed more rapidly toward foreclosure by the disastrous drought across most of North America in the spring and summer of 1988. As of the end of the first half of 1988, some 1,900 counties in thirty-seven states—well over half the counties in the United States—had been declared drought disaster areas by the federal Department of Agriculture. In the northern Great Plains states some 60 percent of this year's grain crop had already been lost. Crop yields nationwide for corn, soybeans, oats, barley, spring wheat, and other grains could drop by 50 percent or more over the summer. By the end of June severe soil erosion had devastated more than 13 million acres of farm and rangeland. Ground moisture had fallen 32 percent below normal, worse than the 1934 low point of the Great Depression's Dust Bowl.

Capitalist domination of the distribution and sale of agricultural products turns natural disasters such as a drought into social catastrophes that ruin many exploited farmers and raise food prices for working people. Meanwhile, enormous profits are reaped by the handful of capitalists who own the giant food processing and marketing monopolies and speculate on the commodities futures markets.

The huge government agricultural subsidies and farm-debt bailouts that have received so much publicity in recent years are designed to profit the wealthy owners of the food monopolies, of bonds and bank stocks, and of the biggest capitalist farms. An example is the 1987 "rescue" of the federal Farm Credit System, which holds one-third of the total U.S. farm debt: Congress authorized $4 billion in bonds that will ensure payment to the capitalists holding the banks' previously issued notes, as well as interest to the coupon clippers who buy up the new securities. The dollar value of the boondoggle for finance capital provided by these misnamed "Farmer Mac" bonds exceeds the earlier federal bailouts of Chrysler, Lockheed, or New York City.

WHILE GUARANTEEING these capitalists against losses, the farm credit banks continue to foreclose on farmers every day. When the federal farm credit bank handling loans in Louisiana, Alabama, and Mississippi was closed by Washington in May 1988—the first one to fail in the seventy-year history of the system—government officials warned that some 40 percent of the farmers with outstanding debts to the institution faced either foreclosure or liquidation of their assets. The remaining 30,000 farmers who are Black are concentrated in this region and are sure to be disproportionately hammered by such a wave of dispossessions.

Government farm subsidy payments have risen from 11 percent of farmers' average income from commodity sales in 1979 to more than one-third today. But the billions of dollars disbursed under these programs end up disproportionately in the bank accounts of the agribusiness capitalists and the rich exploiting farmers. The wealthiest 4 percent of U.S. farm operators take in about 60 percent of total farm income each year, and receive almost a quarter of the federal subsidies. The top 1 percent get 40 percent of total farm income and receive almost 10 percent of the subsidies. The working farmers who account for some three-quarters of U.S. farms, on the other hand, receive only 3 percent of total farm income and less than 20 percent of government payments.[16]

---

16. Despite generally declining interest rates from the late 1980s until early in 1994, the situation facing working farmers described here has not eased substantially. Some two-thirds of all farmers in the United States make the majority of their income from off-farm jobs, in factories or other workplaces. According to the latest U.S. Census of Agriculture, the number of farms in the United States in 1992 dropped to below 2 million for the first time since before the U.S. Civil War in the 1860s. At the same time, farmers and their families make up 70 percent of farm employment (up from 60 percent in 1980), with wage laborers accounting for 30 percent.

Farms with annual sales of less than $100,000 accounted for 83 percent of all farms in 1992 but only 17 percent of total sales. Farms with sales of $500,000 or more, on the other hand, accounted for only 2 percent of farms but 46 percent of total sales. While the price of farmers' land and buildings has risen in recent years from the low point in the mid-1980s, it is still 17 percent below prices earlier in that decade, and the drop would be even greater if adjusted for inflation.

Despite an overall drop in farm indebtedness since the mid-1980s due to lower interest rates, farmers with less than $100,000 in sales owed 43 percent of the total debt while also receiving only 43 percent of total federal farm subsidies. Some 15 percent of federal payments go to the 2 percent of farmers with annual sales of above $500,000. Moreover, the prices paid by farmers for various materials and services they use continued to grow at a faster pace than the prices they received for their produce.

In early 1994 the Clinton administration lifted a temporary, eleven-month moratorium on foreclosures by the federal Farmers Home Administration (FmHA). During the moratorium, 1,800 farmers facing foreclosure did not

Both workers and working farmers in the economically advanced capitalist countries are victims of the intensifying inter-imperialist competition for profits on processed agricultural products. The proceeds from mounting food prices are pocketed overwhelmingly by the capitalists who own the processing, packaging, transport, and marketing monopolies. The rise in the cost of food, which does virtually nothing to raise the income of exploited farmers, is the most regressive tax possible on working people both in urban and rural areas, and both in the United States and worldwide.

In Japan, for example, the capitalist government's restrictions on agricultural imports raise the shelf price of rice, wheat, and beef to between three and six times the world average. The bosses and labor bureaucracy try to convince workers that working farmers are to blame for these high food costs, and in this way hope to weaken workers' understanding of the need for an alliance with exploited farmers.

In Western Europe government price supports now account for nearly 50 percent of annual farm income. As in the United States, these enormous government subsidies benefit finance capital and a handful of capitalist farmers, while the exploited majority find it ever more difficult to make a living on the land. Three-quarters of the farming population in both Europe and Japan have to depend on outside income to make a living.

In most imperialist countries, government agricultural programs also drive farmers to take land out of production, at a time when hundreds of millions of people around the world are desperately in need of food. In the United States, for ex-

---

appeal to the FmHA, while the agency ruled against 692 of the 1,090 farmers who did appeal. Altogether, more than 50,000 farmers were considered overdue on their loans at the time the moratorium was lifted.

For more on the way the capitalist monopolies and government are driving working farmers off the land, see "The Crisis Facing Working Farmers" by Doug Jenness in *New International* no. 4 (spring 1985) and the pamphlet, also by Jenness, *Farmers Face the Crisis of the 1990s* (New York: Pathfinder, 1992).

ample, the amount of land left idle under such government programs in 1987 nearly equaled the combined area of North Dakota and Florida, and even more acreage is to be set aside in 1988. In their drive to boost the profits of the agricultural capitalists and giant distribution and processing monopolies, the imperialist rulers promote famine and malnutrition in a world where farmers using available land and current methods could already produce more than enough fiber and food to provide a plentiful diet and adequate clothing to every human being.

8. Declining real wages and accelerating speedup

To counter the deceleration of capital accumulation, the rulers in the United States and other imperialist countries have sought to boost profit rates by increasing their exploitation of the working class. The value of labor power has been driven down in the United States for the first time since the Great Depression of the 1930s. Speedup has squeezed more profits from working people at the cost of health and safety conditions on the job and in society as a whole. The workweek in manufacturing has reached its highest level since World War II.

Real wages in the United States have been pushed back to their level at the beginning of the 1960s. Most of this drop occurred from the late 1970s on, under the impact first of exploding inflation and then the 1981-82 recession. During the post-1981 rout of the unions, the average annual increase in money wages in new contracts dropped to the lowest level since the 1930s, falling farther and farther behind the rise in the cost of living. Many contracts signed after 1981 actually contained wage freezes or outright cuts in money wages.

As recently as the first half of 1986, for example, 31 percent of the workers covered by contracts signed since 1981 had their wages frozen for the first year; another 10 percent took first-year wage cuts; and nearly one-third received no increase in money wages over the entire term of the contract.

Between 1981 and 1984, unionized packinghouse workers

took pay cuts that brought down their average wage rate from $10.69 an hour to $8.24. Contracts signed in late 1986 and early 1987 froze wages at these levels and, in some cases, instituted two-tier systems that drove starting wages down as far as $6 an hour. Wages of nonunion meatpacking workers have been pushed down even farther to $5 an hour and below.

The 1983 basic steel contract signed by the United Steel Workers gave seven major companies an immediate $1.25 an hour wage cut. This was followed in 1986-87 by company-by-company givebacks in USWA contracts of $3.15 an hour to LTV, $1.96 an hour to Bethlehem Steel, and $0.99 an hour to USX and National Steel. Pay cuts were taken by workers in the copper mines, airlines, and many other industries and workplaces as well.

Today one-third of wageworkers in the United States are paid less than $5 per hour.

Union contracts signed in 1987 marked the first time since 1982 that a majority of settlements included percentage wage increases larger in dollar terms than the previous pact. These pay increases, which averaged only 2.1 percent over the life of the contract, still fell short of inflation, ensuring a further decline in real wages in the years ahead.

Class inequality in the distribution of income in the United States has increased as well. Recent years have been a boom time for millions of middle-class and professional families. Those with incomes in the top 10 percent of the U.S. population saw their reported income increase by 16 percent since 1977 and the top 1 percent saw it leap by 50 percent. Over that same period, however, those below the top 20 percent of the population have seen their real buying power go down. And those in the bottom 20 percent have seen their share in aggregate real income drop from 6.8 percent in 1980 to 4.6 percent in 1986.

Real wage growth in Japan has fallen from nearly 6 percent annually in the 1970s to just over 1 percent since 1979. There has also been a steady growth in Japan of subcontracting labor in manufacturing to temporary workers at wages 30 to 50 percent below the rest of the workforce. Subcontracting now accounts for some 40 percent of workers in Japan's steel industry, and out-sourcing for 75 percent of workers in auto.

Real wages declined throughout the imperialist countries of Western Europe between 1979 and 1985, although there have been small gains in a number of these countries as inflation slowed over the past two years. The number of people living below the official poverty line in Britain rose by 55 percent between 1979 and 1985.

9. Rising unemployment and growing relative surplus population

The capitalists' falling average rate of profit results not only in "surplus" plant, "surplus" food, and other "surplus" capital and commodities, but also in what Marx described as a "relative surplus population." The layoffs of wageworkers and dispossession of agricultural producers proceed at an accelerating pace and outstrip capitalism's capacity to absorb this surplus labor power into new employment. The expanding reserve army of the unemployed becomes a source of pressure used by the capitalists to intensify the labor and hold down the wages of employed workers, and to increase competition among all workers.

"The over-work of the employed part of the working class swells the ranks of its reserve," Marx explained, "while, conversely, the greater pressure that the reserve by its competition exerts on the employed workers forces them to submit to overwork and subjects them to the dictates of capital. The condemnation of one part of the working class to enforced idleness by the overwork of the other part, and *vice versa,* becomes a means of enriching the individual capitalists."[17]

This process has accelerated not just in each imperialist country but worldwide since the onset of the capitalists' accumulation crisis in the late 1960s and early 1970s. In the United States,

---

17. *Capital,* vol. 1, p. 789.

Washington boasts about having reduced unemployment to under 6 percent from its peak of more than 10 percent in 1982, the highest level since 1938. What government spokespeople fail to mention is that this "low" figure remains substantially higher than the average of 4.8 percent for the entire quarter century between 1948 and 1973. Since 1973 joblessness has averaged 7.3 percent. While the annual unemployment rate went above 6 percent only twice between 1948 and 1973, it has dipped below 6 percent only twice for the fifteen years since 1973.

Moreover, the "official" government jobless figure that makes its way into the headlines does not include either the growing numbers of part-time workers seeking full-time employment or the so-called discouraged workers who have given up hope of ever finding a job. The government does issue such figures, however; as of December 1987 unemployment measured in this way was 8.8 percent according to government sources. Adding in immigrant workers, layers of women and young people who would look for jobs if the prospects were better, and others overlooked in government figures, the true unemployment picture at the top of the "Reagan boom" is much grimmer than portrayed in official statistics.

Laid-off workers today are also condemned to spend more time off the job than in the past. The average duration of each spell of unemployment rose from eleven weeks during the twenty-seven years prior to 1974; to thirteen weeks from the 1974-75 world recession through 1981; and to sixteen and a half weeks since the 1981-82 recession. Today more than a quarter of those counted in government jobless figures are out of work more than fifteen weeks, compared to only 15 percent in 1967; and nearly 15 percent today are out work more than half a year, compared to only 6 percent in 1967. Even these figures on the average duration of each *spell* of unemployment understate the evolving picture, since in recent years workers more frequently have several bouts of unemployment over the course of a single year. Of the 10.8 million workers laid off between January 1981 and January 1986, nearly one-third were still jobless at the end of that period and another 30 percent were working for 80 percent or less of their previous wage.

The official unemployment rate for Japan was 2.6 percent in April 1988, well below that of most other imperialist powers. But when part-time workers looking for full-time jobs and the so-called discouraged workers are added in, the figure jumps to more than 8 percent, the same as for the United States. Moreover, in Japan the legal workweek remains forty-eight hours.

Prior to the 1974-75 world recession unemployment was below 5 percent in Spain, below 4 percent in Italy and Britain, below 3 percent in France, and below 1 percent in West Germany. In stark contrast, throughout the *upturn* in the capitalist business cycle since 1982 joblessness across Europe has hovered around 11 percent. In April and May 1988 official jobless figures stood at 19.9 percent for Spain; 15.6 percent for Italy; 13.9 cent for the Netherlands; 10.8 percent for Belgium; 10.3 for France; and 8.8 percent for Britain. In Canada, New Zealand, and Australia unemployment is running at more than 7 percent.

The most devastating effects of capitalism's production of a relative surplus population is in the Third World. Official unemployment rates, while themselves very high, conceal the true enormity of the numbers of human beings who live on the knife-edge of existence without any way to make a living. Major cities throughout the semicolonial countries are surrounded by makeshift neighborhoods of peasant families who have been driven off the land and eke out a meager existence as vendors or doing odd jobs when they can get them. These dispossessed toilers are both peasants who would pour back to the countryside in their millions if arable land and cheap credit were available to them, but at the same time are unemployed workers in the growing ranks of capitalism's relative surplus population.

In India, for example, there are 25 million employed wage-workers, and tens of millions are officially registered as unemployed. But this is out of a population of 800 million! The immensity of unemployment and underemployment in India, both in countryside and city, is completely obscured by official statistics, since the vast majority of its toilers are not even counted in government employment figures.

In Latin America official unemployment across the continent rose by nearly 50 percent between 1980 and 1987, from 47 million to 70 million out of a population of 400 million. According to the International Labor Organization, the percentage of Latin America's toilers who are not even counted on the jobless rolls and scrape by on the margins of economic life jumped from 29 percent in 1980 to 39 percent in 1985.

*   *   *

Given unemployment levels already at a post-1930s high during an upturn in the business cycle, the next international recession will have grave economic and social repercussions throughout the capitalist world. Interimperialist rivalry for dwindling markets will intensify. Price competition will sharpen. Capitalist overproduction and excess capacity will be exacerbated, leading to a new wave of plant closings and layoffs. Investment in expansion of plant and equipment will drop even more steeply than over the past decade. With government and private indebtedness already at an all-time high, bank and business failures will accelerate and defaults on mushrooming corporate and Third World debt will increase. Finance capital will be pushed to greater borrowing and speculation in an effort to pull out of the trough.

Government intervention in this destabilizing process will grow by leaps and bounds. But no alternative economic policies followed by the employing classes or by their states and political parties can avert these consequences of the evolution of the falling average rate of industrial profit. The capitalists are not refraining from major new capacity-expanding investment because they are choosing to divert too much capital into securities markets, real estate speculation, loan sharking, and speeding up production in outmoded factories. The cause and effect are the other way around. The exploiters are sinking their capital into "labor-saving" retooling and speculative paper claims on values because they can get a better rate of return there than from investments in building new factories, installing major new technologies, and hiring on large amounts of additional labor power.

The coming world depression
The capitalists' falling average rate and stagnating mass of profits have undermined the equilibrium of world capitalism. The October 1987 crash on the world's stock markets signaled the consequences: no longer can the exploiters be confident that a major bankruptcy, loan default, crop failure, bank collapse, deflationary slump, stock market dive, or other partial crisis will be buffered and absorbed by the strength of production, investment, and trade in the broader capitalist economy. Today, at this advanced point in the stagnation of capital accumulation, any of these partial crises has the growing potential to spiral out of control and trigger a worldwide depression and a generalized social crisis.

III. THE DYNAMICS OF WORLD REVOLUTION TODAY

THE POLITICAL PERIOD in which we are now living was initiated with Washington's entry into World War II. Its character and trajectory have been determined by the international relationship of class forces and the structure of the imperialist system that came out of that war.

The politics and economics of capitalist development
Our understanding of the interrelationship between the development of the world market and the dynamics of world revolution is grounded in the political continuity of the modern communist workers movement. The initial lessons drawn from this accumulation of class-struggle experience are generalized in the writings of Marx and Engels and in the programmatic con-

quests of the Bolshevik Party and Communist International under Lenin's leadership.

In the opening years of the 1920s the leadership of the Communist International was confronted by a temporary stabilization of the major European capitalist states following the war-precipitated social crisis and tumultuous revolutionary upsurge of 1917-19. The international leadership had to win the new communist parties to understand and carry out a shift in tactical orientation to take account of the changed situation.

At the third Comintern congress in June 1921 the Bolshevik leaders initiated a discussion of the reasons for this shift. This discussion also raised the broader related question of how communists must recognize and act on the interconnected economic phenomena and political events that establish political periods, necessitate conjunctural shifts in tactics, and mark turning points in the long-term development of world capitalism and the class struggle.

A resolution and report on the world economic crisis and the tasks of the Communist International were discussed and adopted by the delegates: "Report on the World Economic Crisis and the New Tasks of the Communist International" and "Theses on the International Situation and the Tasks of the Comintern." Leon Trotsky prepared and presented the report and resolution at that congress on behalf of the Bolshevik leadership. He further developed their major themes eighteen months later in a report to the fourth Comintern congress in December 1922: "Report on the New Soviet Economic Policy and the Perspectives of the World Revolution." In April 1923 he summarized some of the main theoretical points from these Comintern reports and resolutions in a short and condensed letter, which was published later that year under the title "The Curve of Capitalist Development."[18]

---

18. "The Curve of Capitalist Development" is reprinted following this article. For the reports and theses presented by Trotsky to the third and fourth

The 1921 Comintern report explained that in order for communists to assess accurately the current political conjuncture and direction of development of the capitalist world, it is not sufficient to chart the ups and downs of the business cycle: that is, the trade and inventory cycles of recession and recovery that "were inherent in capitalism at its very birth" and "will accompany it to its grave."[19] Nor is it possible to deduce some lawful longer-term cycle, taking place over a number of shorter business cycles, that itself shapes the economic and political prospects of the exploiters and the exploited.

There is no "rigidly lawful rhythm" to the long-term development of world capitalism, Trotsky pointed out in the 1923 article. Capitalist economic cycles, of whatever duration or amplitude, he insisted, "are not fundamental but derivative economic phenomena. They unfold on the basis of the development of productive forces through the medium of market relations." Capitalism, he emphasized, "is not characterized solely by periodic recurrence of cycles—otherwise what would occur would be a complex repetition and not dynamic development."

It is true, Trotsky said, that broad changes in world politics and class relations are rooted "in the changes of the economic foundation" of society "and not anywhere else." But he reminded the delegates of Engels's observation that these underlying economic factors "generally operate a long time in secret before they suddenly and violently make themselves felt on the surface."

Using statistics on production of major manufactured and

Comintern congresses, see Leon Trotsky, *The First Five Years of the Communist International* (New York: Pathfinder, 1972), vol. 1, pp. 174-261, and vol. 2, especially pp. 258-63. Lenin's report at the third and fourth congresses of the Communist International can be found in *Speeches at Congresses of the Communist International,* as well as in volumes 32 and 33 of the *Collected Works.* All these books are available from Pathfinder Press.

19. Trotsky, *The First Five Years of the Communist International,* vol. 1, p. 200.

agricultural goods, the evolution of world trade, and other indices broadly measuring advances in productivity of human labor as the world market expands, Trotsky explained, it is possible to draw a curve that traces the economic development of world capitalism from the Industrial Revolution in the latter part of the eighteenth century to current times. Once this curve has been charted, however, a careful observer will note that its turning points and the length and steepness of its upward, downward, and stagnant segments—corresponding to particular stages or periods in the history of the international capitalist system—depend not solely or even primarily on lawful capitalist economic phenomena.

"As regards the large segments of the capitalist curve of development," Trotsky said, ". . . their character and duration are determined not by the internal interplay of capitalist forces but by those external conditions through whose channel capitalist development flows. The acquisition by capitalism of new countries and continents, the discovery of new natural resources, and, in the wake of these, such major facts of 'superstructural' order as wars and revolutions, determine the character and the replacement of ascending, stagnating, or declining epochs of capitalist development."

THE SHIFTING TRAJECTORY of modern human history has been determined in the last analysis by the uneven and combined development that reflects the extension, and since 1917, also the retreat, of the capitalist mode of production and exchange. The evolution of these capitalist relations cannot be abstracted from the concrete ways that capitalism absorbs and interacts with the various preexisting forms of social organization, exploitation, and oppression drawn into its expanding world domination over several centuries. The capitalist mode of production uses as raw material all the various social relations that capitalism inherits.

Capitalism acts in different ways on different of these materials—for example, on various categories of social labor: indigenous populations living under tribal forms of social organization; former slaves, serfs, or bonded laborers; peasants and other rural toilers; oppressed nationalities that are overwhelmingly working-class; various waves of immigrants; and so on. It forcibly draws the labor of these toilers into the worldwide production and circulation of surplus value, while at the same time maintaining and reproducing important aspects and legacies of precapitalist social relations as adjuncts to its own forms and methods of exploitation and oppression. Most importantly, it creates new combinations from these interactions.

With the victory of the Bolshevik-led revolution in Russia in 1917, prospects for a truly world revolution became a reality for the first time in history. The first workers and peasants republic was a beacon for the world's exploited producers, including throughout the oppressed countries of the colonial world. The triumph in Russia spurred revolutionary movements and the establishment of governments of the toilers throughout the oppressed Asian regions of the old tsarist empire. National liberation struggles against imperialist superexploitation and oppression emerged throughout Asia and growing parts of the colonial world, and these struggles became irreversibly intertwined with the defense and extension of the socialist revolution.

Thus, ever since October 1917 the course of history has been increasingly shaped by the dynamics of world revolution: by the interaction of the class struggle and the testing of political leaderships of the workers and farmers in the imperialist countries, the colonial and semicolonial world, and the workers states. As the 1921 Comintern documents explain, the course of the disequilibrium and equilibrium of world capitalism does "not take place in a social and political vacuum," but involves "the struggle between living forces: the contending classes and their parties."

The history of the world capitalist system throughout most of the twentieth century has been molded by waves of struggles by toilers in countryside and city, in imperialist centers and oppressed countries, against capital and the imperialist system of domination; by the ebbs and flows of these struggles; by their defeats, stalemates, and victories; and by their mutual effects on one another. It has been profoundly changed by workers and peasants overturning capitalist property relations, leading to the establishment of a growing number of workers states outside the world market for capital.

The fundamental characteristics of particular segments in the curve of capitalist development do not repeat in broad outline or new forms those of one or another historical period that came before it. Instead, the characteristics of each period reflect in new and concrete ways the interrelationship of economic, social, and political forces under the changed conditions. New questions are posed before the working class for resolution.

Grasping this dynamic equips that part of the working class that is the communist party to discover not only the character of the conjuncture through which we are living, but also to anticipate sudden leaps that speed up the tempo of world and national politics and change both the rules and consequences of actions in the class struggle. Most importantly, it equips us to organize on the basis of this understanding and prepare consciously to change the world.

Fall of the world's final empire

Today's deepening international capitalist crisis is part of a broader decline: the fall of the world's final capitalist empire —that of finance capital, whose dominant power is U.S. imperialism.

This decline follows on the successive fall of each of the most powerful European colonial empires that arose over the history of world capitalism. Each, for a time, was dominant over the other imperial powers. The explosive rise of rival European empires of finance capital during the closing decades of the nineteenth century and the opening decade of the twentieth resulted in the opening guns of World War I and the slaughter that accompanied that desperate interimperialist war for redivision of the colonies and domination of the exploited nations. The outcome of that war, and the establishment of the Soviet workers and peasants republic in October 1917, gave rise to the conditions that weakened and eventually brought down colonialism in subsequent decades.

In the wake of these events, the U.S. rulers were able to benefit from the weakening of their imperialist rivals. The growing strength of Wall Street and Washington slowed down for a time the decline of the imperialist system. U.S. capitalism, which Lenin called "the only full beneficiary from the war,"[20] emerged in the 1920s not only as the capitalist world's creditor, but as its leading industrial power as well. The basis had been laid for U.S. imperialism to challenge Britain's receding political and military supremacy.

The U.S. rulers bided their time over the following two decades. With the unfolding of World War II, however, they made their decisive move, in the Atlantic and the Pacific both, for world dominance among the imperialist powers. That worldwide bloodbath was the horrible price paid by humanity for the failure of the working-class movement to resolve the crisis of world capitalism and its imperialist system that marked the 1920s and 1930s. This deepening crisis saw two decades of agricultural depression, a decade of deep international industrial depression and mass unemployment, an interimperialist trade war, surging fascist movements, and sharpening imperialist aggression.

At the opening of the 1920s and over the course of the 1930s, the working class waged gigantic struggles that turned the latter half of the 1930s into a prerevolutionary period and posed

---

20. V.I. Lenin, "Report to the Second World Congress of the Communist International," in Lenin, *Collected Works* (Moscow: Progress Publishers, 1966), vol. 31, p. 217. This speech can also be found in John Riddell, ed., *Workers of the World and Oppressed Peoples, Unite!: Proceedings and Documents of the Second Congress* (New York: Pathfinder, 1991), pp. 107-25.

new opportunities and tasks for a world communist movement. As social democratic and Stalinist misleaderships demobilized and disorganized these struggles, however, the failure to register victories—and thus resolve the capitalist crisis to the benefit of the great majority of humanity—opened the road across Europe to defeats of the workers and farmers at the hands of fascist reaction. These defeats were the most crushing in the history of the modern working class.[21]

World War II was the devastating product of those historic defeats. This interimperialist conflict over dominance in the world capitalist market and system of oppression and exploitation was not, as Washington's propagandists claimed, a war to liberate the colonial peoples. Its purpose was to redivide the fruits of domination over them. Substantial layers of the major capitalist ruling classes among the Allied nations, moreover, hoped that the war launched by German imperialism against the Soviet Union would weaken the workers state enough to make possible its overturn and the reimposition of capitalist exploitation over its large toiling population and vast lands.

The transformation of the U.S. workforce during World War II, followed by Washington's victory at the head of the Allied capitalist governments in 1945, prepared the qualitative strengthening of U.S. capitalism's economic preponderance and established its overwhelming military supremacy among the imperialist powers. The propagandists of U.S. capitalism now spoke of an "American century."[22]

---

21. For an account of these struggles, and the betrayal of them by Stalinist and social democratic leaderships, see Leon Trotsky, *The Struggle against Fascism in Germany* (New York: Pathfinder, 1971); *The Spanish Revolution (1931-39)* (New York: Pathfinder, 1973), and *Leon Trotsky on France* (New York: Pathfinder, 1979).

22. In fact, the slogan had been coined as early as 1941, on the eve of U.S. entry into the war, by the U.S. publishing baron Henry Luce. In an editorial in his *Life* magazine February 17, 1941, Luce wrote that the time had come "to accept wholeheartedly our duty and our opportunity as the most powerful and vital nation in the world and in consequence exert upon the world the full im-

The rise of national independence movements during the war weakened the European (and late-arriving Japanese) capitalist empires still further, resulting in the rapid loss of the vast majority of their colonies over the following years. U.S. imperialism moved into the breach, rapidly expanding its economic interests and military influence throughout the former colonies. At the same time, Washington maintained and reinforced direct control over its colony in Puerto Rico and numerous other Caribbean and Pacific islands; consolidated its longstanding economic and military domination over neocolonial regimes throughout Central and South America and in the former U.S. colony in the Philippines; and transformed the colonial possessions of Hawaii and Alaska into states of the union, formalizing its expansion into an arctic and Pacific state, as well.

THIS "AMERICAN CENTURY," however, had already begun to decline before it could arise. A stable historic rise of Washington's world position would have required a reversal of the fall of the European colonial empires. An "american century" had to be a new imperialist century, a new century of international finance capital. It had to be based on an extension of the world imperialist system, not on further retreats and defeats. Only on that foundation could the U.S. rulers' new and dominant position among their capitalist rivals correspond to an overall strengthening of the world imperialism at whose head they stood and with whose fortunes they were inescapably intertwined. By the midpoint of World War II, however, the prospects for such an outcome began to recede:

  • In early 1943 the victory over German imperialism at Stal-

---

pact of our influence, for such purposes as we see fit and by such means as we see fit. . . . It now becomes our time to be the powerhouse from which the ideals spread throughout the world."

ingrad signaled that the Soviet working people, in and out of uniform, had ensured the survival of the world's first, and at that time only, workers state.

• In 1945 the partisan guerrillas under the leadership of the Communist Party of Yugoslavia swept to power over the German occupation army in that country, blocking the establishment of a bourgeois regime and opening the road to the establishment of a workers and peasants government. By 1947 capitalist social relations had been overturned and replaced by nationalized industry, a state monopoly of foreign trade, and a planned economy.[23]

• The Soviet army occupied Eastern Europe in the course of its 1944-45 counteroffensive against the Axis imperialist invasion, and by 1949 capitalist property relations had been abolished in Poland, Czechoslovakia, Hungary, Romania, Bulgaria, Albania, and East Germany.[24]

• The 1945-46 strike wave in the United States blocked the employing class from its goal of rolling back the conquests won by the working class during the second half of the 1930s.[25] While the U.S. labor movement was unable to sustain these battles, capitalist reaction was sufficiently stymied that the door remained open to a new rise by the mid-1950s of the Black rights struggle that had emerged during the closing years of the war. This was the social force that, more than any other, determined the political trajectory of the U.S. class struggle in the following decades. Moreover, the "Bring the Troops Home" movement

---

23. For an account of the establishment of a workers and farmers government in Yugoslavia, see George Fyson and others, *The Truth about Yugoslavia: Why Working People Should Oppose Intervention* (New York: Pathfinder, 1993).

24. For more on the overturn of capitalist rule in Eastern Europe, see Joseph Hansen and others, *Class, Party, and State and the Eastern European Revolution* (New York: Pathfinder, 1969).

25. For an account of the upsurge in strikes following World War II, see Art Preis, *Labor's Giant Step: The First 20 Years of the CIO* (New York: Pathfinder, 1964), pp. 257-370.

among U.S. GIs at the end of World War II blocked Washington's plans to redeploy U.S. soldiers to China to bolster the landlord-capitalist regime there in the developing civil war.[26]

• In 1949 the Chinese revolution tore one-fifth of the world's population from imperialist domination. The new workers and peasants regime successfully turned back Washington's efforts at the opening of the 1950s to reimpose imperialist control over northern Korea and use that as a launching pad to roll back the Chinese revolution. Under the impetus of the mobilization around the war in Korea, a workers state was established in China as well by 1953.

• In 1954 Vietnamese liberation fighters defeated the U.S.-backed French imperialist army, and within two years the new Democratic Republic of Vietnam had become a workers state.

• The failure of combined British and French forces to maintain control over Egypt's Suez Canal in 1956, or to sustain working-class support at home for this effort, marked the final full-scale retreat of Washington's most powerful allies from playing a central role in policing the world imperialist system. Washington, with hundreds of thousands of troops stationed at U.S. bases around the globe, had to shoulder responsibility for that worldwide counterrevolutionary task.

• Over subsequent decades further setbacks have been sustained by the U.S.-dominated imperialist and colonial system in regions throughout the world: Indochina, Algeria, Cuba, Palestine, Ethiopia, the former Portuguese African colonies, Iran, Grenada, Nicaragua, and elsewhere.

New stage in imperialist system

The outcome of World War II marked the opening of a new stage in the history of the imperialist system. The U.S. rulers

---

26. For an account of the Bring the Troops Home movement in the closing months of World War II, see Mary-Alice Waters, "1945: When U.S. Troops Said 'No!'" in *New International* no. 7 (1991).

emerged victorious and dominant among the imperialist powers. But the Soviet Union had survived, and other new setbacks to imperialism—dealt by the rise of the colonial revolution especially—had begun to be inflicted at the very peak of Washington's postwar power, and have continued and extended over the subsequent four-and-a-half decades.

The struggles for national liberation and socialism became even more intertwined in the aftermath of World War II, reinforcing the dynamic set in motion by the October 1917 revolution and its impact throughout Asia and other parts of the colonial world. In China, Korea, Vietnam, and Cuba revolutionary struggles against imperialist domination, against political tyranny, and for land reform took on an anticapitalist direction, led to the establishment of workers and peasants governments, and grew over into socialist revolutions against both foreign and domestic capitalist exploiters.

At the beginning of the 1960s the victory in Cuba opened the socialist revolution in the Americas, right at the doorstep of U.S. imperialism. From the outset, the leaders of the new Cuban workers state sought ways to put both their political authority and the power of the revolutionary government at the service of the international struggle against imperialism. They recognized the growing interpenetration of battles by workers and peasants worldwide against imperialist domination and capitalist exploitation. They took full political responsibility for socialist Cuba's place as a beacon for the oppressed and exploited peoples not only of the Americas, but also of Africa, Asia, and the Pacific. On that basis they integrated Cuba into the Movement of Nonaligned Countries and its leadership.

During its first decade, the Cuban revolution sustained many blows from imperialism and other reactionary forces, including the murder of Ernesto Che Guevara in 1967. Despite these blows, by the latter half of the 1960s the leaders of the Cuban revolution had not only begun to build a mass communist party of the vanguard of Cuba's workers and farmers. They had also begun to use their leadership of a workers state to chart a political course that has advanced the renewal of communist leadership on a world scale for the first time since the Stalinist destruction of the Communist International.[27]

No replacement for U.S. imperialism

The industrial monopoly held by U.S. imperialism coming out of the war rapidly began to erode. By the early 1950s, the Japanese and West German capitalists were modernizing and expanding their manufacturing capacity more quickly than their U.S. rivals. By the mid-1960s this had resulted in renewed price competition and altered the economic balance of forces in the world capitalist market.

This relative decline of U.S. imperialism since the end of World War II, however, has not strengthened its Western European, Japanese, or other imperialist competitors. Nor has it brought any one of them closer to establishing its own predominance in the capitalist world.

Despite intensifying competition for profits on the world market, the rival national ruling classes are chained together in their decline, with the U.S. capitalist rulers at their head. They are bound together by the need to halt the uneven but continuing shift in the world relationship of class forces since World War II to the advantage of the workers and farmers, and to increase the rate of exploitation of the toilers at home and abroad. In advancing these common goals, there is no replacement within the imperialist alliance for Washington's military power, U.S. economic weight, or the dollar as international reserve currency.

The Japanese, German, and other imperialist ruling classes, of

---

27. Lessons of the first decade of the Cuban revolution are discussed in Joseph Hansen, *Dynamics of the Cuban Revolution.* See also the introductions by Mary-Alice Waters to *To Speak the Truth: Why Washington's 'Cold War' Against Cuba Doesn't End* by Fidel Castro and Ernesto Che Guevara, and *Che Guevara: Economics and Politics in the Transition to Socialism* by Carlos Tablada. All three books are available from Pathfinder.

course, seek to advance their own interests against each other and against the U.S. rulers and U.S.-owned monopolies in the world market. Any advantages gained in this regard, however, are temporary and partial when weighed politically against the weakening of the imperialist system as a whole.

This situation is new in the history of world capitalism. The decline of the economic, monetary, political, and military dominance of each previous leading imperial power cleared the way for an already well-prepared successor. These transitions were marked by shifting alliances and wars among the ascending and declining regimes. The victor became the axis of new military and political blocs. Its exports dominated world trade, and its currency world finance.

In the sixteenth and seventeenth centuries the Spanish and Dutch empires, through bloody colonial expansion in the Americas and Asia, accumulated much of the wealth on which capitalism based its initial burst of growth. By the eighteenth century they had been displaced by Britain and France, and by the end of the 1700s British agriculture, banking, and manufacturing capital had laid the foundation for what was to be almost a century and a half of varying degrees of capitalist world predominance before giving way to Wall Street and Washington.

The lack of any alternative to U.S. predominance today is a manifestation of the terminal weakness of finance capital's imperialist system of domination. The policy choices of the U.S. rulers do not represent international leadership by a rising social class, but the pragmatic survival tactics of a wealthy and powerful but declining social class at the helm of a decaying empire. The ruling capitalist families have no historical view, no line of march along which they are seeking to lead society. They have no long-term strategies. They make short-term decisions to deal with the problems at hand, test the waters, and confront further—and always unexpected—problems as defense of their profits and prerogatives require them to do so.

These ruling families have no "new ideas," no "solutions" to the crisis gripping their social system. They select not the leaders they "need," but the leaders they are able to produce. They rely on their national economic weight; the corruption and compliance it can purchase, including within broad layers of the working class; their massive military might; their monopoly of state power; and both legal and extralegal violence against those who resist their exploitation and oppression. On that basis, the capitalist rulers' propagandists, academics, and spokespeople produce not "ideas," but ideological rationalizations backed up by the power of the existing fact.

U.S. strategic military power

The U.S. armed forces are the spinal column of NATO and of the military alliances with imperialist Japan, Australia, and New Zealand, as well as the ultimate sword standing behind the Israeli and South African regimes that serve as imperialist bastions in the Middle East and southern Africa. Washington has 63 percent of the imperialist world's naval tonnage; 46 percent of its land-based and 91 percent of its sea-based jet fighters; and 39 percent of its ground troops.

The U.S. rulers' international military dominance, however, is not based simply on being the most massively armed strategic power within a system of military alliances with other imperialist governments. Nor, like British imperialism in its heyday, does Washington rely primarily on its unchallenged position as the world's leading naval power. Unlike any of its predecessors, the military might of U.S. imperialism reaches directly into every part of the world.

One-quarter of all U.S. forces—some 550,000 troops—are based at nearly 400 U.S. military installations in Western Europe, the Middle East, Africa, the Indian Ocean, Japan, the Philippines, South Korea, Australia, the Pacific islands, Panama, Puerto Rico, and Cuba's Guantánamo Bay. Another 7 to 8 percent of U.S. forces, about 180,000 troops, are on naval patrols in the Persian Gulf and elsewhere around the world. Five of the U.S. military's eighteen standing divisions are in Western Europe, and there are 277 U.S. bases or other installations there, strung from Iceland to Britain and all the way across the continent to Turkey.[28]

The Soviet workers state had begun to construct a nuclear arsenal by the early 1950s to break the monopoly carefully developed by Washington in the years immediately following World War II. In contrast, the economically strongest of U.S. imperialism's competitors—Japan and West Germany—are blocked by historical and political factors from developing nuclear arsenals. Germany's attempted nuclear armament would bring a showdown with the Soviet Union, as well as social upheaval throughout Western Europe. In Japan, whose people were the first victims of the horrors of atomic weapons at the hands of the U.S. rulers, steps to build a nuclear arsenal would so deeply divide the population as to push that society toward civil war.

The British and French imperialists do have their own nuclear arsenals, as does the Israeli regime. The rulers of the South African apartheid regime have some nuclear weapons as well. These subsidiary arsenals, despite the very real dangers they pose to the world's working people, do not lessen the de-

---

28. Since the disintegration of the Moscow-dominated Warsaw Pact military alliance at the opening of the 1990s, Washington has decreased the size of its military forces stationed abroad, especially in Europe. At the same time, the U.S. rulers have stepped up demands that their rivals in Europe and in Japan take on more of the financial burden and political risks of policing the world on behalf of imperialist interests. U.S. imperialism, however, remains determined to preserve its global military predominance, including deployment of substantial U.S. troops and matériel on every continent and in every major ocean and sea.

Since 1987, the U.S. armed forces have reduced the number of active duty troops by more than 20 percent. The numbers stationed abroad have dropped from over half a million to some 306,000, and now comprise some 18 percent of all U.S. military personnel, down from a quarter. Two standing U.S. army divisions are currently based in Europe, with the Sixth Fleet operating in the Mediterranean. In Asia the Marines maintain divisions in the Pacific and at a base in Okinawa, as well as the Seventh Fleet in the Indian Ocean, and the U.S. Army has divisions in South Korea and Hawaii.

pendence of the entire imperialist system on Washington's strategic nuclear arms and delivery systems.

U.S. military supremacy rules out a repetition of interimperialist conflicts such as the First and Second World Wars, despite mounting economic and political tensions among the rival national ruling classes and their states.[29] In addition, the imperialists are aware that the previous two world wars were fought at a heavy price to international finance capital: the Russian revolution; Chinese revolution; the overturn of capitalist property relations in Eastern Europe, North Korea, China, and Vietnam; and national liberation struggles that exploded across Asia and the Pacific, Africa, Central and South America, and the Caribbean.

Moreover, the nuclear standoff with the Soviet Union also compels the imperialist rulers to shelve for the foreseeable future their historic goal of rolling back the workers states and reestablishing capitalist exploitation over the peoples of those countries.

Instead, policing Asia, the Pacific, Africa, Latin America, and the Caribbean has been the focus of imperialism's efforts to hold back the world revolution over the past four decades. It is in the colonial and semicolonial countries that the most massive and brutal imperialist military power has been used since World War II—from Korea to Algeria, from Kenya to the Dominican Republic, from Vietnam to Angola, from Palestine to Ireland, from Nicaragua to the Congo, from the Suez Canal to the Persian Gulf, from Grenada to New Caledonia.

ALL THE IMPERIALIST ruling classes are dependent on the massive presence of U.S. ground, air, and naval forces on every

---

29. For a discussion of the fundamental shift in the postwar world political situation that once again began posing the prospect of interimperialist war, see "Imperialism's March toward Fascism and War" later in this issue, as well as the lead article in *New International* no. 7, "The Opening Guns of World War III."

continent and in every ocean to maintain the world capitalist order against struggles for national liberation and social justice by workers and peasants. A few of Washington's imperialist allies still play a direct military role in this counterrevolutionary effort, although limited to regions near their own borders or under their colonial rule either now or in the recent past. France operates brutally in this way vis-à-vis Chad and a few other former African colonies, as well as in New Caledonia and its other Pacific and Caribbean colonies (Tahiti, Guadeloupe, Martinique, Guyane); Britain in the Malvinas and Ireland; Israel in the Arab lands surrounding its occupying niche; and South Africa in Namibia, Angola, Mozambique, and elsewhere in southern Africa.

Even in these cases, as soon as conflicts become far-reaching, U.S. military power is decisive. Without Washington's direct military involvement in transport, logistics, matériel, and intelligence, for example, British imperialism could not have fought, let alone won, the war to hold on to the Malvinas. It was for this reason that former U.S. secretary of defense Caspar Weinberger was decorated in 1987 by the queen of England. The political obstacles to massive, U.S.-organized assistance to South Africa's apartheid regime have made it impossible for Pretoria to stand up militarily in southern Angola to the combined forces of the Cuban volunteers, Angolan army, South West African People's Organisation, and the African National Congress.

A number of European capitalist governments, having lost their last colonial holdings in the 1960s and 1970s, have been reduced to playing little or no independent military role in the Third World compared to the major imperialist powers. This is true of the Belgian and Portuguese rulers, for example. Together with other smaller imperialist countries, some of which never had their own colonies, they now contribute to the defense of world capitalist interests primarily through political and military complicity with U.S.-organized overt and covert operations.

In addition, not even the most strongly armed and politically servile of imperialism's neocolonial client states are reliable as stable military surrogates for Washington, nor can they be. The past decade alone, for example, has seen the overthrow of the shah of Iran; the demise of the Marcos dictatorship in the Philippines; the growing instability of the South Korean regime; a debt crisis shaking the governments of Brazil and Argentina; and a political-economic crisis threatening any stable role for the Mexican ruling class.

Only the military forces of U.S. imperialism itself are capable of patrolling every region of the earth. Washington can and will continue to pressure its allies to pick up more of the costs for this mounting military effort. It must and will pull back from forward military positions around the world that are less and less sustainable economically and politically. But this will not fundamentally alter the military equation among the imperialist powers. While the imperialist ruling classes will keep getting pushed back by advances in the world revolution, they can never give up their attempt to preserve the greatest possible portion of the globe for capitalist exploitation.

The deepening economic crisis will increase imperialist pressures toward war, as workers and peasants organize struggles to defend themselves against intensifying attacks on their social conditions and national sovereignty. The most decisive victories for the world revolution since World War II have all been in the semicolonial countries. But wars fought in these countries by the imperialists—even if successful—have neither reversed the fundamental decline of their world system nor brought them long-term stability. Nor have bloody triumphs for international finance capital in the Third World brought it closer to overthrowing the workers states, where capitalist property relations have been abolished.

Moreover, Washington's historic defeat in Vietnam severely undercut support among working people in the United States for such military aggression. It reinforces such attitudes in other imperialist countries. It creates important obstacles to the use of imperialist military might in Central America and the Caribbean, elsewhere in the Americas, Asia, the Pacific, and Africa.

In addition, growing opposition to nuclear arms among working people throughout Western Europe in particular, as well as the United States and other imperialist countries, has become a powerful objective political factor limiting the military options of Washington and its allies. It threatens the imperialists with unexpected and explosive reactions to the deployment of nuclear weapons and delivery systems and the movements of nuclear-armed ships and submarines.

U.S. economic power and the dollar

In addition to Washington's military power, the enormous size and weight of the U.S. market and productive capacity also preclude any replacement of U.S. imperialist dominance in the capitalist world. The conditions of production, finance, and trade in the United States are the primary determinant of the direction and prospects of the entire international capitalist economy. This remains true to a much greater degree than for any other imperialist country.

The relative decline of U.S. capitalism increases the vulnerability of all the imperialist economies to partial crises. No other power, however, has the economic size to serve as a counterweight that could salvage the equilibrium of the world capitalist system.

Despite the rapid end of the industrial monopoly of U.S. imperialism that came out of World War II, the annual output of U.S. capitalism today remains three times that of its closest competitor, Japan. The U.S. share of world exports has fallen from 15 percent at the beginning of the 1960s to around 11 percent in the mid-1980s. But this frequently cited figure overstates the erosion of U.S. economic power, since it leaves out commodities produced and exported by U.S.-owned factories in other countries.

U.S.-owned corporations today produce 17 percent of the exports on the world market, roughly the same as two decades ago. In 1985, for example, U.S.-owned affiliates in other countries sold $410 billion in goods to buyers where they are located and another $294 billion in exports, while exports from the United States itself totaled $216 billion. The big majority of commodities produced in the United States are sold on the U.S. market, and U.S. capital has often found it more profitable to produce overseas for sales on foreign markets.[30]

The enormous size of the U.S. economy can be gauged by how much it buys, as well as how much it sells. The U.S. market alone absorbs some 25 percent of the goods imported by all the imperialist countries combined. The United States, for example, makes up half the international market for consumer electronics, and 25 to 30 percent of world purchases of auto parts.

The economic power of U.S. imperialism that stands behind the dollar precludes its replacement as the international reserve currency in capitalist trade and finance. At the end of 1987, more than two-thirds of the foreign exchange reserves of all the world's governments were held in U.S. dollars, while 15 percent were held in West German marks and 7 percent in Japanese yen.[31]

The U.S. rulers are even able to wield the historically declining dollar as a club in their economic competition against their imperialist rivals. In 1987, for example, the central banks of other imperialist governments bought up $130 billion in dollars to help bolster the plummeting value of the U.S. currency and defend the competitiveness of their own exports. Together with dollars bought over previous years, Tokyo, Bonn, London, and other rivals of U.S. imperialism ended up sitting on more

---

30. As described in the 1994 article later in this issue, U.S. imperialism's cost-cutting drive enabled it since the latter 1980s to regain the edge on its imperialist rivals. Between 1985 and 1994, the U.S. rulers' market share of world exports (not including exports by U.S. affiliates abroad) rose from 11 percent to 14 percent, while the world market shares of Japan and of Germany and other European Union countries all declined.

31. At the end of 1993, dollars made up some 61 percent of reserves with both the German mark and Japanese yen comprising marginally higher percentages than in 1987.

than $450 billion of the depreciating currency at the end of 1987. But doing so was a lesser evil for Washington's rivals than allowing a free-falling dollar to endanger the entire international monetary system.

In this way, the weight of U.S. capitalism is successfully brought to bear on its competitors to shore up the commanding, even if slipping, U.S. share in the division of the international pool of surplus value produced by the world's toilers. The rivals of the U.S. ruling class mobilized their own national capital to aid the additional accumulation of capital in the United States. That is one of the ways that interimperialist competition works today, in a situation where Wall Street and Washington retain their predominant position and intensifying conflicts among the rival ruling classes cannot be resolved by war as they were twice before in this century.

This balance of forces among the capitalist powers cannot be substantially altered by agreements among the 12 Western European governments that make up the European Community, popularly called the European Common Market. The EC is scheduled to end all internal barriers to trade, labor, and capital flows by 1992, creating a common market of some 350 million people. But the 1992 goal is already in trouble, as rival capitalist interests jockey to protect their own profits.

Competition among the dozen European ruling classes will intensify, not abate, with the next world recession or explosion of inflation, let alone a more devastating social and economic crisis. The rival national capitals will not give up their separate states, which protect their interests against each other and above all against the working people off whose labor they grow wealthy.

Without a common European state there can be no common currency to rival the dollar, nor common monetary and financial policies. Whatever their efforts to ensure a wider European market for their goods and capital, the German exploiters will never mortgage their profits to the fortunes of the French economy, the French to the fortunes of the British, the British to the Portuguese, Danish, Spanish, or Greek. Thus no single European currency has any prospect of supplanting these various "coin of the realm," let alone replacing the dollar as the world's reserve currency.

The U.S. rulers, for their part, are already responding to the prospect of greater rivalry from a European common market by pushing for one of their own with the Canadian capitalists. U.S. finance capital is also trying to use Mexico's debt burden as a club to bludgeon the government of that semicolonial country—already the third largest market for U.S. exports—to open its doors even wider to U.S. imperialist penetration and domination.[32]

Effects of post–World War II expansion and international penetration of capital on class structure in the capitalist world

In the closing years of World War II, the international relationship of class forces shifted to the detriment of imperialism. Important victories have been won since then by the toilers of Asia, the Pacific, Africa, and the Americas. In a few semicolonial countries working people waged revolutionary struggles that established workers and peasants governments, put an end to imperialist domination, and culminated over a number of years in the expropriation of the landlords and capitalists.

Cuba is the outstanding example of the gains that are made possible by this socialist course. Not only does Cuba's economic and social development stand in stark contrast to the rest of Latin America and other Third World countries, but the leadership of the Cuban revolution has been decisive in beginning

---

32. While formal barriers to trade and commerce in the European Community were eliminated January 1, 1994, commitment to a common currency has been postponed a further five years, with London and Copenhagen granted the right in advance to "opt out." The North American Free Trade Agreement, a pact signed by the governments of the United States, Mexico, and Canada reducing duties and other restrictions on the cross-border flows of commodities and capital, also took effect January 1, 1994.

the renewal of communist leadership on a world scale. These advances have been made in the face of enormous obstacles resulting from the legacy of centuries of colonial and semicolonial oppression and ongoing imperialist economic and military pressures.

The overwhelming majority of countries in the semicolonial world, however, remain dominated by the world capitalist market and oppressed by the imperialist system. Most are saddled with neocolonial governments that represent domestic exploiting classes subservient to varying degrees to imperialism. The operation of the law of value, combined with the policies of finance capital and its various state powers, have maintained and reinforced the division of the capitalist world—first called attention to by Lenin, and later by the Communist International—into a handful of imperialist countries and the great majority of oppressed and exploited countries.

Since World War II there has been an expansion of manufacturing in the semicolonial countries and a substantial differentiation in rates of development, including significant industrialization in a few cases. Despite these changes, not a single one of the semicolonial countries has crossed the bridge into the ranks of the industrialized imperialist states, even as a junior partner.

The oppressed countries of Asia, Africa, the Pacific and the Americas

The big majority of working people in the colonial and semicolonial countries remain on the land. In the oppressed countries of Africa and Asia more than two-thirds of the population still live and toil in the countryside. In Latin America and the Caribbean the figure is one-third for the region as a whole, although many countries still have 40 to 70 percent of the population in rural areas (Barbados, Haiti, Honduras, Guatemala, Bolivia, Ecuador, Dominican Republic, Paraguay, Nicaragua, Costa Rica, El Salvador, and others). Agricultural commodities and raw materials account for some 80 percent of export earnings from the semicolonial countries, compared to less than a quarter for the imperialist countries.

In many of the oppressed countries the majority of the rural toilers work the land under semifeudal or other precapitalist or semicapitalist conditions, bound to village chieftains or wealthy landholding families. In other countries bourgeois "land reforms" have brought the toilers under more directly capitalist forms of exploitation: wage laborers working for a pittance on plantations owned by local landlords or imperialist-based corporations, while scratching out subsistence on a tiny plot; tenant farmers paying money rent to these same landholding exploiters; or independent commodity producers working as debt slaves for local or foreign capitalists who lend them money and hold their mortgage, sell them farming supplies, and purchase their product to resell at a profit.

Whatever the form of exploitation of these rural toilers, a growing portion of the wealth produced by their labor ends up in the hands of imperialist finance capital. Sometimes the landholders themselves are capitalist-owned businesses in the United States, Canada, Western Europe, Japan, Australia, or New Zealand. For commodities such as coffee, cotton, cocoa, pineapple, tea, bananas, sugar, and others, between 60 to 90 percent of the trade on the world market is controlled by three to six imperialist-owned monopolies. Even much of the wealth initially extracted from the toilers by domestic capitalists and landlords ends up being drained from these countries through interest payments and unequal trade relations, becoming part of imperialism's superprofits.

Throughout the semicolonial world two processes intermesh. Millions of toilers are still being drawn out of precapitalist social relations on the land into the capitalist rents and mortgages system and rural wage labor. At the same time, millions of others are being driven off the land into swollen slums where they join a growing urban proletariat, and from which many migrate in search of work to more economically advanced semicolonial countries or one of the imperialist centers.

The expansion of industry and commerce in many of these

countries has also created a growing employed urban proletariat. Workers—whose average wages and conditions are well below those of workers in any of the imperialist countries—have formed unions; many have become seasoned fighters in labor and political struggles.

While layers of capitalists in parts of the Third World have been able to break into the international capitalist market for manufactured goods—not only for light consumer items and durables, but also steel, automobiles, trucks, computers, and ships—not a single one of these countries has seen the growth of a home market sufficient to absorb a significant portion of what the domestic industrialists produce. The majority, usually a big majority, of workers and peasants simply have such a low standard of living that the consumer market among the bourgeoisie and relatively small middle classes cannot even approach making up for it. The majority of toilers are often not part of the modern sectors of the economy, not fully part of a modern class structure.

UNLIKE THE IMPERIALIST POWERS, most countries with semicolonial economic structures do not even have a single wholesale market price for most agricultural commodities, nor a single average rate of industrial profit of domestic capitalists. Stock and securities markets, to the degree they exist, have not taken on the function described by Engels of centralizing the accumulation and redeployment of domestic agricultural, industrial, and commercial capital. This is a barrier to the mobilization of the various local pockets of national capital on a substantial enough scale to contribute to sustained economic development comparable to that in the advanced capitalist countries.

A great deal of attention has been focused by the big-business press on a handful of semicolonial countries in Latin America and Asia—Brazil, Mexico, South Korea, Taiwan, Hong Kong, and Singapore—that have managed to increase their share in world industrial production by a few percentage points in the more than forty years since the end of World War II. For the rest of the semicolonial countries, however, the total share in world industrial output has fallen over this same period. Moreover, even in the so-called newly industrializing countries, the economic and social conditions of working people drastically limit the home market.

The proliferating U.S.- and other imperialist-owned assembly plants (*maquiladoras*) that are allegedly "developing" northern Mexico, for example, pay workers $3 to $5 per day. In Brazil and South Korea average wages of workers employed in manufacturing are well below $1.50 an hour.[33] The expansion of manufacturing in these countries has been predicated on dispossession of the peasantry and superexploitation of the growing proletariat, which has driven down average real wages, not on developing a broad working class capable of purchasing a wide range of consumer goods and durables.

In none of the cases where neocolonial governments have carried out what have been billed as "land reforms" has the result been a thoroughgoing land distribution and state provision of cheap credit. As a result, nowhere in these countries has there developed a broad, modern class of small farmers whose income and living standards on average are equal to that of skilled workers. Instead, a thin layer of well-off farmers has been created and the superexploitation, dispossession, and pauperization of the toiling rural majority has increased.

This lack of a broad home market puts the capitalists in these countries at a severe disadvantage in the intensifying trade competition, on the world market. It makes the economies of these countries particularly vulnerable to inflation, recessions,

---

33. As a result of a wave of hard-fought strikes in the late 1980s and early 1990s, industrial wages in South Korea increased more than 55 percent between 1987 and 1991, while industrial wages in Brazil continued to decline, ending the 1980s lower than at the beginning of the decade. Wage increases slowed by 1993 in South Korea, and industrial strikes in 1994 have been at the lowest level since 1987.

monetary fluctuations, trade restrictions, and other factors that slash demand for imports in the capitalist world. Imperialism, nonetheless, continues to accelerate the export-orientation of agriculture and industry, both native and foreign-owned. The semicolonial countries, most of them originally with substantial acreage of rich soil and plentiful forests and water resources, have been transformed into importers of food, clothing, and other basic necessities.

THE IMPERIALIST-OWNED monopolies reap profits at both ends—from the exports whose distribution, transport, insurance, and financing they control; and from the industrial and consumer goods that Third World countries must import. Most neocolonial governments are expanding so-called free trade zones, where imperialist-owned companies can exploit workers virtually free from regulation and pay little if any taxes on the profits squeezed from their labor. Finance capital also promotes large-scale organized tourism in many of these countries, aimed at visitors from the imperialist centers and controlled by syndicates of local and foreign monopolists dealing in hotels, restaurants, gambling, drugs, and prostitution.

Over the past decade, the imperialist bankers and international financial agencies have introduced even greater distortions into the economic structures of Third World countries, in order to boost export and tourist earnings that can be channeled into interest payments on the ballooning foreign debt. Imperialist-sponsored "development" projects have resulted in disastrous overplanting of farmland and overcutting of forests. This is responsible for the creeping Sahara that is devastating much previously arable cropland in northern Africa; a growing threat to the forest and river networks of Central America; the virtual deforestation of much of Haiti; and the accelerating destruction of the Brazilian rain forests.

The mounting debt trap exacerbates every aspect of imperialist domination of the oppressed countries, blocking economic development and condemning hundreds of millions of people—the big majority of the toiling population of the capitalist-dominated world—to brutalizing economic and social conditions.

• While 85 percent of the people of the capitalist world live in the semicolonial countries, they receive only about 20 percent of its total income.

• More than 60 percent of the world's population lives without electricity.

• On the African continent some two-thirds of the population is illiterate, ranging to above 90 percent in some countries. In the oppressed countries of Asia some 40 percent of adults cannot read or write, once again reaching above 80 percent in several cases. In Central and South America illiteracy runs at about one-quarter of the population for the continent as a whole, and above 40 percent in some countries.

• Infant mortality—which in the United States averages some 11 deaths during the first year of life for every 1,000 births—averages 125 per 1,000 on the African continent, going well over 200 in several countries there. In the semicolonial countries of Asia the rate is about 90 per 1,000 births, with several countries at nearly 200. In Central and South America the average figure is 50 deaths for every 1,000 births, going over 100 in a few countries.

• Five million children die from diarrhea every year and two million from measles, the overwhelming majority of them in the Third World.

• The caloric intake for the peoples of the semicolonial countries is 36 percent lower on average than in the United States, and daily consumption of protein is more than 45 percent lower. Two million people in the world die of starvation each year.

The United States and other imperialist countries

The labor force in the United States today is more than double its size at the opening of World War II. The structure and composition of the working population have seen qualitative changes since the Great Depression.

• The demand for labor power created by the massive expansion of military-related production during World War II drew in millions of working people from the countryside, which had been devastated by two decades of depression conditions. This resulted in a sharp 20 percent drop in the farm population between 1940 and 1945, the largest and fastest shift in U.S. history.

The accelerating development of the productivity of agricultural labor since then has resulted in the proletarianization of millions of members of farm families. Today the percentage of the labor force engaged in agriculture has dropped to below 3 percent from more than 15 percent in 1940.

On top of these changes, a majority of working farmers today are forced by economic necessity to work a full- or part-time job, and many belong to industrial unions. The gap between the general living and social conditions of workers and exploited farmers in the United States is narrower today than ever before.

• Over the past thirty years the percentage of gross domestic production accounted for by manufacturing has remained roughly the same. In 1987 some 25 million workers were employed in manufacturing, mining, and construction, a 43 percent increase since 1946.

The rising rate of surplus value in manufacturing since 1941—that is, the percentage of value produced by labor that goes to the bosses as a surplus instead of to workers as wages —and the long-term growth in the mass of profits made possible a faster growth rate of sales, clerical, and "service" jobs (government, wholesale and retail trade, schools, hospitals, offices, etc.) relative to employment in plants, mines, and mills.

Since the mid-1970s the capitalists have destroyed values in outmoded industrial plant and equipment by writing off a major hunk of excess capacity, and have slowed investment in new plant and equipment. As a result, the rate of hiring of additional labor power has been reduced as well. A world depression will result not only in massive unemployment in mining and manufacturing, however. It will come as a devastating blow to sectors of the economy that generate no new value for the capitalists, leading to millions more layoffs.

The creeping crisis of the past fifteen years has already witnessed major layoffs of workers in health, education, and other vital social services. The firing of up to 15,000 employees from Wall Street securities outfits in New York following the October 1987 crash provides a taste of what another stock market or banking collapse would mean for working people employed in a broader range of financial institutions around the country, let alone the many other commercial sectors of the economy that would be rocked by such an event.

• During World War II hundreds of thousands of working farmers, sharecroppers, and tenant farmers who were Black poured into industry, as the massive expansion of production created opportunities to escape the economic devastation that had wracked the rural South for decades. Following the war, Blacks continued to be driven off the land and migrated in growing numbers to cities both in the North and throughout the South looking for jobs.

The prolonged postwar acceleration of capital accumulation, combined with gains won through civil rights battles against Jim Crow segregation in the 1950s and 1960s, broke down further employment barriers. Among employed male workers who are Black, the percentage holding industrial jobs went up from 17 percent in 1940 to 40 percent in 1971. Workers who are Black today comprise 11 percent of the labor force and some 15 percent of the workforce in industry. Chicanos and Puerto Ricans also make up a substantially larger percentage of the industrial working class than before World War II.

These workers who are part of oppressed nationalities continue to face racial and national discrimination in hiring, in job upgrading, and in the workplace and labor movement—a reality that gives their labor power a lower than average value in the working class. The racist inequalities confronting workers who are Black, Chicano, Puerto Rican, Chinese, American Indian, or from other oppressed nationalities and national minorities are constantly reproduced and reinforced by the capitalist job market, and are used by the employers to keep the working class divided and thus weakened.

This is the objective basis for the fact that only labor's fight for affirmative action quotas can forge a strong and united working-class movement capable of defending the exploited producers against the effects of today's employer attacks and the much deeper social crisis and capitalist offensive that lie ahead.

• The last quarter century has witnessed the greatest immigration of workers to the United States since the early 1900s. In the mid-1960s, at the peak of the postwar expansion, U.S. capital was rapidly drawing in new labor power, so Congress loosened immigration quotas to expand the reserve army of labor and hold down wages. As the decline in the average industrial rate of profit accelerated over the next decade, the employers sought to cut costs and found even greater need for a pool of workers who could be intensely exploited through low wages, long hours, and substandard job conditions.

Over this same period, the dispossession of peasants and mounting unemployment and underemployment throughout the semicolonial world was leading millions to emigrate in search of a way to make a living. They were joined by others fleeing the terror of U.S.-backed dictatorships in many countries.

By keeping these workers in a pariah status as "aliens" and "illegals," the employers attempt to create a broad, permanent layer of the working class with few political or social rights. These workers face systematic discrimination on the basis of language, skin color, and nationality, as well as the constant threat of harassment or deportation by "la migra." The threat of such victimization often serves as a barrier to immigrant workers exercising their right to fight for union protection or social and medical services.

During the 1970s some 6.6 million immigrants came to the United States, about two-thirds of them with documents; as many as nine million more are expected by the end of the 1980s. In 1987 more than 600,000 documented immigrants entered the United States. That figure, which does not even count many scores of thousands of additional immigrants who entered the United States without papers, is more than were accepted by all other governments in the world combined last year.

In contrast to the turn of the century, when the big majority of immigrants to the United States were from Europe, more than 90 percent now are from Asia, Mexico, Central and South America, the Caribbean, and the Pacific islands. Today a language other than English is spoken at home by 11 percent of the U.S. population; in almost half these homes the language is Spanish.[34]

Other imperialist powers have also drawn in immigrant labor in growing numbers over the postwar period. While most immigrants to Canada came from Eastern and Southern Europe until the 1960s, the majority over the past quarter century have come from the Caribbean, Asia, and Latin America.

Despite measures throughout Western Europe in the mid-1970s to restrict a further influx of workers from the semicolonial world, the size of the immigrant population has continued to grow. France today has a higher percentage of foreign-born

---

34. In Los Angeles County, which has the largest concentration in California of immigrants from Latin America, the percentage of Latinos rose from 28 percent in 1980 to 38 percent in 1990; the percentage of Asians rose from 6 percent to 10 percent.

In the November 1994 elections, Proposition 187—which would deny basic rights to education, health care, and other social services to undocumented workers and their children—was adopted by a 3-2 margin. The capitalist politicians who campaigned for the reactionary measure appealed to the economic insecurity and growing resentments in the middle class and layers of the working class, including to Latinos and Blacks.

workers than the United States. In addition to continuing immigration to the cities of Britain by working people from the Caribbean and the Indian subcontinent, there has also been a new wave of Irish immigration, as imperialist superexploitation and British colonial oppression have worsened conditions in Northern Ireland.

In addition to the indigenous oppressed Maori population in New Zealand, there has been a mounting immigration of toilers from throughout the Pacific islands over the past two decades. Workers of non-European origin make up a large and growing percentage of the industrial working class in New Zealand. A "white Australia" policy was openly on the books of that country's government until the 1960s, but there has been growing immigration over the past quarter century from Asia, the Middle East, the Pacific, and Latin America, as well as a continuation of the longer-standing influx from Europe. The majority of these immigrants to Australia are workers, many of them industrial workers.

JAPAN, where overall immigration has been smaller than in the other largest imperialist powers, is nonetheless approaching a million foreign-born residents, with some 700,000 from Korea alone. A new and bigger wave of immigration has been growing there during the latter half of the 1980s, mostly from Southeast Asia, India, and Pakistan. In addition, three million people of Japanese national origin comprise a pariah "Burakumin" caste subject to discrimination and superexploitation.

Even smaller imperialist centers such as Iceland have imported immigrant labor in recent years and have begun to develop, even if still on a much reduced scale, similar patterns for the exploitation of immigrant workers.

Immigrants live and work in especially large numbers in the giant proletarian centers of these imperialist countries—New York City, London, Paris, Berlin, Los Angeles, Montreal, Auckland, Sydney, Stockholm, Toronto, Miami, Amsterdam—giving

these cities a multinational, multilingual, and increasingly cos-
mopolitan character. One-quarter of New York's population is
foreign-born. More than 700,000 residents of London are
Black or Asian. Half of all elementary school students in Amsterdam are non-Dutch, and young people of Turkish origin
make up a growing percentage of students in West Berlin
schools. Arab and African workers are a large component of
the Paris proletariat, and an even greater percentage of the
working class in Marseilles and much of southern France.

• The incorporation of women into the labor force in the
United States took a leap forward during World War II. The entrance of five million women into civilian and military jobs
raised their participation rate from 25 percent of the labor
force in 1940 to 36 percent in 1945. Despite a dip during the
immediate postwar demobilization and industrial reconversion,
the percentage of women in the labor force never dropped
back to its prewar level. The accelerated rise in female employment that began in 1941 has continued ever since.

Not only did women provide a growing percentage of labor
power drawn in by U.S. capital during the long expansion, but
the pace of their incorporation into the labor force actually increased as the crisis of capital accumulation grew over the past
two decades and the bosses sought ways to drive down the price
of labor power. From the mid-1960s to today, women have been
hired for over 60 percent of the new jobs created in the United
States.

In 1987 nearly 70 percent of women between the ages of sixteen and twenty-five were in the labor force in the United States,
and 45 percent of workers were women. The number of years
that a woman remains in the workforce on average has risen
sharply, as well. Today a young woman getting her first job can
expect to work for more than twenty-five years of her life, up
from twelve years in 1940. There has also been a sharp increase
in the participation in the workforce of married women with
children under eighteen. In 1950, 22 percent of these women
worked. In 1987 some 70 percent of married women with chil-

dren six to seventeen were in the labor force, and nearly 85 percent of women who are divorced. For women with children under six, the percentage was 56.8 percent for married women in 1987 and 70 percent for those who are divorced. And 51.9 percent of women with children less than a year old are in the labor force today, compared with 31 percent as recently as 1976!

Full-time, year-round workers who are women in the United States are now paid on the average 64 percent of what is made by similarly employed workers who are male—up from 59 percent a decade ago. While the relative price of female labor power has risen in the last few years in the United States under the impact of women's affirmative action gains, the value of female labor power remains substantially lower than that of adult males. This has been true throughout the entire history of capitalism, in every country. It continues to be lower today because of the historical legacy of women's oppression inherited by capitalism, perpetuated and reproduced by its social relations of production, and reinforced by bourgeois ideology.

WORKERS WHO ARE FEMALE do not take home smaller paychecks because their "jobs don't pay well." To the contrary. It is the bosses who "don't pay well," and they are able to keep wages low by preserving certain jobs as segregated bastions of cheaper female labor power. This superexploitation is possible *because these jobs are held by women, not because they are "dull and repetitive" or "low-paying jobs."*

As women fight successfully to break down the barriers of sex segregation on the job, however—as they did during the labor shortage of World War II—this situation begins to change. The influx of millions of women into the workforce and unions has brought a growing proportion of women into social and political life. They have become part of the working class in a qualitatively new way, thus increasing their self-confidence and fighting capacities and that of the working class as a whole.

With the rise of struggles for equal rights in the 1970s, a broader vanguard layer of working women once again battled their way into jobs previously held largely, sometimes almost solely, by men. These include unionized industrial jobs in coal mining, steel, oil refineries, transportation, auto assembly lines, and construction. Women in such jobs generally found themselves working alongside men receiving equal wages for equal work and taking home paychecks substantially larger than they had received in previous jobs. During the 1970s there was, for the first time in this century, a small but real decline in the indices used to measure sex segregation on the job.

The 1981-82 recession and the employers' subsequent restructuring of sectors of industry cut into some of these gains won by women in desegregating employment, but did not reverse them. Women workers have been largely successful over the 1980s in maintaining their position in industry. Like millions of others, of course, many of these industrial workers who are women have found themselves in recent years holding different jobs than a decade ago, with lower pay, worse conditions, and longer hours. The much deeper downturns ahead will lead to renewed and sharper attacks on job desegregation as part of the assault on the working class.

Every manifestation of sex segregation in the workplace is a barrier to women's equality and working-class unity. This underlines the need to include the fight to enforce affirmative action quotas to defend and extend women's conquests in employment and job equality as a central part of the struggle by the labor movement to protect workers' living and working conditions. Only through such social and political battles led by the working-class movement can the historical gap between the value of labor power of men and women be closed and women's equality eventually be achieved.

The incorporation of women in the workforce has increased in all the imperialist countries since World War II and, as in United States, even accelerated since the onset of the world capitalist crisis in the mid-1970s. As of 1983, for example, 72 percent of working-age women in Denmark were in the workforce; 77 percent in Sweden; 67 percent in Norway; 60 percent in Canada; 58 percent in Britain; 57 percent in Japan; 50 percent in Belgium, France, and Germany; 52 percent in Australia; 47 percent in New Zealand; and 40 percent in Italy.

As elsewhere, the value of women's labor power in these countries is lower than that of men's. In Britain, for example, women's pay averages 75 percent of men's, and 40 percent of women categorized as "full-time manual workers" earn less than 100 pounds per week, compared to only 6 percent of men in such jobs. In New Zealand women make on average 73 percent what men take home. In Japan working women are paid only about half what the average male worker is paid. Throughout the imperialist countries, moreover, women hold a disproportionately large number of newly created part-time or temporary jobs.

Women are moving into the workforce in growing numbers in semicolonial countries as well. In Latin America the percentage of women who are wage or salaried workers grew from 17.9 of women in 1950 to 26.6 percent in 1980. A study of the so-called free trade zones in the Third World found that some 80 percent of the workers in these imperialist-owned factories are young women. By hiring a largely female workforce, the capitalist owners reap the benefit of lower wages along with the tax breaks and other inducements wrung from neocolonial regimes. The majority of the more than 350,000 workers in the largely U.S.-owned maquiladora assembly plants in Mexico along the U.S. border are women, many of them making as little as 40 to 60 cents an hour.[35]

---

35. For a further assessment of the changes in women's social conditions since World War II, and the employers' offensive against these gains, see the introduction by Mary-Alice Waters to Joseph Hansen, Evelyn Reed, Mary-Alice Waters, *Cosmetics, Fashions, and the Exploitation of Women* (New York: Pathfinder, 1986) and the three-volume collection edited by Waters, *Communist Continuity and the Fight for Women's Liberation: Documents of the Socialist Workers Party, 1971-86* (New York: Pathfinder, 1992).

New forces for world workers movement

These irreversible changes in class structure brought about by the international expansion and penetration of capital have important consequences for workers and farmers.

On an international scale, the expansion of the capitalist rents and mortgages system and wage labor in the countryside continues to draw millions of exploited rural toilers more tightly into the world capitalist market, both as peasants and farmworkers. At the same time, growing numbers of working people from the Third World continue to be driven off the land and drawn by capital into the mines, mills, and factories not only in the nations of their birth but in the imperialist countries as well.[36]

The effects of increasing exploitation do not fall in an undifferentiated way on all layers of the toiling population. Workers in much of the semicolonial world are already living under depression conditions that, on the whole, are only a growing premonition to working people in the imperialist countries.

Within the imperialist countries workers who are Black, workers of other oppressed nationalities, immigrants, youth, and layers of working-class women have been hit most heavily by the creeping social crisis that is already under way. But it is not only these sections of the working class that have been affected. Large layers of working farmers have been ruined and dispossessed. Cutbacks in social spending by capitalist governments have reinforced the workings of the law of value in shifting the distribution of income even more lopsidedly to the benefit of the ruling rich and moneyed middle classes. And the employers' profit drive has fueled an ideological offensive against women aimed at pushing back gains in their fight for equality in employment and on the job.

---

36. For more on the rents and mortgages system, see Doug Jenness, "The Crisis Facing Working Farmers," in *New International* no. 4 (1985), especially pp. 110-13 and 123-27.

All these factors intensify competition among working people and initially set back the willingness and capacity to think and act in class terms—to identify "we" as the exploited toilers, whether currently employed or unemployed, and regardless of skin color, national origin, sex, age, or job category; and to recognize "they" as our common class enemy, the imperialist ruling families and capitalist exploiters both in the countries where we ourselves live and work and elsewhere around the world.

Yet the toilers of the oppressed and oppressor countries are more intertwined today than ever before in an integrated capitalist world market. We increasingly cross swords with the same imperialist-owned monopoly corporations. Transactions that determine our lives and livelihoods are conducted on the same stock, bond, and commodities markets. Our common future is threatened by the debt crisis that finance capital has inflicted on the semicolonial world. The effects of the deepening capitalist crisis, and the worldwide depression that it will inevitably bring, will drive down the living and job conditions of all working people. But they will also create the objective basis, and an ever-greater need, for a common international fight if the struggles on any front are to be victorious.

The workings of the world capitalist system continue to bring masses of new workers into the labor force throughout the imperialist countries: immigrants escaping the unlivable conditions in their homelands; women who must go to work to support their families and who want to have a more independent and less restricted life; members of farm families driven off the land. In the United States workers who are Black, Latino, or Asian already make up nearly a quarter of the workforce.

Changes such as these give "national" working-class traditions less and less reality and weight. What does it mean today to speak of a "typical U.S. worker"? A "French" worker? A "British" worker? A "Dutch" worker? A "New Zealand" worker? A "Canadian" worker? A "German" worker? Or a "European" or "North American" worker?

The working class in the imperialist countries is qualitatively different in composition from the working class that faced the Great Depression and took part in mass struggles between labor and capital. The working class today can no longer be described in national terms without excluding a decisive and growing part of the class itself. It is far more multinational. Workers of different national origins, with different first languages, and of different skin colors more and more often work alongside each other, and gain common experiences in struggles against the employers. The employed working class is far more female than ever before as well.

In preparing for the class battles that inevitably lie ahead, the eyes of communists must not turn back to various "national" working-class traditions of the 1930s, nor to reactionary illusions of some "North American" or "European" consciousness of tomorrow. Instead, our eyes must turn toward the realities of the working class and its allies in the 1990s, and the international fighting course that must be explained, generalized, and led in every country in today's world.

Prospects for reversing the falling rate of industrial profit and preparing a new acceleration of capital accumulation

To reenter a road of accelerating and self-feeding capital accumulation, the exploiters must inflict crushing defeats on the working class; drive under giant quantities of the weakest and most outmoded capitals at home and abroad in a ruthless competition for markets and profits; and invest in new industries and technologies that qualitatively expand their productive capacity.

This course would require the capitalists to jack up the rate of exploitation of the working class to a degree that could only be achieved by longer hours of work and intense speedup. To accomplish this, in turn, would require chronic unemployment and defeats of the unions on a massive enough scale to sap workers' confidence, intensify competition and deepen divisions among them and with their allies, diminish their level of organization, and thus destroy their capacity to fight. These defeats would need to be international in scope, extending from the imperialist countries throughout the Third World.

Finance capital would have to destroy excess capital and productive capacity not only through sweeping shutdowns of outmoded facilities, but above all through unrelenting destruction of rival *capitals* at home, in other imperialist countries, and throughout the semicolonial world. The resulting elimination of capitalist firms, including very large ones, would further accelerate the concentration and centralization of capital, both on a national and international level.

The capitalists would have to open up major new markets, realize enormous masses of profits through increased sales, and speed up the turnover of capital. They would have to find new ways to drive down further the costs of raw materials, energy, and plant and equipment.

Only by attaining these goals could the capitalists restore a high enough average rate of profit and accumulation of mass of profits to launch and sustain a major wave of investment in construction of new factory capacity and a massive computerization, let alone "robotization," of whole sectors of industrial production. Only on that basis could a new ascending period of capitalist expansion be prepared, partial crises absorbed, surging inflation avoided, and the business cycle moderated.

The thirty-year accelerated expansion of U.S. capitalism that began in 1941 created a substantial enough aristocratic layer in the U.S. working class to fasten a class-collaborationist officialdom on the labor movement; extinguish the embers of the broad proletarian social movement that had begun to take shape through the struggles that built the industrial unions and fought racism and reaction; eliminate the need for the rulers to move outside imperialist democracy in order to maintain stable political control; and foster the gutting of union power that continues to this day. With a time lag, a process with increasingly similar elements took place throughout the imperialist countries over the postwar years.

Despite this grave weakening of the labor movement, the toll that the international profit system has exacted from working people worldwide through and following the 1974-75 and 1981-82 recessions falls far short of the blows that the capitalists must deal to living standards and conditions of work as preconditions for launching and sustaining a new wave of capital accumulation. Nor have the rulers been able to impose the draconian reorganization of class relations and degree of additional social devastation on the peoples in the colonial and semicolonial countries that would be necessary to collect the Third World debt.[37]

To judge the capitalists' prospects for preparing a new acceleration of capital accumulation, it is useful to look at a number of their possible options. Several are factors that played a significant role in the initial capital accumulation that gave rise to the world dominance of industrial capitalism by the opening decades of the twentieth century. Others have either played a role, or are often perceived to have played a role, in helping the capitalists pull out of previous capital accumulation crises. Still others are factors that under certain historical and political conditions have the potential to give a powerful boost to the capitalists' average rate of industrial profit.

In reviewing these various options, we need to answer the question of whether or not they can work given the class structure and relationship of forces in today's world.

Nuclear power

From the late 1940s through the 1960s, the "peaceful use of the atom" was presented throughout the capitalist world as a virtu-

---

37. The political consequences of the failure by the leaderships of the organized labor movement and popular organizations in Latin America to take up the Cuban government's call for a campaign to demand cancellation of the debt is discussed in "Defend Cuba, Defend Cuba's Socialist Revolution" by Mary-Alice Waters, published elsewhere in this issue. How international finance capital averted a potential banking collapse in the latter half of the 1980s by "securitising" the unpaid loans as other forms of paper assets ("Brady bonds") is described in "Imperialism's March toward Fascism and War."

ally unlimited economic boon. Nuclear power was going to drastically lower energy costs across the board and result in a general increase in the average industrial rate of profit. The massive investments necessary to construct and outfit the reactor plants—given their long-term profit potentials—would further stimulate economic expansion.

Instead, over the past two decades nuclear power has ended in a debacle. The politics of nuclear power became the opposite of what had been expected by the capitalist rulers. As a result, it has proven to be an economic disaster for them. Nuclear power has met growing public opposition, as accidents such as those at Three Mile Island in the United States and Chernobyl in the Soviet Union have put a spotlight on its unalterable catastrophic dangers. On top of the ever-present threat of a meltdown, nuclear reactors day in and day out produce mounting radioactive wastes (22,000 tons in the United States as of 1987) that remain life-threatening for tens of thousands of years and cannot be safely stored or disposed of.[38]

Popular opposition to nuclear power has become a permanent political factor throughout the imperialist countries. It has cut deep into industry profits by forcing the shutdown or cancellation of many plants and steeply increasing capital costs to cover additional safety equipment and procedures. The capitalists have increasingly concluded that nuclear power is a losing proposition. No new plants have been ordered in the United States since 1978, and more than 100—some near completion—have been canceled. Only three are currently scheduled to be completed and opened after 1989, and all of these are in jeopardy from challenges to their operating safety.[39]

---

38. For a concise account of nuclear power's special hazard to health, safety, and human life, see Fred Halstead, *What Working People Should Know about the Dangers of Nuclear Power* (New York: Pathfinder, 1981).

39. Five years later, as of the end of 1993, there were still no new nuclear power reactors on order in the United States and only one more had been completed and licensed for operation over that period. This trend is not lim-

There is massive overcapacity in the U.S. nuclear reactor manufacturing industry, which now produces almost entirely for plants being foisted onto semicolonial countries. Especially following the Chernobyl disaster, capital investment in nuclear power has slowed across most of Western Europe, and the debate over phasing out existing reactors is under way in many countries. Even in France, where nuclear power accounts for 65 percent of electrical generation, the industry faces a $32 billion debt.

Because of the change in consciousness about its irremediable dangers, nuclear power cannot be made profitable. While the wealthy owners of utilities monopolies are now organizing to recoup some of their colossal outlays through tax breaks, higher rates, and accounting write-offs, there is no way for them to transform a massive loss into a profitable new source of expanded productive capacity. They are now waging a battle within finance capital as a whole to share out the losses, not divide the profits, of four decades of investment in nuclear power.

In the 1950s and 1960s, the capitalists anticipated that nuclear energy would bring a drastic lowering of the circulating costs of constant capital (that is, the costs of raw materials, in this case, energy). Instead, by the closing decade of the twentieth century the nuclear industry and related public utilities

---

ited to the United States, as indicated by an article headlined "Concern over lull in plant construction" in a special supplement on the world nuclear industry in the November 21, 1994, *Financial Times* of London. It reported that no nuclear power plants are under construction anywhere in Western Europe except France, "and even it is close to the end of its programme." The International Atomic Energy Agency estimates that nuclear power's market share in energy production worldwide will drop from 17.5 percent in 1993 to between 13 and 15 percent by the year 2000.

So long as the capitalists hold power, however, they will not conclude once and for all that nuclear power is a losing proposition. The political fight will have ebbs and flows with the course of the class struggle and capital's energy and profit needs.

were saddled with an enormous increase in the fixed costs of constant capital (that is, the costs of nuclear plant and equipment). Much of this capital has been simply written off, with many reactors mothballed in recent years. At the same time, the "promise" of nuclear power has left a long-term legacy to humanity of tens of thousands of tons of deadly radioactive wastes, as well as hundreds of useless concrete-and-steel monuments to the truth of Marx's insight into capitalism's tendency to transform the forces of production into forces of destruction.

A new gold rush

The opening of major new goldfields in California and Australia in the late 1840s and in South Africa and Alaska in the 1890s were among the factors that enabled the capitalists during the nineteenth century to pull out of two deflationary segments of the curve of capitalist development. The discovery of gold deposits in Brazil or elsewhere today cannot play the same role.

In the nineteenth century gold mining had not yet been monopolized by a handful of major capitalist producers. Today the owners of a few giant trusts mine and market gold using the same profit criteria as capitalists in other sectors of production. Extraction costs and world price calculations, not "discoveries," now dominate gold production. On the basis of those cost and profit decisions, the mining monopolists determine how much gold to produce, how many miners to hire or lay off, and how much of their output to hold back from sales.

There will be no more unforeseen "gold rushes" that lower the value of gold enough to flood the capitalist world with money, driving up prices and profits across the board.

Revolution in capitalist agriculture

At the origins of capitalism, as Marx discovered and explained, the new exploiting class "conquered the field for capitalist agriculture, incorporated the soil into capital, and created for the urban industries the necessary supplies of free and rightless proletarians."[40] The capitalists did this primarily through massive expropriations of small agricultural producers, as well as the takeover of church and other feudal landholdings.

Hundreds of years later capital is still dispossessing rural producers, both in the imperialist countries and throughout the semicolonial world. Most of the world's best land has already long been concentrated in the hands of the exploiters, however. Wealth amassed through further expropriations is nowhere near sufficient to empower a broad new surge of capital accumulation.

Rapid mechanization and adoption of new farming methods following World War II led to an explosion of agricultural production in the United States and other imperialist countries, helping to stoke the capitalist expansion. But the ruling capitalist families cannot look to a repetition of this today. The world capitalist market already faces chronic overproduction of agricultural commodities, which has led to intensified price competition and large-scale protectionist measures. Despite conjunctural ups and downs, agricultural prices will remain depressed throughout the coming years of deepening economic and social crisis.

Contributing to the production of this glut of farm commodities for export will be more and more nations throughout the Third World, whose workers and peasants will at the same time suffer and die in growing numbers from malnutrition and starvation, from a profit famine created by finance capital.

A 'Marshall Plan' for the semicolonial countries
Between 1948 and 1952 the U.S. rulers provided billions of dollars in long-term loans that were used to rebuild the foundation for renewed industrial production and stabilization in war-ravaged capitalist Europe. The capitalist expansion over the subsequent two decades rapidly narrowed the large initial post-

---

40. *Capital,* vol. 1, p. 895.

war gap between the U.S. and Western European industrial rate of profit and resulting mass of profits.

Today, imperialist governments, banks, and international finance agencies have foisted hundreds of billions of dollars in loans on the semicolonial countries. Not only has it proved impossible, however, for the local bourgeoisies to reproduce there the successes registered in postwar Europe, but the opposite has occurred. The gap between the economic strength of the imperialist and semicolonial countries has widened. The Third World debt is not a blessing preliminary to a historic expansion, but a trap that shuts tighter and tighter preliminary to a devastating crisis. No better confirmation than these contrasting experiences could be given of the fact that debt is a *social relation,* one that varies in its effects depending on the relative power of lender and borrower.

At the beginning of the 1960s the U.S. government announced with great fanfare the Alliance for Progress, which was presented as a road to economic and industrial development for Latin America. A quarter century later the balance sheet is clear from the deteriorating economic and social conditions throughout the Americas. The Alliance for Progress allotted $20 billion in "development funds" spread over ten years, while in just the past seven years there has been a substantially larger net drain of wealth from Latin America to the imperialist ruling families through debt payments and capital flight.

More recently, Washington's Caribbean Basin Initiative was trumpeted in the early 1980s as a road to development and a "democratic" alternative to the Cuban, Nicaraguan, and Grenadan roads. But the CBI, which was supposed to open the U.S. market to increased imports from the Caribbean, has instead been followed by a 30 percent decline in imports from the region.[41]

---

41. Whatever the fluctuations, export income from the region's long-standing leading exports—sugar, rum, and bananas—has been permanently undercut

Imperialist domination of the semicolonial countries prevents the development of a class structure and value of labor power capable of supporting an internal market that can meet the profit needs either of a broad developing local bourgeoisie or absorb massive imports of capital and commodities from the imperialist countries. These semicolonial class relations permit the emergence of isolated pockets of prosperity, layers of very wealthy export- and service-oriented capitalists, and a narrow middle class. But there neither is nor can be a large-scale middle class, employed proletariat, and relatively well-off population of small farmers able to purchase a range of consumer durables, let alone cars or houses, on a level comparable to the imperialist countries.

Moreover, the semicolonial world has been a relatively shrinking, not a growing market for the owners of the imperialist monopolies as well. Sales by U.S.-owned corporations to these countries actually declined from 36 percent of total exports in 1975 to 32.5 percent in 1986.[42]

THE SEMICOLONIAL COUNTRIES were hit hard by the recessions in 1974-75 and, even more so, 1981-82. Capitalists in these countries, heavily dependent on revenues from exports, have faced contracting world markets and intensifying competition

---

by the combination of falling prices and declining market share, as London and other governments in the European Union have refused to continue granting preferential market access to their former Caribbean colonies. No shift in the terms of trade can reverse the consequences of this accelerating plunder. As in the rest of the capitalist countries in the Third World, the workers and farmers will have to establish their own revolutionary government in order to reorganize agriculture, expand industrial development, and join in the worldwide fight for socialism.

42. As explained in the 1994 article later in this issue, U.S. exports to Latin America and several semicolonial countries in Asia expanded in the opening years of the 1990s. In 1993 nearly 40 percent of U.S. exports went to buyers in Third World countries.

from imperialist-owned businesses. While in 1975 goods produced in the Third World accounted for 40 percent of U.S. imports, that slipped to just over 30 percent by 1986. This has dealt a heavy blow to economic growth in all the semicolonial countries, even the relatively best-off.

Between 1979 and 1984, annual growth in industrial production for South Korea, Taiwan, Singapore, and Hong Kong slumped to only 15 percent of the 1966-73 growth rate. For Brazil and Mexico average industrial growth rates for 1979-84 fell to 20 percent of the 1966-73 levels. Growing unemployment, underemployment, and worsening living conditions—in city and countryside alike—have been the result for hundreds of millions of workers and peasants.

In the early and mid-1970s the ruling classes of the semicolonial countries with large oil resources succeeded in wresting a bigger piece of the pie from the owners of the imperialist energy monopolies. The illusion that any of these ruling classes would join the ranks of international finance capital, or that increased oil revenues would undergird durable economic and social development in these countries, let alone make them lesser members of the imperialist "family of nations," rapidly evaporated.[43]

Capitalist producers in the imperialist countries responded to rising energy prices by stepping up domestic oil exploration

----

43. The Saudi monarchy, for example, was even pointed to by some in the radical movement in the 1970s as an example of rising "Arab finance capital." Today the reactionary Saudi rulers face a severe financial crisis, with their reserves having fallen to some $15 billion from more than $120 billion in the early 1980s. Their friends in Washington and other imperialist countries thanked them for their services rendered during the 1991 Gulf War by hitting up the royal family for a $55 billion contribution to the effort, which the regime is now struggling to pay off with the help of a line of credit from J.P. Morgan & Company of Wall Street. What's more, Riyadh is stretching out the payments to Boeing and McDonnell-Douglas for the Clinton administration–engineered $6 billion commercial aircraft deal, which is described more fully in "Imperialism's March toward Fascism and War."

and production, intensifying price competition, and capturing a growing share of the world market. The workers and peasants of the oil-producing semicolonial countries did not benefit widely or long from the windfall of their domestic exploiting classes, while the conditions of toilers elsewhere in the semicolonial world have been worsened by rising energy prices.

Far from being potential engines of capital accumulation able to help bail out the world capitalist system, the semicolonial countries are already sustaining the heaviest blows from the economic downswing that began two decades ago. Interest payments on the mounting foreign debt eat up more and more wealth produced by the toilers, erecting further obstacles to economic development and leading the national bourgeoisies to drive down living standards further.

The next world recession will cut even more deeply into already contracting markets for exports from the semicolonial countries and worsen still more their terms of trade with the imperialist exploiters. Above all, the growing debt peonage of the nations of the Third World can provide the detonator for a worldwide crisis in which the working people of all continents will be the victims.

The Marshall Plan *has* been repeated. Its main result has been the debt crisis in the semicolonial world. And it has been a disaster for the vast majority of the workers and peasants of these countries.

The Soviet, Eastern European, and Chinese markets

Despite the enormous combined population of the Soviet Union, China, and the Eastern European workers states, an increased opening of their markets to commodities and capital from the imperialist countries will not resolve the deepening crisis of world capitalism.

First, trade with the workers states currently represents only a tiny share of total U.S. imports and exports. In 1975 trade with these countries accounted for under 2 percent of U.S. foreign sales and purchases, and dropped to 1.3 percent in 1986. Capital investments in these countries, while larger today than a decade ago, account for an infinitesimal percentage of U.S. or other imperialist holdings abroad.

While such trade and investment may grow in the future, even by large amounts in dollar terms, these economic links cannot undergo a qualitative change without a matching shift in social relations in the Soviet Union, China, and other workers states. This is particularly true for any extensive increase in capital investment, which, unlike increased markets for trade alone, could conceivably make a substantial difference to the imperialists in accelerating their rate of capital accumulation.

As a precondition to any qualitative increase in imperialist penetration of the workers states, the state monopoly on foreign trade would have to be substantially dismantled. The ruble and other currencies would have to become convertible on world money markets, making these countries vulnerable to speculation, fluctuating prices, and large-scale cyclical and structural unemployment.

Above all, the governments in the workers states would have to lift control over the investment of capital and exploitation of labor power by the imperialists. These regimes would have to permit workers' wages, conditions, and hours to be set by the capitalists without extensive regulation. They would have to open their soil, forests, and other resources to the monopolies on a massive scale. They would have to allow the capitalists to make decisions on the distribution and reinvestment of profits and—most fundamentally—allow capital flows to be determined by the market, not the plan.

Short of such measures, international finance capital will continue to seek markets and investment concessions in the workers states, but these economic ties will be much riskier and less attractive on the whole than those in countries where capitalist property relations prevail.

As the crisis produced by the political monopoly of the privileged bureaucratic castes deepens in the Soviet Union, Eastern Europe, and China, the governing strata in these deformed and degenerated workers states have begun to implement limited aspects of some of the above measures. They cannot and will not carry out the full complement, however, for two important reasons.

First, to do so would amount to a suicide pact. The castes would be agreeing to officiate over the destruction of their own power. It is one thing for the bureaucratic layers to share a greater portion of the trough from which they derive their own material benefits and comforts; it is quite another to permit imperialism to steal the trough outright.

Second, and most importantly, whatever further steps the Stalinist misleaders take to reimpose the methods of capitalist exploitation, they will not be able to carry out such a program on a broad scale without a political confrontation with growing layers of the working class and rural toilers. Any effort to break the plan and reintroduce the market as the determinant of industrial investment would rapidly lead to devastating economic and social consequences for the workers and peasants that would yield revolutionary uprisings and civil war.

For well over half a century the workers states and their social conquests have proven stronger than these privileged bureaucracies, and this will not cease to be the case during a period when their political stranglehold is weakening.

Not only will world imperialism be unable to bail itself out on the backs of working people in the Soviet Union, Eastern Europe, and China. But the convulsions throughout the capitalist world will shatter the plans of the bureaucratic castes, including their reactionary illusions and hopes in world capitalism, and deepen the crisis of their regimes.

A new technological revolution

Can the exploiters reverse the current deceleration of capital accumulation by investing in a massive expansion of new, automated industrial capacity?

In the wake of the 1974-75 recession and the deeper down-turn in 1981-82, the capitalists managed to destroy a substantial amount of capital, ridding themselves of a great deal of out-moded plant and equipment no longer competitive on the world market. They have invested in substantial amounts of "la-bor-saving" advanced technology to refurbish existing produc-tive capacity, speed up production, and cut wage costs. They have rolled back work rules and reorganized the labor process at the expense of health and safety on the job. They have ex-panded the reserve army of the unemployed and pushed down the value of labor power. They have instituted limited cost-cut-ting measures, such as "just-in-time" inventory systems to re-duce warehousing expenses and speed up the turnover time of capital.

Despite these accomplishments, the employers remain far from establishing the preconditions to begin preparing massive capital investments in the construction of new factories and a major expansion of the automation and computerization of production. For that, they need to drive up the rate of exploita-tion of the working class much further and begin on that basis to anticipate an ascending average rate of profit.

"Robotization" could accelerate a capitalist expansion, but it cannot cause one. Large-scale "robotization" of industry under capitalism could only occur as a product of a devastating on-slaught by the employers on the conditions of the working class. It would serve not to lessen the overwork of the toilers but to in-tensify exploitation to the greatest possible degree. Living labor alone creates the mass of surplus value from which profits are de-rived, and the capitalists seek to use every advance in science and technology to extract more and more labor time from the brain and muscle of the producers.

Moreover, there is an irresolvable contradiction between enor-mous chronic unemployment and devastated living standards of the working population that must inevitably accompany "roboti-zation" under capitalism, and the exploiters' inability to realize profits unless they can find buyers for the massively expanded quantities of commodities that automated production would entail.

Capitalist "robotization" is a reactionary fantasy. It is only realizable assuming fascist-like defeats of the working class and its organizations.[44]

Workers will have their chance
Neither past sources of rapid capital accumulation nor other options can enable the imperialist ruling classes to restore the long-term accelerating accumulation of world capitalism and avert an international depression and general social crisis.

The harder times confronting growing layers of working people, and the more devastating shocks that lie ahead, do not mark the difficult birth of a new world capitalist order. Instead, they register the wrenching decline of the more and more overheated and underpowered imperialist system forged under the dominance of Wall Street and Washington during and following World War II.

The period in the history of capitalist development that we are living through today is heading toward intensified class battles on a national and international scale, including wars and revolutionary situations. In order to squeeze more wealth from the labor of the exploited producers, the capitalists will step up attacks on wageworkers, small farmers, and peasants *the world over.*

The employers will attempt to weaken and where possible smash the unions, in order to radically alter the relationship of class forces between capital and labor. The imperialist ruling

---

44. The computerization pressed by capitalists in recent years is *not* a fantasy; it is a cost-cutting measure that has boosted capitalist profits in the short run. As explained in "Imperialism's March toward Fascism and War," however, this increase in spending on constant capital—without an increase in productive capacity and, above all, without the hiring of more workers to produce more surplus value—ends up reinforcing the falling rate of profit and retarding capital accumulation.

classes will seek to intensify the debt peonage of the oppressed nations and demand ever greater economic, political, and military subordination of the colonial peoples to the profit needs of international capital. They will continue to look for opportunities to weaken the states where capitalist relations have been overturned, laying the groundwork for eventual moves to retake these parts of the globe for direct exploitation.

These attacks will be met by growing resistance by working people around the world—from fights for jobs and a shorter workweek, to revolutionary national liberation struggles. The capitalists will stop at nothing to try to defend their profits and prerogatives, and will shove aside bourgeois-democratic forms of rule as it becomes necessary to fight to maintain their power.

Before the exploiters can unleash a victorious reign of reaction, however, the workers will have the first chance. The mightiest class battles of human history will provide the workers and exploited farmers in the United States and many other countries the opportunity to place revolutionary solutions on the order of the day.

Revolutionary Continuity

Marxist Leadership in the United States

Farrell Dobbs

Forging a leadership to advance the class interests of the toilers in the United States. From pre-Civil War struggles by workers and small farmers, to Radical Reconstruction and the labor battles of the 1870s and '80s. From the efforts to build a Marxist left wing in the pre–World War I Socialist Party to the Russian revolution and formation of the Communist Party.

Revolutionary Continuity
The Early Years, 1848-1917
$16.95

Revolutionary Continuity
Birth of the Communist
Movement, 1918-1922
$16.95

Available from Pathfinder. See front of magazine for addresses.

World War II and the failure of the 'American Century'

The Socialist Workers Party in World War II
Writings and Speeches, 1940-1943
JAMES P. CANNON

Preparing the communist workers movement in the United States to campaign against wartime censorship, repression, and antiunion assaults. $22.95

Fighting Racism in World War II
C.L.R. JAMES, GEORGE BREITMAN, EDGAR KEEMER, AND OTHERS

A week-by-week account of the struggle against racism and racial discrimination in the United States from 1939 to 1945, taken from the pages of the socialist newsweekly, the *Militant*. $20.95

The Struggle for Socialism in the 'American Century'
Writings and Speeches, 1945-1947
JAMES P. CANNON

The challenges posed by the post-World War II labor upsurge, the rapid expansion of openings for the communist movement, and the subsequent ebb in face of the stabilization of U.S. capitalism and the employers' antilabor offensive and witch-hunt. $22.95

Speeches to the Party
The Revolutionary Perspective and the Revolutionary Party
JAMES P. CANNON

Writing in the early 1950s, Cannon discusses how a proletarian party can resist the conservatizing pressures of the emerging capitalist expansion and anticommunist witch-hunt. He discusses Washington's failure to achieve it's goals in the Korean War, why the U.S. rulers reined in Joseph McCarthy, and how class-conscious workers under these conditions carried out effective union work and political activity to build a communist party. $20.95

FROM PATHFINDER. WRITE FOR A FREE CATALOG.

Join Now!
PATHFINDER READERS CLUB

Pathfinder is an international publisher of books and pamphlets by revolutionary leaders in the fight against capitalism and the oppression and exploitation it engenders and reinforces.

Joining the Pathfinder Readers Club gives you easier access to more than 500 titles by Karl Marx, Frederick Engels, V.I. Lenin, Leon Trotsky, Rosa Luxemburg, Ernesto Che Guevara, Fidel Castro, Malcolm X, Farrell Dobbs, James P. Cannon, Joseph Hansen, George Novack, Evelyn Reed, Nelson Mandela, Thomas Sankara, Maurice Bishop, Eugene V. Debs, and others.

- Readers Club members receive a **15 percent discount** on books and pamphlets at any Pathfinder bookstore around the world.
- You get **even higher discounts** on special selected titles and new releases.
- And membership costs only US $10 a year.

To join anywhere in the world, contact the Pathfinder bookstore nearest you (see front of magazine for distributors' addresses), or send US$10 to Pathfinder, 410 West Street, New York, NY 10014.

The Changing Face of U.S. Politics

Working-Class Politics and the Trade Unions

BY JACK BARNES

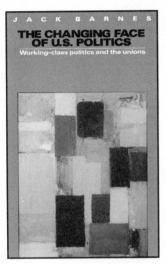

A handbook for workers coming into the factories, mines, and mills, as they react to the uncertainty, turmoil, and brutality of capitalism in the closing years of the twentieth century.

It shows how millions of workers, as political resistance grows, will revolutionize themselves, their unions, and all of society. $19.95

Trade Unions in the Epoch of Imperialist Decay

By LEON TROTSKY, with an introduction by FARRELL DOBBS

Featuring: Trade Unions: Their Past, Present and Future
by Karl Marx

"Apart from their original purposes, the trades unions must now learn to act deliberately as organizing centers of the working class in the broad interest of its complete emancipation. . . . They must convince the world at large that their efforts, far from being narrow and selfish, aim at the emancipation of the downtrodden millions."—*Karl Marx, 1866.*

In this book, two central leaders of the modern communist workers movement outline the fight for this revolutionary perspective. $14.95

FROM PATHFINDER. SEE ADDRESSES ON PAGE 2

THE CURVE OF CAPITALIST

DEVELOPMENT

by Leon Trotsky

June 21, 1923

IN HIS INTRODUCTION to Marx's *Class Struggles in France,* Engels wrote:

> In judging the events and series of events of day-to-day history, it will never be possible for anyone to go right back to the final economic causes. Even today, when the specialized technical press provides such rich materials, in England itself it still remains impossible to follow day by day the movement of industry and trade in the world market and the changes which take place in the methods of production, in such a way as to be able to draw the general conclusion, at any point of time, from these

---

This letter, published in the Soviet Union in 1923, first appeared in English translation in the May 1941 Fourth International, *a predecessor of* New International. *It is included in the collection Leon Trotsky,* Problems of Everyday Life *(New York: Pathfinder, 1973). Leon Trotsky was a central leader of the Soviet government and Communist Party, of the Red Army that defeated the landlord-capitalist forces in the 1918-21 civil war, and of the early Communist International. He led the opposition in the Soviet Union and Comintern to the betrayal of Lenin's communist course by the rising parasitic layers in the state and party bureaucracy headed by Joseph Stalin. Forced into exile by Stalin in 1929, Trotsky continued organizing to build a world communist movement until his assassination in 1940 by the Kremlin's secret police.*

very complicated and ever changing factors: of these factors, the most important, into the bargain, generally operate a long time in secret before they suddenly and violently make themselves felt on the surface.

A clear survey of the economic history of a given period is never contemporaneous; it can only be gained subsequently, after collecting and sifting of the material has taken place. Statistics are a necessary help here, and they always lag behind. For this reason, it is only too often necessary, in the current history of the time, to treat the most decisive factor as constant, to treat the economic situation existing at the beginning of the period concerned as given and unalterable for the whole period, or else to take notice of such changes in this situation as themselves arise out of events clearly before us, and as, therefore, can likewise be clearly seen.

Hence, the materialist method has here often to limit itself to tracing political conflicts back to the struggles between the interests of the social classes and fractions of classes encountered as the result of economic development, to show the particular political parties as the more or less adequate political expression of these same classes and fractions of classes.

It is self-evident *that this unavoidable neglect of contemporaneous changes in the economic situation, of the very basis of all the proceedings subject to examination, must be a source of error.*[1]

These ideas, which Engels formulated shortly before his death, were not further developed by anyone after him. To my recollection they are rarely even quoted—much more rarely than they should be. Still more, their meaning seems to have

---

1. Karl Marx, *The Class Struggles in France, 1848-1850,* (New York: International Publishers), pp. 9-10. Our emphasis—L.T.

escaped many Marxists. The explanation for this fact is once again to be found in the causes indicated by Engels, which militate against any kind of finished economic interpretation of *current* history.

It is a very difficult task, impossible to solve in its full scope, to determine those subterranean impulses which economics transmits to the politics of today; and yet the explanation of political phenomena cannot be postponed, because the struggle cannot wait. From this flows the necessity of resorting in daily political activity to explanations which are so general that through long usage they become transformed into truisms.

As long as politics keeps flowing in the same forms, within the same banks, and at about the same speed, i.e., as long as the accumulation of economic quantity has not passed into a change of political quality, this type of clarifying abstraction ("the interests of the bourgeoisie," "imperialism," "fascism") still more or less serves its task: not to interpret a political fact in all its concreteness, but to reduce it to a familiar social type, which is, of course, intrinsically of inestimable importance.

But when a serious change occurs in the situation, all the more so a sharp turn, such general explanations reveal their complete inadequacy, and become wholly transformed into empty truisms. In such cases it is invariably necessary to probe analytically much more deeply in order to determine the qualitative aspect, and if possible also to measure quantitatively the impulses of economics upon politics. These "impulses" represent the dialectical form of the "tasks" that originate in the dynamic foundation and are submitted for solution in the sphere of the superstructure.

OSCILLATIONS of the economic conjuncture (boom-depression-crisis) already signify in and of themselves periodic impulses that give rise now to quantitative, now to qualitative changes, and to new formations in the field of politics. The revenues of possessing classes, the state budget, wages, unemployment, proportions of foreign trade, etc., are intimately bound up with the economic conjuncture, and in their turn exert the most direct influence on politics. This alone is enough to make one understand how important and fruitful it is to follow step by step the history of political parties, state institutions, etc., in relation to the cycles of capitalist development. By this we do not at all mean to say that these cycles explain *everything:* this is excluded, if only for the reason that cycles themselves are not fundamental but derivative economic phenomena. They unfold on the basis of the development of productive forces through the medium of market relations. But cycles explain a *great deal,* forming as they do through automatic pulsation an indispensable dialectical spring in the mechanism of capitalist society. The breaking points of the trade-industrial conjuncture bring us into a greater proximity with the critical knots in the web of the development of political tendencies, legislation, and all forms of ideology.

BUT CAPITALISM is not characterized solely by the periodic recurrence of cycles—otherwise what would occur would be a complex repetition and not dynamic development. Trade industrial cycles are of different character in different periods. The chief difference between them is determined by quantitative interrelations between the crisis and the boom period within each given cycle. If the boom restores with a surplus the destruction or constriction during the preceding crisis, then capitalist development moves upward. If the crisis, which signals destruction, or at all events contraction of productive forces, surpasses in its intensity the corresponding boom, then we get as a result a decline in economy. Finally, if the crisis and boom approximate each other in force, then we get a temporary and stagnating equilibrium in economy. This is the schema in the rough.

We observe in history that homogeneous cycles are grouped in a series. Entire epochs of capitalist development exist when a number of cycles are characterized by sharply delineated booms and weak, short-lived crises. As a result we have a sharply rising movement of the basic curve of capitalist development. There are epochs of stagnation when this curve, while passing through partial cyclical oscillations, remains on approximately the same level for decades. And finally, during certain historical periods the basic curve, while passing as always through cyclical oscillations, dips downward as a whole, signaling the decline of productive forces.

It is already possible to postulate a priori that epochs of energetic capitalist development must possess features—in politics, in law, in philosophy, in poetry—sharply different from those in the epochs of stagnation or economic decline. Still more, a transition from one epoch of this kind to a different one must naturally produce the greatest convulsions in the relationships between classes and between states. At the Third World Congress of the Comintern we had to stress this point[2]—in the struggle against the purely mechanistic conception of capitalist disintegration now in progress. If periodic replacements of "normal" booms by "normal" crises find their reflection in all spheres of social life, then a transition from an entire boom epoch to one of decline, or vice versa, engenders the greatest historical disturbances; and it is not hard to show that in many cases revolutions and wars straddle the borderline between two different epochs of economic development, i.e., the junction of two different segments of the capitalist curve. To analyze all of modern history from this standpoint is truly one of the most gratifying tasks of dialectical materialism.

Following the Third World Congress of the Comintern, Professor Kondratiev approached this problem—as usual, painstakingly evading the formulation of the question adopted by the congress itself—and attempted to set up alongside of the "minor cycle," covering a period of ten years, the concept of a "ma-

2. See "Report on the World Economic Crisis and the New Tasks of the Communist International" in Leon Trotsky, *The First Five Years of the Communist International*, (New York: Pathfinder, 1973), vol. 1, pp. 174-226.

jor cycle," embracing approximately fifty years.[3] According to this symmetrically stylized construction, a major economic cycle consists of some five minor cycles, and furthermore, half of them have the character of boom, and the other half that of crisis, with all the necessary transitional stages. The statistical determinations of major cycles compiled by Kondratiev should be subjected to careful and not over-credulous verification in respect both to individual countries and to the world market as a whole. It is already possible to refute in advance Professor Kondratiev's attempt to invest epochs labeled by him as major cycles with the same "rigidly lawful rhythm" that is observable in minor cycles; it is an obviously false generalization from a formal analogy.

THE PERIODIC RECURRENCE of minor cycles is conditioned by the internal dynamics of capitalist forces, and manifests itself always and everywhere once the market comes into existence. As regards the large segments of the capitalist curve of development (fifty years) which Professor Kondratiev incautiously proposes to designate also as cycles, their character and duration are determined not by the internal interplay of capitalist forces but by those external conditions through whose channel capitalist development flows. The acquisition by capitalism of new countries and continents, the discovery of new natural resources, and, in the wake of these, such major facts of "superstructural" order as wars and revolutions, determine the character and the replacement of ascending, stagnating, or declining epochs of capitalist development.

Along what path then should investigation proceed?

To establish the curve of capitalist development in its nonpe-

---

3. Nikolai D. Kondratiev was a professor at the Agricultural Academy and the head of the Business Research Institute of Moscow after the revolution. In 1930 he was arrested by Stalin's political police as the alleged head of an illegal Peasants Labor Party and exiled to Siberia.

riodic (basic) and periodic (secondary) phases and breaking points in respect to individual countries of interest to us and in respect to the entire world market—that is the first part of the task. Once we have the fixed curve (the method of fixing it is, of course, a special question in itself and by no means a simple one, but it pertains to the field of economic-statistical technique), we can break it down into periods, depending upon the angle of rise and decline in reference to an axis on a graph. In this way we obtain a pictorial scheme of economic development, i.e., the characterization of the "very basis of all the proceedings subject to examination" (Engels).

Depending upon the concreteness and detail of our investigation, we may require a number of such schemas: one relating to agriculture, another to heavy industry, and so on. With this schema as our starting point, we must next synchronize it with political events (in the widest sense of the term) and we can then look not only for correspondence—or to put it more cautiously, interrelationship between definitely delineated epochs of social life and the sharply expressed segments of the curve of capitalist development—but also for those direct subterranean impulses which unleash events. Along this road it is naturally not at all difficult to fall into the most vulgar schematization and, above all, to ignore the tenacious internal conditioning and succession of ideological processes—to become oblivious of the fact that economics is decisive only in the *last analysis.* There has been no lack of caricature conclusions drawn from the Marxist method! But to renounce on this account the above indicated formulation of the question ("it smells of economism") is to demonstrate complete inability to understand the essence of Marxism, which looks for the causes of changes in social superstructure in the changes of the economic foundation, and not anywhere else.

At the risk of incurring the theoretical ire of opponents of "economism" (and partly with the intention of provoking their indignation) we present here a schematic chart which depicts arbitrarily a curve of capitalist development for a period of

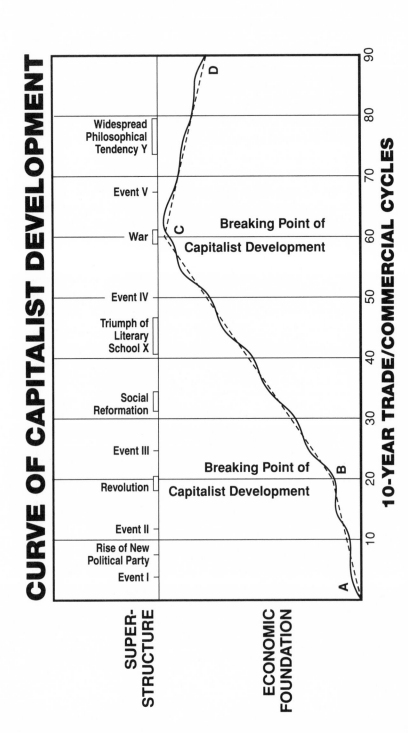

CURVE OF CAPITALIST DEVELOPMENT

SUPER-STRUCTURE

- Widespread Philosophical Tendency Y
- Event V
- War
- Event IV
- Triumph of Literary School X
- Social Reformation
- Event III
- Revolution
- Event II
- Rise of New Political Party
- Event I

ECONOMIC FOUNDATION

Breaking Point of Capitalist Development

Breaking Point of Capitalist Development

A B C D

10-YEAR TRADE/COMMERCIAL CYCLES

10 20 30 40 50 60 70 80 90

ninety years along the above-mentioned lines. The general direction of the basic curve is determined by the character of the partial conjunctural curves of which it is composed. In our schema three periods are sharply demarcated: twenty years of very gradual capitalist development (segment *A-B*); forty years of energetic upswing (segment *B-C*); and thirty years of protracted crisis and decline (segment *C-D*). If we introduce into this diagram the most important historical events for the corresponding period, then the pictorial juxtaposition of major political events with the variations of the curve is alone sufficient to provide the idea of the invaluable starting points for historical materialist investigations. The parallelism of political events and economic changes is of course very relative. As a general rule, the "superstructure" registers and reflects new formations in the economic sphere only after considerable delay. But this law must be laid bare through a concrete investigation of those complex interrelationships of which we here present a pictorial hint.

I n the report to the Third World Congress, we illustrated our idea with certain historical examples drawn from the epoch of the revolution of 1848, the epoch of the first Russian revolution (1905), and the period through which we are now passing (1920-21).[4] We refer the reader to these examples. They do not supply anything finished, but they do characterize adequately enough the extraordinary importance of the approach advanced by us, above all for understanding the most critical leaps in history: wars and revolutions. If in this letter we utilize a purely arbitrary pictorial scheme, without attempting to take any actual period in

---

4. In addition to the Third Congress report cited earlier, a discussion of the 1848 revolutions, the 1905 revolution in Russia, and the period opened by the October 1917 revolution can be found in Mary-Alice Waters, "Communism and the Fight for a Popular Revolutionary Government: 1848 to Today," in *New International* no. 3 (1984).

history as a basis, we do so for the simple reason that any attempt of this sort would resemble far too much an incautious anticipation of those results flowing from a complex and painstaking investigation which has yet to be made.

At the present time, it is of course still impossible to foresee to any precise degree just what sections of the field of history will be illuminated and just how much light will be cast by a materialist investigation which would proceed from a more concrete study of the capitalist curve and the interrelationship between the latter and all the aspects of social life. Conquests that may be attained on this road can be determined only as the result of such an investigation itself, which must be more systematic, more orderly than those historical material excursions hitherto undertaken.

In any case, such an approach to modern history promises to enrich the theory of historical materialism with conquests far more precious than the extremely dubious speculative juggling with the concepts and terms of the materialist method that has, under the pens of some of our Marxists, transplanted the methods of formalism into the domain of the materialist dialectic, and has led to reducing the task to rendering definitions and classifications more precise and to splitting empty abstractions into four equally empty parts; it has, in short, adulterated Marxism by means of the indecently elegant mannerisms of Kantian epigones. It is a silly thing indeed endlessly to sharpen and resharpen an instrument to chip away Marxist steel, when the task is to apply the instrument in working over the raw material!

In our opinion this theme could provide the subject matter for the most fruitful work of our Marxist seminars on historical materialism. Independent investigations undertaken in this sphere would undoubtedly shed new light or at least throw more light on isolated historical events and entire epochs. Finally, the very habit of thinking in terms of the foregoing categories would greatly facilitate political orientation in the present epoch, which is an epoch that reveals more openly than ever before the connection between capitalist economics, which has attained the peak of saturation, and capitalist politics, which has become completely unbridled.

I promised long ago to develop this theme for the *Vestnik Sotsialisticheskoi Akademii*.[5] Up to now I have been prevented by circumstances from keeping this promise. I am not sure that I shall be able to fulfill it in the near future. For this reason I confine myself in the meantime to this letter.

---

5. Bulletin of the Socialist Academy, the Soviet periodical in which this appeared in 1923, under the subtitle "A Letter to the Editor in Place of the Promised Article."

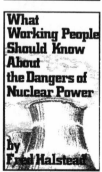
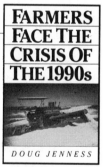

COSMETICS, FASHIONS, and the EXPLOITATION of WOMEN

Joseph Hansen, Evelyn Reed, and Mary-Alice Waters

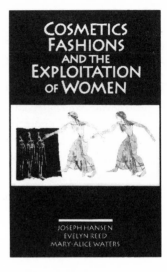

How big business promotes cosmetics to generate profits and perpetuate the oppression of women. In her introduction, Mary-Alice Waters explains how the entry of millions of women into the workforce during and after World War II irreversibly changed U.S. society and laid the basis for a renewed rise of struggles for women's equality. $12.95

PROBLEMS of WOMEN'S LIBERATION

Evelyn Reed

Explores the social and economic roots of women's oppression from prehistoric society to modern capitalism and points the road forward to emancipation. $12.95

COMMUNIST CONTINUITY and the FIGHT FOR WOMEN'S LIBERATION

Edited with an introduction by Mary-Alice Waters

How did the oppression of women begin? Who benefits? What social forces have the power to end the second-class status of women? This three-part series helps politically equip the generation of women and men joining battles in defense of women's rights today. 8½ x 11 format. 3 vols. $30.00

On the EMANCIPATION of WOMEN

V.I.Lenin

Writings and speeches by the central leader of the Russian revolution on the fight for women's equality and the struggle for socialism. $4.95

THE FIGHT AGAINST FASCISM

The Struggle against Fascism in Germany
Leon Trotsky

Writing in the heat of struggle against the rising Nazi movement, a central leader of the Russian revolution examines the class roots of fascism and advances a revolutionary strategy to combat it. $28.95

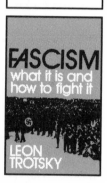

Fascism: What It Is and How to Fight It
Leon Trotsky

Why fascism was able to conquer only in those countries where social democratic and Stalinist parties blocked workers and their allies from utilizing a revolutionary situation to remove the capitalists from power. Booklet. $3.00

The Spanish Revolution (1931-39)
Leon Trotsky

Analyzes the revolutionary upsurge on the land and in the factories leading to the Spanish civil war and how the Stalinists' course ensured a fascist victory. $27.95

What Is American Fascism?
James P. Cannon and Joseph Hansen

Workers leaders assess Father Charles Coughlin's Social Justice movement and Mayor Frank Hague's dictatorial antilabor regime in Jersey City in the 1930s, and the anticommunist crusade led by Sen. Joseph McCarthy in the 1950s. 8½ x 11 format. $8.00

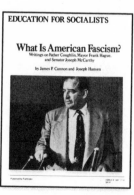

The Fight against Fascism in the U.S.A.
FORTY YEARS OF STRUGGLE
DESCRIBED BY PARTICIPANTS
James P. Cannon and others

Lessons from the fight against incipient fascist movements since the capitalist crisis and labor radicalization of the 1930s. 8½ x 11 format. $8.00

FROM PATHFINDER. SEE FRONT OF MAGAZINE FOR ADDRESSES.

The Teamster Series

IMPERIALISM'S MARCH TOWARD
FASCISM AND WAR

by Jack Barnes

I. WORKING-CLASS LEADERSHIP AND YOUTH

OVER THE PAST SEVEN YEARS, some of the biggest political changes in the last half century have occurred. A new —and descending—segment in the long-term curve of capitalist development was signaled by the October 1987 crash of the world's stock markets. A few years later the Stalinist appara- tuses throughout Eastern Europe and in the Soviet Union came tumbling down, one after another. Then, a war against Iraq that Washington sought to portray as a glorious military victory end- ed up sharpening the conflicts of the imperialist world order. At the opening of the 1990s capitalism entered a worldwide depres- sion for the first time since prior to World War II.

The most important political consequences of this increas- ingly compressed and volatile development of world capitalism, and the practical conclusions that communist workers and youth must understand in order to orient their activity, are true not just for the 1990s. They are true from now until the most fundamental economic, social, and political questions facing humanity have been settled in historic class battles between the revolutionary working-class movement and the forces seeking

---

This report was discussed and adopted by the Socialist Workers Party's August 1994 national convention. It is based on talks given by SWP national secretary Jack Barnes at educational conferences in Chicago (April 1994), New York (March), and Miami (February).

either to maintain or to impose capitalist rule in countries the world over.

How the working class responds in the years ahead to the political consequences of this accelerated dialectic of world capitalism will determine whether or not imperialism's march toward fascism and war can be stopped. That, in turn, depends on the forging of a communist leadership from the ranks of the most class-conscious and self-sacrificing working-class fighters the world over. It depends, in the most immediate sense, on the efforts today by the still relatively small forces who are committed to the perspective of building mass revolutionary proletarian parties—battalions of an international communist movement—that can lead workers and their allies in winning power from the capitalist rulers, founding a workers and farmers government, and opening a socialist road away from the cataclysm into which capitalism will otherwise drag humanity.

In discussing the next, modest steps that can and must be taken in order to advance in this direction, I want to begin by looking at the current stage of the upturn in the business cycle in the United States coming out of the 1990-91 recession. I start here because the hiring that has been under way in industry since the latter half of 1993 provides an opportunity like we haven't had for years to strengthen the communist movement in important ways. This is the first significant round of hiring throughout the country by manufacturing, mining, and freight transportation employers since the recovery officially began in April 1991. For its first two years, this upturn in the United States had commonly been called the "jobless recovery." Payrolls were actually lower two years into the upturn than when it began. (We should never forget that a recovery of *profit* rates and cash flow is what defines a capitalist recovery.)

Big business measured its success during those two years by chopping down the number of shifts; by intensifying work; by laying off employees; by cutting or freezing wages; by restructuring plants; by selling unprofitable divisions; and by computerizing administrative, financial, and commercial procedures.

Employers tested how many additional hours the existing workforce would accept before putting up serious resistance. The major dailies and business press harped on the "graying," the aging of the industrial working class, especially in the auto plants, steel mills, the mines, and elsewhere in heavy industry. If you didn't get a job at Wal-Mart or McDonald's, the commentators said, then you weren't likely to be working alongside any young workers. The picture they painted was a caricature, but it was based on a real slowdown in industrial hiring in the late 1980s and early 1990s.

The 1990-91 recession and stagnant job growth in the opening years of the recovery reinforced pressures on the communist movement that have their origins in blows dealt to the working class and labor movement by the capitalists during the 1980s. In face of the employers' attacks on living and working conditions, and saddled with a class-collaborationist misleadership, the unions remained in retreat, despite some important strikes and other rank-and-file resistance. In the closing years of the decade, the workers and farmers government in Nicaragua went down to defeat as the leadership of the Sandinista National Liberation Front politically succumbed to domestic and imperialist class pressures. Stalinism's defeat of the revolution in Grenada in 1983 and the setback in Nicaragua left Cuba as the only living socialist revolution anywhere in the world whose example of communist leadership could be looked to, learned from, and believed in.

FEWER YOUNG FORCES were being attracted to the communist movement and the average age of the membership was rising in the Socialist Workers Party. There was a decline in the nationwide spread of our movement as a number of SWP branches closed to release cadres to reinforce branches in other areas. Young people repelled by the evils of capitalism they saw all around them had a harder time figuring out a political course along which to organize themselves and others to fight these ills.

It was harder for them to see how struggles they were involved in were intertwined with the fight for a different social system, for socialism. It was even harder for them to see how they could link up with a social force, with the working class and labor movement, that had the power to bring about change. It was harder yet for them to connect up with a broader tradition of struggle, with a communist movement that organizes to have a presence all over the country and incorporates lessons of battles by the oppressed and exploited throughout modern history.

But over the past year we have begun to see evidence of a change. Assessing this change and making the necessary and appropriate adjustments is the challenge before the entire international communist movement.

Expanded hiring opportunities

First, expanded hiring has begun in industry, including where the Socialist Workers Party has fractions—in United Mine Workers–organized construction jobs building new coal mines, in rail, auto, steel, electrical machinery, and elsewhere. A new generation of workers is getting hired, many of them for their first time in an industrial job or, frequently, in a union job. Communist workers have the chance to be among these new hires and go through experiences with them on the job, in the unions, and as part of world and U.S. politics that affects us all. And we have the responsibility to organize to take advantage of this opportunity.

A real, conjunctural expansion of the capitalist economy is under way in the United States right now (as well as in Australia, New Zealand, Canada, and Britain and a number of other European countries). That does not contradict the fact that world capitalism has entered a depression. Ups and downs in the business cycle will continue. We should not be afraid to use the capitalists' term for what is happening: it is an *expansion.* The U.S. rulers are expanding production and expanding their profits. They are expanding their use of weakened union contracts to sidestep hiring provisions and take on younger workers at lower wages. They are especially expanding the market share they can take back from their capitalist rivals abroad. They are expanding their use of muscle to gain an edge on rival capitalists, and wannabe capitalists, around the world.

What is important to us is not that the average age of production workers in many auto or steel plants remains higher than it was ten or fifteen years ago. That's true. It's also true that many young people are still being hired by McDonald's and Wal-Mart and temp agencies. What we have our eyes on, however, is the fact that in more than six straight months of employment growth from September 1993 through today, a total of some 100,000 workers were hired into manufacturing jobs in the United States—and there appears to be no letup.

But we don't have to rely solely on statistics. Workers here this weekend from a number of regions around the country report that in recent months auto plants they work in, or where they have friends, are putting on third shifts. They report that a round of hiring has gone on in mine construction, and that jobs have opened in big steel mills that haven't taken applications for years. We have been slower than we would like to have been in responding to this shift and recognizing its importance to the revitalization of our union fractions, but the facts are not a secret to a party composed largely of industrial workers.

At the very time this hiring has been going on, big business has continued to "downsize," announcing layoffs at a record clip of 3,100 per day so far this year. A substantial majority of the layoffs over the past year or so have been among middle managers and salaried office employees. But manufacturing jobs also declined for most of the first twenty-eight months of the upturn, and factory workers continue to be laid off in particular industries and regions. In today's depression conditions, unemployment levels remain high by the standards of a post–World War II recovery, especially when you take account of those forced to work temporary or part-time jobs and those who have given up looking for work for the moment and are thus not counted in government jobless figures.

But since the closing months of last year more workers have

been hired into the plants, mines, and mills than have been laid off, and the hiring is still growing as we approach mid-1994. That is important for the working class and the unions right now. And it is very important for the small communist vanguard of our class.

The downsizing, the cost cutting, the retrenchment in capacity-increasing investment by the owners of industry is dead serious. But we should never lose track of why the capitalists are laying off employees, shedding whole sections of industry, and slashing prices sometimes to the point of near bankruptcy. They are doing so in order to take back enough market share from their capitalist rivals to begin hiring workers to produce a lot of goods to make more profits. That is the goal of the downsizing. The ones that don't reach the goal go under; the ones that do, hire.

What is important to communist workers are not the average figures for hiring any given month. What is important is staying on top of the hiring that is going on and finding ways to get in on it.

Young people challenge capitalism's evils

The second change we have noted over the past year is the growing number of young workers and students who are beginning to react against the devastating social and political consequences of the world capitalist disorder. The steps taken by young people in several cities in the United States in the opening months of 1994 to begin organizing a nationwide socialist youth organization is a product—in fact, the most important product—of these stirrings.

About 100 young people from across the country have gathered here in Chicago, in conjunction with this socialist educational conference of some 300 participants, to discuss signing up to be part of an organizing committee to launch a nationwide young socialists organization. A couple of months ago, four young socialists—two from New York, two from Minneapolis/St. Paul—initiated an organizing committee with the aim of calling together this broader meeting in Chicago. Coming out of this conference, there will be some twenty young socialists groups carrying out political activity and studying communist books and pamphlets in cities and on several campuses around the country. Through their efforts to reach out to other young fighters in their areas and elsewhere, they plan to organize a founding conference of a young socialists organization.[1]

This development reflects the fact that more young people today than in quite a while are becoming interested in politics and are willing to fight. They hate the consequences of capitalism they see around them and throughout the world. They hate the racism, the police brutality, the attacks on women's rights, the destruction of the environment, the unemployment, the wars and threats of war. They are convinced all this is getting worse, not better. Some are becoming interested in socialism and want to join together with other like-minded fighters. These young fighters want to link up with workers and youth in Cuba waging the battle to maintain the foundations of the socialist revolution there. They want to be part of a worldwide movement with young fighters from South Africa. Wherever there is resistance to oppression and exploitation, they want to join the battle. Above all they are inspired by and respond to the discovery of powerful forces in this country or anywhere in the world who, they have reason to believe, are moving in the same political direction.

We see evidence of such discontent in other parts of the world too. In March, for example, young workers and students

---

1. A second meeting of young socialists was held in Oberlin, Ohio, in August 1994 as part of an international socialist conference coinciding with the 37th national convention of the Socialist Workers Party. Some 100 participants in the youth meeting voted to take the name Young Socialists, issued a call for a founding conference of an international socialist youth organization, and elected a National Committee to lead their political activity between that meeting and their next international gathering.

in France dealt another blow to the anti-working-class policies of the government. For weeks, as the *Militant* newsweekly has been reporting, they mobilized all across France in the hundreds of thousands—backed by millions of working people and by all three major trade union confederations—calling on the government to withdraw its plans to cut the minimum wage for workers aged twenty-five and under. Through these struggles, they forced the regime of Prime Minister Edouard Balladur to back down. Just a few months earlier, in October 1993, Air France workers had shut down both the Charles de Gaulle and Orly airports near Paris, forcing the government to back off its antilabor plans to privatize Air France and ram through thousands of layoffs and other concessions. The Balladur government had planned to use Air France as the launching pad for a new round of assaults on jobs, wages, working conditions, and the union movement.

This resistance has weakened the ability of the French capitalist rulers to advance their strategy to strengthen the franc and protect their world market share and profit margins against German, U.S., British, and other capitalist rivals. The squeeze on the working class that has been tightening for more than a decade—under "Socialist" and conservative cabinets and presidents alike—was loosened a bit. The bosses' sanctimonious calls for "just a bit more sacrifice" had worked for so long that they became overconfident and started to make mistakes. Now they've had to start making panicky concessions and retreating from stated plans, at least for the moment. But in doing so they encourage other working people to resist and thereby undermine the stability of their profits and even of their government.

Young people in South Korea have been in the news too. As we meet here today, Korean students and young workers are demonstrating in Seoul against Washington's deployment of Patriot missiles in the South. The U.S. rulers are having a hard time finding many in South Korea who are willing to risk provoking a war against the Democratic People's Republic of Korea, since the result could be rapid and massive defensive assaults by the Pyongyang government against cities in the South.

Growing numbers of workers and youth in Korea see through Washington's cynical hypocrisy in demanding that the North Korean government halt the construction of medium-range missiles; they know that the U.S. armed forces have maintained massive, deadly ground- and sea-based air power—including missiles ready for launching—on the Korean peninsula and elsewhere in the region for decades. It was U.S. imperialism that completely leveled Pyongyang and many other Korean cities during the Korean War, and Washington remains the only world power ever to have used nuclear weapons—against the people of Hiroshima and Nagasaki in Japan. Many Koreans also know that the Japanese government has been stockpiling plutonium, that Tokyo's goal is to develop its own nuclear arsenal despite official denials, and that its missiles will be pointed among other places at the coveted Korean peninsula.

South Korean capitalists themselves are fearful that Washington may someday trigger a war that will result in the destruction of their plants and equipment in a matter of days. Growing numbers of youth are morally and politically repelled by the prospect of a military assault on the North by those in Washington who engineered the division of their country nearly half a century ago. Korea remains the last of the nations brutally divided by the victorious powers in World War II—through the connivance of U.S. imperialism and the Stalinist bureaucracy in Moscow. Millions of young people in Korea—whether or not they are pro-communist and regardless of their views about the regime in Pyongyang—aspire to throw off U.S. imperialist domination once and for all and restore Korea's sovereignty and national unification.

Recognizing and acting on what has changed
When revolutionary workers have been carrying out political work for some time under relatively difficult conditions, it is often hard to recognize when these conditions start to change. This is true for at least two reasons.

The first reason may sound funny, but we would be foolish to ignore it. It is the fear that if we turn out to be wrong about some perceived opportunity, if we exaggerate it, then we are just going to end up being disappointed, and that will make things even more difficult.

For the past few years, the slowed pace of political activity has made it difficult for the communist workers movement to win and integrate a new layer of young workers and students. So it is a responsible attitude for revolutionists to avoid jumping to conclusions about what might be momentary or accidental developments. Take advantage of any political opening, we say to ourselves. Join demonstrations and other protests that take place; take part in whatever resistance there is on the job; go onto campus to meet whoever we can; get socialist literature around as broadly as possible to explain scientifically that what appear to be distinct social evils are endemic to the capitalist system, and to present the socialist alternative. But let's not assume every break we happen to get marks some broader change in politics that we need to analyze and adjust our overall work and priorities to. Otherwise, we'll just start jumping around, instead of basing what we do on an objective, thought-out understanding of politics and a disciplined and sustainable, a proletarian, approach to organization. We will end up frittering away our accomplishments and disorganizing our work.

Such caution is grounded in a good trait—a sound, conservative trait in experienced communist workers.

There is a second reason why it can be difficult to recognize when something important is changing in politics. We have a harder time judging such changes in the short or medium term when they are taking place—as they are today—in a situation where longer-run trends in the other direction have not yet been reversed. There can and will be sudden shifts and explosive political developments in the class struggle. But that is not happening right now, and no competent leader would pretend to predict the date such developments will occur. At what point then, we ask ourselves, do we recognize that enough changes are accumulating, even if on a smaller scale, to necessitate an adjustment in what we are doing?

This is the question we need to discuss, to talk out together, today. We need to assess the two phenomena we have just described—the increased hiring and expanded political openings among youth. And then we must decide what we should do about this new situation—from the newest member of the communist movement to the person who has several decades of political experience.

We are obligated to ask ourselves the question: Is there a basis in the objective economic and political situation for what we see happening? Do we have good reason to believe these changes are substantial enough, and will last long enough, for communist workers and revolutionary-minded youth to reorganize, substantially if necessary, in order to take advantage of them and recoup lost ground?

Youth and the communist movement

No central leader of the modern communist movement, since its origins a century and a half ago, has ever believed it was possible to build a communist organization without attracting growing layers of young fighters—from various class origins and with a wide range of initial political experiences—to the working-class movement. We should remember that the founding document of the first international revolutionary workers organization, commissioned at a convention in London in November/December 1847, was drafted by two people still in their twenties.

That document, which has become known as the Communist Manifesto, was written by Karl Marx at age twenty-nine and Frederick Engels at age twenty-seven. It was written, moreover, by people who at the time had relatively little experience in the workers movement. Marx and Engels had both started out in politics as students who were revolutionary democrats, part of a broader radicalization of youth in Germany at that time.

From the outset Marx and Engels were capable, committed,

energetic, and hard-working—very hard-working—and disciplined in their work. They organized their lives around fighting for what they believed in, instead of insisting that what they believed in was less important than their personal priorities and comfortable lives. In all these ways, they were like millions of other young people over the decades and throughout the world.

BUT MARX AND ENGELS later explained something very important about their political evolution, so there could be no misunderstanding. Over a number of years in the mid- and late 1840s, these two young rebels had come into increasing contact with groups of revolutionary-minded workers, not only in Germany but in Paris, Brussels, London, and elsewhere. Marx and Engels explained that if they had not been able to find, and be found by, such an organized group of experienced, revolutionary workers, there would have been no beginnings of a communist movement in the mid-nineteenth century—or at least these two young revolutionists would not have been part of it, and the movement would have been weaker.

The workers who recruited Marx and Engels had already been organizing for years to fight capitalism and its effects on the lives of their class. They had been wounded in battle. They had spent time in prison. They knew about cops and provocateurs—part of the real world that any revolutionist must confront and learn how to handle. Many of their ideas and organizational procedures were stamped by the conspiratorial methods and petty-bourgeois utopianism and leftism that dominated radical politics among workers in the decades following the French revolution—something that left them vulnerable to the very provocateurs they sought to combat.

But these revolutionary workers were truly the vanguard of the rising working class at that time. In the 1830s they had suffered some defeats, and by the late 1840s they had been through lean times. They needed an infusion of young fighters and a renewal and rejuvenation of their proletarian institutions. For the young Marx and Engels, joining this organization of revolutionary-minded workers was a necessary step in recognizing themselves as actors in history who, in order to be effective in politics, needed to be part of the vanguard movement of a class.

Toward the end of his life, Engels described the lasting impact of his first encounter with three of the workers leaders who subsequently recruited him and Marx to the Communist League in 1847. "They were the first revolutionary proletarians whom I met," Engels wrote, "and however far apart our views were at that time in details—for I still owned, as against their narrow-minded egalitarian communism, a goodly dose of just as narrow-minded philosophical arrogance—I shall never forget the deep impression that these three real men made upon me, who was then still only wanting to become a man."[2]

The Communist League was the first modern revolutionary workers organization. It armed the working-class movement with scientifically formulated, written ideas that would never die as long as class society exists—no matter how many communists died in battle, from one generation to the next, fighting to act on those ideas. The program and strategy first codified in the Communist Manifesto keep being enriched in light of lessons from class-struggle experience by workers and our allies. No capitalist state, no reactionary movement of the exploiters, no matter how strong for a period of time, will ever succeed in destroying that programmatic continuity, because it is based on the actual historic line of march of the working class.

Those of you who have read and studied the Communist Manifesto recently have undoubtedly been struck by the discipline, the knowledge, the plain hard work that must have gone into drafting it. We're all impressed by the depth of its understanding

---

2. "On the History of the Communist League" (1885), Marx and Engels, *Selected Works*, vol. 3, p. 175. Also in Marx and Engels, *Collected Works*, vol. 26., p. 314.

of history, its insight into the condition of the working class and of the exploited classes that came before it. But there is also a striking freshness to its language, an openness, a reaching out to fighters against every form of despotism and oppression. It has an "in your face" tone not only toward the exploiters and oppressors but especially toward those in the workers movement who would adapt to and apologize for these privileged classes.

Marx and Engels were in their mid-twenties when they first linked up with experienced worker cadres. These proletarian leaders collaborated with the two young revolutionists for several years and read and learned from their political writings on topics such as free trade and protectionism, as well as their polemics against petty-bourgeois socialists like Proudhon and others.[3] On the basis of this common experience over several years, Marx and Engels accepted the assignment at the Communist League congress in late 1847 to draft the world program of an international organization made up of workers from across Europe. It took that process of recruitment to give birth to the manifesto of the international Communist League and the movement that would be built around it. It took the energy and the ability of young revolutionists to look freshly and clearly at the biggest questions of politics and organization confronting the working class, combined with the experience of working-class cadres who were leaders of an already-existing revolutionary workers movement.

Radicalization and political polarization among youth

The history of this century has shown that before large workers struggles become generalized and begin building on and reinforcing each other, layers of youth start rebelling against the most brutal and dehumanizing consequences of capitalism's

---

3. See, for example, "The Poverty of Philosophy" and "Speech on the Question of Free Trade" by Marx and "The Communists and Karl Heinzen" by Engels in *Collected Works*, vol. 6, as well as other writings from that collection from 1845-48.

economic and social contradictions. Whatever their starting point, and however confused and eclectic their initial views may be, some of these radicalizing young people begin giving serious consideration to the idea that capitalism is at the root of the problem and begin thinking of themselves as socialists. They become more attracted to the activity of socialist organizations and more open to proposals by communist workers about what needs to be done. The years leading up to the 1905 and 1917 revolutions in Russia, the initial manifestations of the mass labor radicalization in the United States in the 1930s, the rebirth of the revolutionary movement in Cuba in the late 1940s and early 1950s, the South African youth rebellion in the mid-1970s—in all these cases and others, the beginning of political stirrings among youth was a sign that more powerful social forces were changing underneath.

There is nothing mysterious about this pattern; it has a material basis in the social condition of youth. Young people are less tied down with jobs, families, and other responsibilities. For a relatively brief period, they are often freer than their elders simply to react against the evils of capitalism all around them. What they see happening seems more and more unbearable. Their entire lifetime is ahead of them. They don't want to live in a world like that. They reject the hypocrisy of bourgeois values and of the preachers, politicians, "personalities," and professors who defend these values.

More and more young people are appalled by the brutality of capitalist social relations. They don't want to be complicit in tolerating the degradation of human beings and destruction of nature that multiply year by year. Something is terribly wrong, and they want to be part of doing something about it. They begin trying to understand what is causing these things that they find more and more intolerable. They start reading books, magazines, and newspapers that they hope can provide some explanations. They begin looking for political movements or organizations that seem to know what's happening and have proposals about what to do.

In the absence of revolutionary working-class leadership, this rebelliousness of youth takes spontaneous forms. Some want to protest, to take to the streets, to demonstrate. Others pick up a rock and throw it at some symbol of the existing order, at a building, at a cop. Such frustration and spontaneity can easily become the seedbed of ineffective ultraleftism, of individual terrorism. If the working class does not move into action and appears incapable of leading broader and broader social forces toward resolving the crisis, then the anticapitalist radicalism of young people can lead layers of them to the right, to link up with reactionary forces emerging out of the parties and institutions of bourgeois society. Such layers of radicalized youth hold the established "political class" in contempt and turn to the streets to put pressure on the "decadent" and "disgusting" spokespeople for the rulers.

In fact, what is happening among young people on the campuses today is above all a political *polarization*. For every young person attracted to the communist movement right now, another one or two are attracted to various reactionary and rightist outfits, including some ultrarightist ones. And this is happening among students from a wide variety of backgrounds, given the growth of middle-class layers among Blacks and other oppressed nationalities and national minorities in the United States (and in other imperialist countries, as well). In a period of deepening social crisis, radical right-wing groups initially grow more rapidly than communist organizations or class-struggle-oriented currents, since the right emerges directly out of bourgeois politics and its existing political formations.

Radicalizing young people begin reacting to something more than just capitalism's evils. They begin sensing its weaknesses. They begin to recognize that the capitalist rulers, despite their posturing, are *not* all-powerful. They are not what they pretend to be. They don't have a stable future. Something can be done about the consequences of their rule, if a strong enough social force can be mobilized against them. Young people begin looking for such social forces, and if they don't find them in the working-class movement, some will turn to other class forces and their radical demagogy. In this way, as well, what's happening among youth is a preview of the coming polarization of the rural population, women, and layers of the middle classes.[4]

This is why it is important for communists to reach out and seek to politically convince every young rebel we can, before he or she becomes committed to crank ideas, is pulled toward the radical right, or simply comes to terms over time with capitalism and sinks back into workaday life in bourgeois society. Those we can win to the revolutionary movement right now are not large in numbers, but they are spread all over the United States. A nationwide socialist youth organization is needed so they can get to know each other, discuss politics together, learn to work with and lead each other, make decisions democratically, and then act in a collective way to carry out what they've decided.

An accurate look at the objective situation

This brings us back to the question we posed a bit earlier: Are we right about what has begun to change among growing numbers of young people? We must take this question seriously, especially since socialists and other revolutionary-minded people want very much for the answer to be yes. So we should ask ourselves: Are there objective developments in the world, are there shifts in politics, that can explain a receptivity to socialist ideas among a small but expanding layer of young people today?

---

4. For a discussion of how rightist movements seek to appeal to working farmers, see "The Crisis Facing Working Farmers" by Doug Jenness in *New International* no. 4, pp. 114-115, as well as the article "Farmers' Struggle: Who Are Its Allies?" by Jenness, writing under the pen name Chester Nelson, in the February 25, 1983, issue of the *Militant*. The susceptibility to fascist and other reactionary demagogy among substantial layers of women—especially women in the middle classes and those who are not working jobs and part of the labor movement—is discussed in the same issue of *New International* in "The Revolutionary Perspective in the United States," p. 70, as well as in the introduction by Mary-Alice Waters to the book *Cosmetics, Fashions, and the Exploitation of Women* (New York: Pathfinder, 1986), pp. 3-27.

We can dispense with one potentially easy explanation for such a change: there are currently no ascending social protest movements or even big battles by the unions that would account for a new openness to anticapitalist ideas. We have to dig deeper. But as we do so, we come up against a problem. Given the rapidity of developments since the October 1987 crash of the world's stock markets, we find ourselves at a conjuncture in world politics where it's not possible, I think, for the socialist movement to make accurate political judgments without a levy of youth. That might sound like an extreme statement, but I am convinced it is true. It makes sense to most people why it would be impossible for a socialist organization to maintain a certain level of activity if it ceases drawing in young members. But I am raising something different: that we cannot *think* about the world clearly today without the beginnings of motion toward a youth organization.

Why is this so? Because in addition to the experience and continuity without which any communist organization will go off the rails politically, there are also points in history at which so much is changing so rapidly that even the best fighters will be disoriented unless they can break from habits of thought developed in the past and see the world through the eyes of a generation just awakening to political life. The developments I noted at the beginning of this talk mark such a moment in history: the October '87 crash; the collapse of the Stalinist apparatuses, with the acceleration of the forces of capitalist restoration and the deepening social and class polarization; the Gulf War; the opening of the first world depression since the thirties.

To thinking people in their late twenties or older, these register giant political shifts. The way you previously looked at the world must now be adjusted. But to young people who are just coming into politics, this is the only world political situation they've ever known and functioned in. This is what they take as a given.

Similarly, young workers in the plants and mines today have a different starting point than older workers. The blows that have been dealt by the employers to the working class and unions over the past fifteen years are part of the experiences that workers have to draw on in order to function in politics and the working-class movement today. Anyone active in the labor movement during that period has lived through retreats and defeats, through frustrating stalemates and partial victories, that have affected growing numbers of workers in different job situations and union locals. It would be next to impossible not to internalize certain cautious conclusions from these experiences.

But this pattern doesn't weigh nearly so heavily on workers who have been in a workplace one, two, or three years. They don't act on the basis of some perception of what the labor movement has gone through over the past decade and a half. That is not how they judge opportunities and responsibilities to fight some new probe by the employers, *today*. By itself, of course, this doesn't change the relationship of class forces, but it opens up new possibilities for resistance to the unceasing capitalist offensive against the working class and unions. And it opens new space for those who grasp these possibilities as their starting point.

We're able to draw these conclusions because in the United States we have been successful in winning a small levy of young fighters over the past year. This not only confirms our initial judgments but allows us to be more accurate about the openings before us.

What is it, then, about today's world that leads us to believe that growing numbers of youth will *continue* to rebel against the existing order and be attracted toward the socialist movement?

In answering this question, we should step back and begin, as Marxists always do, not with labor but with capital. If we understand capital's flows and capital's problems, then we will be able to understand labor's possibilities and how to take advantage of them.

We should remember that we in the communist movement are by no means the only ones to take note of a big shift in world politics in recent years. Many bourgeois political figures and commentators have also done so; it's now even common to speak of a "new world disorder."

Virtually everyone but us, however, puts the turning point in 1989-90, with the fall of the Berlin Wall and the collapse of Stalinist regimes throughout the former Soviet bloc. We're the only political current that starts with capitalism, with the 1987 stock market crash and what it signaled about the new stage in the tendency of world capitalism to decline and about the heightened class tensions and political polarization its crises would unleash. This is the only framework in which it is possible to understand and intervene in the unfolding of world politics and the class struggle today, including the factors that lie behind the "failure of socialism" and prevent the transformation of this "socialism" into a stable capitalism.

II. DEFLATION AND DOWNSIZING

WE'VE ALREADY DISCUSSED the fact that we've entered the third year of an upturn in the capitalist business cycle in the United States that is only now beginning to result in substantial job creation. This kind of shallow and sluggish recovery is and will be normal for depression conditions. The generations that have grown into adulthood and political life since the end of World War II, however, are living through something new, something outside the previous direct experience of any of us.

The capitalists in the United States and in other imperialist powers are not putting capital into a major expansion of productive capacity, as they did from the 1950s into the 1970s. For nearly two decades the capitalists have faced an accelerating crisis of declining profit rates, as explained in the Socialist Workers Party's 1988 resolution, "What the 1987 Stock Market Crash

Foretold."[5] Capitalists are driving to cut costs—"downsizing," "resizing," or "reengineering" in current business jargon—instead of expanding productive capacity, because they can't secure a competitive rate of return on investment in capacity-expanding plant and equipment.

Both within the United States and throughout the world capitalist system, price competition is intensifying among capitalists, as they contend over limited markets. As a result, there will be a tendency toward deflation, with prices of many products falling. The capitalists continue to fear a deflationary collapse like the one that marked the opening years of the Great Depression of the 1930s. The massive rents—the above-average profits—commanded by the manufacturers of major name-brand products have become much more difficult to extort, in many cases evaporating, as these goods are forced to compete for market share as just one more commodity alongside others.

This is the opposite of what has happened in the imperialist world during the conscious lifetime of most adults today. During these years, mammoth imperialist trusts competed for world markets by expanding, by taking on new capacity, by building new factories and adding new machinery. Those sectors of capital that *prepared the best for growth* reaped the biggest rewards. That's the way it worked for the first two and a half decades following World War II, until the engines began gradually running down in the late 1960s and mid-1970s. It no longer worked that way in the 1980s, but the emerging new reality was largely hidden by a massive balloon of debt, which set the stage for what's happening today—the "great de-leveraging," as they say.

During the prolonged capitalist expansion, big manufacturers in the United States and other imperialist countries used their domination of markets to establish brand names. They competed for market share through advertising for product-name recognition. They didn't compete for your business by

<hr>

5. Published elsewhere in this issue.

slashing prices. You knew the brand name and were convinced, rightly or wrongly, that it was a better product. Many of us grew up in the heyday of Borden's Elsie the Cow, Philip Morris's Marlboro Man, Procter & Gamble's Pampers, Kellogg's Corn Flakes, and so on. The brand name often became synonymous with the product itself. In large parts of the country a "Coke" *was* what you called soda pop, whatever the flavor or whoever made it. Kleenex was the name for tissue paper. Scotch tape was cellophane tape. Those were the only names I knew for these products when I was growing up.

Why did we buy Kleenex instead of other tissue, even if it cost more? Because we recognized that name, which had established a monopoly position in the market. The makers of Kleenex collected a brand-name rent. And when you added it up on a world scale, the rent was huge.

But that's all coming to an end. There is stiffening price competition for market share today. You won't stop smoking if the price of Marlboros go up; you'll switch to another brand. You won't stop eating corn flakes for breakfast if Kellogg raises the price; you'll pick up the generic brand of corn flakes.

The competition is even stiffer for big new markets the capitalists are opening abroad. The emerging middle class in China may like drinking Cokes and Sprites. But the Chinese can make soda pop too, and not just aimed at the growing middle class. The average person in China who will be able to afford a soft drink now and again will be happy to buy one for a third the price of a Coke. Peasants coming into the city won't leap to brand names.

Of course, Coca-Cola will fight for a market in China. The front cover of Coca-Cola's third-quarter report to its stockholders last year featured a full-color photograph of a young woman on a bicycle in Beijing with a bottle of Sprite in her hand. "China is one of the Company's fastest growing emerging markets," Coca-Cola told its shareholders. In the first nine months of 1993, it said, it had expanded its sales by nearly 25 million cases, "or the equivalent of creating a market generating current annual volume the size of Ireland."

But we should remember that Coca-Cola's dream depends not on the thirst of a billion. It depends on a stable, growing middle class, buffered from class strife, that will spend its disposable income on brand names advertised and distributed by imperialist-based corporate giants.

Capitalist overproduction

If you read or listen to the business news, you'll hear the phrase: "Sears took a 'one-time charge' of $1.3 million this quarter." Or Philip Morris, or Borden, or NCR, or others. That is simply an accounting phrase for the consequences of mounting capitalist overproduction. It registers the large-scale devaluation and destruction of capital—turning products into cut-rate commodities, as owners seek to clear their inventories at the best returns possible under the circumstances.

Interest rates are low in the United States, even with the small hikes in February and late March by the Federal Reserve Board. They've been dropping in capitalist Europe and Japan too. But even if real interest rates hit zero or drop below (as they have at various times in this century, taking inflation into account), capitalists won't borrow to invest in new plants and equipment unless they can turn a higher rate of profit by doing so than by using their money capital in other ways.

Why would capitalists take out a loan to invest in a new factory, if the upshot is not only that they have to pay back the loan—even at little or no interest—but also that they end up losing money on their investment? The answer is, they won't and they aren't. Businesses aren't taking the loans. Only twice in this century in the United States have commercial and industrial loans declined for three consecutive years—1934 to 1937, and 1991 to 1993. That fact alone is worth thinking about.

The big Merrill Lynch brokerage and investment banking firm put out a year-end report in late 1993 entitled "The Meek Inherit the Earth." It painted a picture of the world capitalist economy that is scary from the viewpoint of their class. The report said that profit rates continue to decline and outlets for profitable investment in expanded production continue to shrink in the major industrialized countries. Barriers to the expansion of capital continue to proliferate, the report said, although not in those words. In this situation, it advised that the road to profits was what the employing class calls "increased productivity"—that is, squeezing fewer workers to produce more value at lower wages, while cutting down other production costs as well.

"The long postwar business cycle resembled, in retrospect, a vast Monopoly game," said the Merrill Lynch report. "Demand went in one direction, up, and investment, often financed with the house's money, debt, followed." (Many of us, I'm sure, have played the game of Monopoly, where the winner is the player able to obtain the most cash and rapidly turn it into hotels and other profitable rental properties.)

"These dynamics are in the process of reversal," the report said. "The 1990s are clearly behaving differently. As the economy enters its third year of expansion, deflationary forces continue to lurk. . . . We think the rules of Monopoly have changed. The reckless acquisition of productive assets and relentless pursuit of growth now entail distressingly low returns. Growth retailers find competition omnipresent as retail inventories consistently outpace sales, airlines face relentless price wars and bankers have difficulty finding a good loan.

"In the current world," the report concluded, "consumption patterns are changing, corporate profit growth is slowing, returns on investment are declining, and the pressure to downsize, improve asset utilization and increase productivity are unrelenting. . . . In the 1990s, smaller is better, things go backwards, the meek inherit the earth."

Except for the fact that biblical meekness is not a characteristic of finance capital—during boom or bust—this picture is largely accurate, and not just for the United States but across the imperialist world.

All that downsizing accomplishes in and of itself, however, is to put greater pressure on the rate of profit, as the bosses seek to make more off the labor of relatively fewer workers. It also poses a sharper threat to outstanding loans and to assets of all kinds whose paper values are bloated. What the capitalists call downsizing limits the expansion of the mass of surplus value and increases as a percentage of capital that portion that Marx called constant capital—the portion laid out for everything other than wages for labor power. And that puts further downward pressure on profit rates. It's not only an important theoretical question; it's one with utmost practical implications right now.

THE ONLY WAY the capitalists can increase surplus value to the degree they need is by drawing more workers, more labor power, into expanded production; lengthening the workday and intensifying speedup alone won't do the job for them. Expanded production, in turn, requires more hiring and greater expenditures of capital on new factories, more and more productive machinery, and additional parts and raw materials. Conjuncturally that is what we're seeing right now in the United States, as well as in other countries to a lesser degree.

When an upswing begins, on whatever scale, the working class and unions are in a stronger position to fight for better wages and conditions, and to reconquer some ground taken by the bosses in leaner times. There's already evidence of increased labor resistance in the United States, as we'll discuss later on.

The current upswing in the business cycle doesn't change the bigger picture we're describing. Cost-cutting does not further the self-expansion of capital, which is the only thing that can open up a prolonged period of relatively crisis-free capitalist development such as we saw for some twenty-five years beginning in the late 1940s. When capitalism is expanding in that way, the working class and labor movement can slowly but surely wrest economic and social concessions from the employing class, as well as more democratic rights.

But that's not what's in store for our class today. That period is behind us.

Few of the biggest names you know in capitalist industry in the United States are expanding productive capacity. Instead, they are holding down costs on what they do produce and competing harder to sell it. Those that do this the best can boost their profits in the short run and counteract some of the downward pressure on their rate of profit. Caterpillar, for example, is succeeding in the short run in producing construction equipment at less cost in order to undercut Komatsu and other competitors and take more worldwide market share away from them. (Worker-bolsheviks, like other thinking workers, are painfully aware of how the Caterpillar bosses have done this by targeting working conditions and union rights. The initial success of the Caterpillar bosses has whetted their appetite for deeper assaults on the United Auto Workers membership.)

Right now, those being hit hardest by the downsizing and cost cutting of the biggest U.S. corporations are not industrial workers, not primarily those who produce surplus value for the employing class. The employers are increasing the mechanization, and computerization, of all sorts of unproductive jobs—unproductive in the Marxist sense of producing no added value for the employing class. The capitalists are cutting costs by computerizing aspects of retail and wholesale trade, banking, and insurance and by laying off employees in these sectors. Lower-level managerial personnel and technical, commercial, and other salaried employees are facing permanent layoffs in record numbers. If you spend some time in parts of the country where IBM, for example, has been the dominant employer for a quarter century, you read in the newspapers every week about what's hitting layers of workers who thought they and their families had permanently escaped into the middle class. The layoffs are taking a devastating toll on big sections of the population in entire small cities and towns.

While downsizing does cut costs for individual capitalist firms, however, it doesn't necessarily raise profit rates. A lot of businesses became more efficient each year that passed during the depression of the 1930s, but their profit rates kept going down.

They could only reverse that by fundamentally expanding their rate of production and how much they were able to sell. It was preparations for the second world imperialist slaughter, the massive economic mobilization during the war itself, and the sweeping reconstruction of the vast destroyed productive capacity of their rivals in Europe and Japan that both brought the U.S. capitalists out of the deep 1937-38 downturn and laid the basis for the postwar expansion that put the depression behind them.

Explosion of paper values

Big business in the United States and other imperialist countries doesn't need a lot of money circulating in the economy right now. Since businesses are not expanding, banks aren't making a lot of loans; they are finding more lucrative ways to turn a profit. When corporations sell new issues of stock today, they use their revenues from these sales to pay off debt, not to build new factories. Although they can't analyze it scientifically, capitalists know in practice that those who have the cleanest balance sheets today have the best chance of survival—the opposite of how it has been for several decades.

The biggest threat to the stability of the capitalist economy right now is not inflation, as it was fifteen or twenty years ago, but the possibility of accelerating deflation. Many prices are actually going down, and the overall inflation rate—some 3 percent annually (or lower) in much of the imperialist world—is the lowest for any extended period of time since the 1950s through the early 1960s.

The prices of what Wall Street calls commodities—oil, farm products, base metals and other raw materials for industry —have been at very low levels, dropping by more than half since 1980. Despite an increase during the opening months of 1994, these prices are still in the low range historically.

Commercial real estate prices plummeted by half in the late 1980s and early 1990s, too. Capitalists who couldn't make what they considered satisfactory profits by investing in expansion of manufacturing capacity poured their excess capital, among other places, into a massive overbuilding of skyscrapers, shopping centers, and office complexes. By the opening of the 1990s, however, vacancy rates in downtown areas of major cities were at extraordinarily high levels. Big commercial landlords stopped demanding rent payments from hard-pressed business tenants, competing to hold onto lessees until conditions turned up. I'm not talking about your landlord or mine; our landlords will bounce us out if we don't pay the rent. But that's not what businesses face. This collapse in real estate prices is true not just here in the United States, but in Britain and Japan as well.

Economic collapse lurks behind such deflationary trends. This is what a business cycle upturn is like in a depression —high levels of unemployment and of part-time and temporary work, even in periods of renewed hiring; downward pressures on prices.

The deflation affects our class in a particular way. Our real wages and family income have been declining since the opening of the 1970s, as our take-home pay failed to keep up with rising prices, even as inflation slowed after 1982. In recent years, however, employers have often simply been freezing our wages or cutting our hourly wage rates outright. They can't use inflation to rob us these days as easily as they did in the earlier period; that's not what's happening.

What is happening? Banks aren't very interested in your or my money right now. Have you tried to open up a bank account lately? What do they offer on an interest-bearing checking account—one and a half percent or something? Or on a savings account—two to two and a half percent? Less than the rate of inflation. They don't want our money. They've even begun closing more and more neighborhood branches.

Banks these days aren't much interested in banking—that is, what we think of as normal banking business, attracting deposits and making loans. There are some 2,500 fewer banks in the United States today than there were in the middle of the 1980s. And the trend continues toward bigger and fewer. Banks grow wealthier by borrowing cheap from the government and then buying bonds from the same government that pay them a higher interest rate. (Talk about welfare queens!) And they engage in the ever-expanding international currency speculation.

That's what your friendly local bankers have been doing. And that's what they will keep doing so long as the dollar remains strong, inflation and long-term interests rates stay down, and there's not a political explosion somewhere in the world that upsets the apple cart.

1994 stock market slide

But if not much money has been created by banks loaning money in recent years, it has been created in another, hidden way—by the massive floating of securities. Up until February of this year, when the stock market began another slide, the 1990s had witnessed an explosion of stock prices in the United States. Stock markets in most other advanced capitalist countries soared in 1993 as well. The notable exception was the three-year-long collapse of the stock market in Japan, which has turned back up a bit for the first time this year. Ultimately risk capital and ownership rights, as Engels describes in his appendix on the stock exchange in volume 3 of Marx's *Capital*,[6] are the means the ruling class uses in the capitalist epoch to profit from the domination of piles of capital.

Every day giant blocks of shares of stock are bought and sold on Wall Street and other paper markets around the world, along with bonds—interest-bearing government and corporate debt—and, in recent years, more and more "financial products" derived from stocks and bonds ("derivatives," as they are called). Massive amounts of capital will suddenly start flowing into a fast-food chain called Boston Chicken. Then into Snapple beverages, or Celestial Seasonings. Gambling stocks have

---

6. See "The Stock Exchange" in volume 3 of *Capital* (New York: Penguin, 1976), pp. 1045-47 (this edition is identical to the one printed for several years under the Vintage imprint), and the discussion of it in "What the 1987 Stock Market Crash Foretold," the 1988 SWP political resolution.

been among the biggest "growth stocks" the past year—shares of ownership in riverboat casinos, giant Las Vegas hotels aping Egyptian sphinxes, gambling rip-offs on Indian reservations, corporations running state lotteries. Holders of capital even start buying up paper claims on future business activity—not ownership of stocks or bonds themselves, but claims on what might happen to the price of these pieces of paper in the future. And capitalists borrow massively to do all this, on the premise that the market value of this paper can only go up.

So, on the one hand, a massive bubble grows on the stock market—a hidden form of inflation embedded in enormous amounts of money tied up in stocks held by the bourgeoisie and better-off middle classes, and more and more leveraged by gigantic borrowing. On the other hand, disinflation threatens to turn into a deflationary collapse. This explosive contradiction builds up.

Peasants throughout the history of commodity circulation have developed a social intuition that senses these speculative bubbles and the dangers of their collapse. They take what small savings they have out of currencies and start buying up gold jewelry, pieces of jade, hunks of valuable metal—anything they might be able to sell someday—and stash it away. A similar mentality may soon start growing among many owners of capital in imperialist countries, with special urgency among relatively smaller and more vulnerable holders: "Should I get my money out of stocks and riskier bonds right now and put it into 'things'?" The danger is that instead of just shuffling borrowed money among various hands, a large-scale sell-off and implosion of paper securities can coincide with rising paper values of commodities, threatening a collapse of production and trade.

Of course, this is their problem, not ours. But workers shouldn't forget one thing that is our problem: that also floating inside the credit bubble are all the promises to working people about "guaranteed" pensions upon retirement, about "secure" medical plans. Billions of dollars in all these "fringe benefit" funds have been poured into the stock market too.

Our futures are suspended inside the bubble! Never think that you have a pension, that you have a medical plan. What you have is the capitalists' *promise* of a pension, the *promise* of a medical plan. You have a *promise* based on the "value" of the paper holdings in a "trust." And trust it you should not!

W E MAKE NO PREDICTION about how big that bubble can grow or about when it will explode. But that growing contradiction, that impending catastrophe built right into this stage in the longer-term rhythms of the declining capitalist system, is what the 1987 collapse of the world's stock markets pointed to as a coming attraction.

We've gone through another stock market slide in early 1994, although not nearly as sharp as the crash in 1987. Wall Street stock prices, as measured by the Dow Jones Industrial Average, dropped by nearly 400 points from their high in late January, almost 10 percent, before turning back up again a bit—and that's just what happened to the stock of thirty of the most highly rated corporations. The index of share prices of 6,000 companies fell more than 15 percent from the high point.

For the past couple of years, the wealthy in the United States seemed to be riding high. Their downsizing and cost cutting was bashing their rivals in other imperialist countries. They were speeding up production, extending the workweek, and pushing back workers' wages, benefits, and job conditions. Interest rates were lower than in nearly fifteen years. Both the stock and bond markets were booming. It didn't seem like they would ever go down. Billions were being made on Wall Street, including "with other people's money," as the saying goes—including a lot of workers' pension fund money.

There didn't seem to be any way to lose. The sky was the limit. They could borrow ten times what they owned to buy stocks, bonds, and other securities, because the market would only go up and they could cover the loan. They could borrow fifty or a hundred times what they owned if they were buying government bonds, because these were "safe" and would only go up. The professional Wall Street trading freaks forgot the real world. They even had a little chant they would holler after a particularly good day: "Five and five in ninety-five!"—that is, by 1995 long-term interest rates would drop to 5 percent and the Dow Jones stock average would shoot over 5,000 points. And all this was based on historically low levels of investment in capacity-expanding plant and equipment or hiring of new labor power![7]

In mid-February a panic gained momentum on Wall Street and in other paper markets after the U.S. Federal Reserve Board raised short-term interest rates by a few tenths of a point. Big holders of stocks and bonds began selling and scrambling for buyers, and prices went into a skid. That's when a lot of them had to pay their dues for living a lie. Somebody finally said, "Oh, by the way, the price of those bonds didn't go up this month, they went down. So you owe me ten times, or a hundred times, what you bought them for, because that's what I lent you to buy them." That happened to growing numbers of Wall Street traders.

Panics happen in the history of capitalism. Today we can see small but sharp elements of the heat lightning of what the next one may look like. Marx and Engels explained the objective basis of such panics. From the standpoint of the capitalist, Engels wrote in a note in *Capital*, "The production process appears simply as an unavoidable middle term, a necessary evil for the purpose of money-making. . . . This explains why all nations characterized by the capitalist mode of production are periodically seized by fits of giddiness in which they try to accomplish the money-making without the mediation of the production process."[8]

---

7. *Business Week* commented in its cover story a few weeks later in April 1994 that "In hindsight, these strategies embodied too much leverage, contained much more risk, and were much less hedged than their creators had figured."
8. *Capital*, vol. 2, p. 137.

More and more derivatives, fewer and fewer workers. *¡Qué milagro!* But trying to steady themselves from such giddy heights can turn the "miracle" into its opposite.

Greed *and* fear drive the capitalist paper markets, and have from their outset. For the past half decade greed has driven them, and greed could save the capitalists from any little disturbance that came along. Just have confidence, borrow what you need, buy while the market is dipping and wait for it to shoot back up.

I N UNDERSTANDING the social psychology of how capitalism actually works, we shouldn't lose sight of what's sometimes called the "greater fool theory." A reasonable person can ask: "How can something be sold for such a high price? It's clearly not worth that. Why would anyone pay such a price?" But the answer is simple: They'll pay it because they're confident that someone else will come along and pay them *even more* for it. Capitalism has functioned that way from its very earliest days. For a while in Holland in the 1600s, during what became known as the "tulipomania," a single tulip bulb could be sold for the equivalent of several thousand dollars!

If there was a fool who would pay that for a tulip bulb three centuries ago because he figured a greater fool would pay him a thousand dollars more the next day or next week, the scale of the phenomenon has become infinitely greater with the modern-day dominance of finance capital and speed-of-light communications. Today trillions of dollars are traded on the world's stock, bond, commodities, and currency markets each day. What's more, you can borrow the money to make the purchase, multiplying your returns—or your losses. Why get out of Boston Chicken when its stock price shoots up to $45, if you think someone will buy it from you next week at $55? This is not a joke. It's not an aberration. It is the genuine social psychology of how stock, bond, and other paper markets work, without which capitalism can't function.

But when the confidence of the owners of paper disappears, when a greater fool can no longer be found, that's when the panic hits. It turns out you're the greatest fool. Everything that once appeared fine-tuned goes up for grabs. Fear then replaces greed as the dominant sentiment among those who buy and sell paper to collect, as rents, part of the surplus value that we produce with our labor. The prices paid for stocks and bonds just the previous week—or the previous day or previous hour—only "made sense" because those who held capital were willing to believe that's what those pieces of paper were worth. The beliefs, fears, and hopes of the ruling class become objective factors in the short-run evolution of capitalism.

What we've seen in the opening months of 1994 in the world bond markets is a little foretaste of that kind of panic. That is another reflection—like larger numbers of young people beginning to react against the evils of capitalism—of the weaknesses building up underneath the imperialist world order.

The politics of economics

We should always remember that big *political* explosions in the world—not just stock market collapses, banking crises, sudden shortages, and so on—will continue to trigger economic and social catastrophes in the capitalist world.

In the imperialist epoch above all, as Lenin and Trotsky taught us, politics is concentrated economics; economic phenomena don't simply run their course irrespective of class struggles, wars, and revolutions. Major shifts in the curve of capitalist development have been triggered by developments outside the economy per se, or rather, outside the lawful operations of the capitalist business cycle.[9] Neither we nor anyone else has any timetables. No one can know beforehand what combination of economic and political developments may set off such a catastrophe—al-

---

9. See "The Curve of Capitalist Development" by Leon Trotsky, and "What the 1987 Stock Market Crash Foretold," both printed elsewhere in this issue.

though history gives us good reason to believe that wars and preparations for war will be a weighty element.

We have nothing to take back from the SWP's 1988 resolution and the accompanying popular pamphlet, *An Action Program to Confront the Coming Economic Crisis.* Capitalism is becoming more and more vulnerable to a worldwide crisis that will bring in its wake mass unemployment, ruination of working farmers, homelessness, destruction of small businesses, and impoverishment on a scale not experienced since the 1930s. It will devastate the Third World, the majority of whose toilers have already faced a deterioration of economic and social conditions for almost a quarter century. And it will open a new stage in the social and political crisis of the imperialist countries.

Millions of working people today believe that such a prospect is a distinct possibility. They are already being shaken by the instability inherent in the evolution of world capitalism. This explains the receptivity to revolutionary literature even before the onset of such a social catastrophe or major class battles.

The "lack of stability," wrote Bolshevik leader Leon Trotsky in the 1920s, "the uncertainty of what tomorrow will bring in the personal life of every worker, is the most revolutionary factor of the epoch in which we live." The "tranquil mode of existence" of the labor officialdom for nearly a quarter century prior to World War I, Trotsky wrote, had "also exerted its influence upon the psychology of a broad layer of workers who are better off."

All that was changed, Trotsky explained, by the economic and social crisis of capitalism that the rival ruling classes of North America, Europe, and Japan had failed to resolve through the worldwide slaughter they had inflicted on humanity. The resulting "absence of stability drives the most imperturbable worker out of equilibrium," Trotsky wrote. "It is the revolutionary motor power."[10]

---

10. Trotsky, *First Five Years of the Communist International* (New York:

III. HISTORIC SHIFT IN WORLD CAPITAL FLOWS

WE NEED TO LOOK at where capital is flowing in the world today—from where and to where. That will help us understand more concretely the effects of these capital flows on international politics and prospects for the class struggle.

Throughout most of this century, a substantial majority of imperialist capital invested abroad has gone to other advanced capitalist countries. This has been true even as large amounts of capital were exported to colonial and semicolonial countries to reap superprofits from the exploitation of rural and urban toilers. Especially since the end of World War II, U.S. capital has flowed in huge quantities into Canada, Europe, Japan, Australia, and New Zealand. Capital from various Western European countries has flowed throughout capitalist Europe, to North America, and to Japan and elsewhere in Asia and the Pacific. Japanese capital has flowed into the United States and Europe, as well as to Australia and New Zealand.[11]

Since the beginning of the 1990s there has been a substantial shift in this balance toward greater U.S. and other imperialist investment in the most industrialized countries of the Third World, as well as into parts of Central and Eastern Europe. As the Merrill Lynch research report cited earlier put it, from finance capital's point of view, "the primary flow of capital . . . will be to the developing world and the primary source of above average returns in the 1990s will be there." (The change noted in the first half of the sentence is a fact; the second half of the sentence is a hope.)[12]

Pathfinder, 1972), vol. 1, pp. 233-34.

11. Some 80 percent of the assets of U.S. companies abroad, for example, are in Western Europe, Canada, Japan, Australia, and New Zealand.

12. The percentage of foreign direct investment flowing to Third World

For the first time in U.S. history, in the opening years of the 1990s the United States has become a net exporter of capital. U.S. capital is flowing overseas, especially to Latin America and elsewhere in the Third World, in search of the kinds of profit rates that are harder and harder for the exploiting classes to achieve within the United States.

Throughout its history the United States has been a net importer of capital. During the latter half of the nineteenth century, the U.S. ruling families imported massive amounts of foreign capital to help finance the building of industry and the railroads. In the closing decade of the last century, as the United States emerged as an imperialist power, U.S. capitalists began exporting growing amounts of capital abroad in competition with its rivals for markets and for sources of cheap labor and raw materials. Since U.S. imperialism's triumph in World War II, moreover, it has been the world's single largest exporter of capital.

Throughout this entire period, however, even larger amounts of capital continued to flow into this country, given the absolute size of the U.S. economy and internal market and the predominance of Wall Street in international stock, bond, and currency trading. During the 1980s capitalists in Japan, Germany, Britain, the Netherlands, and elsewhere bought up billions of dollars in U.S. treasury bonds. They bought up real estate and built or purchased factories here as a wedge into the U.S. market. And billions of dollars poured in from interest payments extracted to "service" the Third World debt. Now, over the past few years the pace of this influx of capital into the United States has slowed, as Japan and much of capitalist Europe has been mired in recession and as interest rates have fallen in the United States. At the same time, U.S. capital has been pouring beyond its national boundaries at an increasing clip.

---

countries in 1993 was nearly 40 percent, up from an annual average of around 20 percent in the 1980s. New annual foreign capital investment in these countries more than doubled between 1990 and 1993.

The capital pouring into semicolonial countries from the United States and other imperialist countries today is not primarily more of the enormous, parasitic bank loans we saw in the 1980s—although the Third World debt has nonetheless risen from $1.2 trillion in 1987 to $1.5 trillion in 1993. Servicing that debt—that is, paying blood money—remains an enormous burden, exacted by bourgeois governments in Latin America, Africa, and Asia from the wealth produced by brutal exploitation of the workers and peasants. But loans from commercial banks and international financial institutions have dropped from more than 80 percent of the imperialist capital flowing into Third World countries at the opening of the 1980s to about 25 percent today.

Instead, nearly 75 percent of imperialist capital in Third World countries last year went into buying up stocks and bonds on what are becoming known as the "emerging markets." The biggest flows are into equity capital, that is, into the purchase of stock in big companies in Asia, Latin America, and the Middle East (aside from South Africa, very little capital flows into sub-Saharan Africa today). U.S. capitalists not only construct their own factories and build up other businesses in these countries. They buy stock in privately owned companies, or in formerly state-owned enterprises that bourgeois governments are "privatizing," that is, auctioning off to the highest bourgeois bidders. For the imperialists, buying up these shares is a stepping-stone to directly taking over and running these factories and other businesses. But it takes some time to pressure the semicolonial bourgeoisies to give up ownership and control, so a lot of imperialist capital still takes the form of purchasing massive blocks of stock.

WHETHER IN THE FORM of new imperialist-owned factories or shares of stocks on the "emerging markets," however, the big majority of this capital flows into just a handful of the most industrialized Third World countries—Argentina, Brazil, Mexico, Korea, Taiwan, and a few others. And it flows into only a small number of potentially lucrative businesses within these countries, such as oil, telecommunications, construction conglomerates, and banking.

The imperialists' goal is simple. In the framework of a falling rate of industrial profits at home, they want to superexploit cheap labor in the Third World—and to a lesser degree in the workers states in Eastern Europe and the former USSR—and turn these countries more and more into surplus-value-producing platforms. Their goal is to keep exporting capital to these countries at higher and higher returns.

The bourgeoisies in these countries allot big tax and other government subsidies to the imperialists, seeking in this way to stabilize their own rule and further enrich themselves.

Capital flows to Latin America are heavily dominated by U.S. imperialism, although its Japanese and European competitors have made inroads. The domestic and overseas exploiters continue seeking to profit from the consequences of the political defeats and setbacks that have been dealt to the workers movement in Latin America over nearly three decades. The influx of capital goes hand in hand with increased privatization, new assaults on the wages and working conditions of workers, stepped-up assaults on poor and landless peasants, devastation of the social wage affecting broad layers of the middle classes as well as workers, and the ravaging of mineral resources, forests, the air, lakes, and rivers.

In terms of new investments in Asia, including China, Japanese capitalists have overtaken their U.S. rivals in recent years. Most of this involves the construction of Japanese-owned factories in these countries, spurred by the fact that the so-called Japanese miracle has come to an end. As competition with U.S. business stiffens, capitalists in Japan are under mounting pressure to build export platforms and exploit cheap labor elsewhere in Asia to hold their own. This aggressive course is accelerating as we meet and discuss here today.

The export of capital to Russia and Eastern Europe is particularly important to the bourgeoisies of Germany and elsewhere in capitalist Europe, although U.S. businesses remain the largest single exporter of capital into manufacturing and trade in the region. While some ventures have brought lucrative returns to particular capitalists, profits from these investments have fallen far short of the imperialists' initial expectations for the political and economic reasons we've discussed before.[13] German capitalists in particular have been squeezed, having paid a huge political blood price to Moscow during the Gorbachev period in the form of massive low-interest loans. Germany's capitalist rulers, moreover, are still far from recovering from the burden of "digesting" the workers state in eastern Germany following unification in 1990, and they are just now beginning a slow and hesitant upturn from Germany's sharpest recession since World War II.

The opening of markets and export of capital to Central and Eastern Europe and the former USSR will neither reverse the declining rate of profit in the imperialist centers nor bring economic and social stability to these weak and grossly deformed workers states.

While the German capitalists will continue to pursue their historic goal of dominating Central Europe, their dream of the deutsche mark's stability and unchallenged ascendancy from the North Sea to the Urals has already been set back a good ways.

U.S. gains an edge on imperialist rivals

Germany remains the key to Europe; there's no doubt about that. No other European imperialist power—not France, not Britain, and certainly not others—will surpass its industrial and

---

13. See in particular "How U.S. Imperialism Lost the Cold War," the resolution adopted by the 1990 convention of the Socialist Workers Party, and "Imperialism's Deadly World Disorder" by Jack Barnes, an April 1993 talk presented to regional socialist educational conferences in Greensboro, North Carolina, and Des Moines, Iowa. Both will appear in *New International* no. 11. See also "The Opening Guns of World War III" by Jack Barnes, in *New International* no. 7.

trading prowess. As the German rulers continue pressing to bridge the gap between their economic strength and the limitations that still exist on the use of their military might abroad, however, they will come up against an unassailable fact: U.S. imperialism's economic and military power remain permanent and weighty factors in European politics.

No European capitalist government can be an effective military power on a world scale without Washington's involvement and assistance. None attempting a global military operation will escape the reality brought home to the British expeditionary force during its war against Argentina in the early 1980s to regain control of the Malvinas Islands. Without direct logistical and surveillance support from the U.S. Navy and other armed forces, British imperialism could not have fought, much less won, that war.

With the partial exception of the United Kingdom, the capitalist powers throughout Europe are three or four years behind the U.S. rulers in "downsizing," cost cutting, and imposing what the employers call "labor flexibility." They are behind their U.S. rivals in extending workers' hours. They are behind in slashing wage rates, implementing multi-tier wage agreements, and gutting the social wage. They are behind in undermining work rules and health and safety guidelines. They are behind in expanding part-time work, bringing in nonunion temporary workers at lower wages with no benefits, contracting out work to nonunion outfits, slashing vacation time, and imposing other antilabor measures.

As we observed six years ago in "What the 1987 Stock Market Crash Foretold," there is not and will not be a substitute for the dollar as the predominant currency of world trade, investment, banking, accounting, payment, and reserves. At the same time, the deepening crisis of world capitalism means that the dollar itself is a less and less stable and reliable unit for the owning classes of the world. It will never again be the world currency it was from the time of Washington's victory in World War II until Nixon was forced to end its convertibility into gold in 1971. The almighty dollar was humbled forever by the weakening of U.S. imperialism coming out of the Vietnam War, the related war-fueled inflation, and the relative advance of capitalist Japan and Germany as manufacturing and trading powers.

Since the closing years of the 1980s, however, U.S. imperialism has scored substantial further gains over the capitalist powers it defeated in World War II. The relative position of U.S. imperialism vis-à-vis its chief rivals in Europe and Asia has once again strengthened. If Japanese and German imperialist interests kept buying U.S. treasury bonds in the mid- and late 1980s, that was not a sign of their strength. It simply registered the enormous size of the U.S. capitalist economy, which sucked in capital from throughout the world, as well as the falling relative valuation of the dollar against the mark and the yen. Competition and conflict is rising among *all* the imperialist powers, but the contest revolves above all around the United States, Germany, and Japan. The losers in World War II, just like the losers in the first interimperialist slaughter a quarter century earlier, are once again having to fight the enormous pressures of the victor.

This is the opposite of how the world has often been portrayed by bourgeois politicians, press commentators, and the labor officialdom in the 1970s, '80s, and even into the '90s. Novels, movies, and docudramas (the self-serving soap operas of the TV intellectual) have all sounded the alarm against the rising economic power of Japan. Soon no one was going to be able to buy a car, a television, or a laptop computer that wasn't made in Japan. Japanese capital was buying up U.S. real estate and factories at a dangerous rate, we were told. They bought Rockefeller Center, a national landmark! Would there be any "American-owned" land left in Los Angeles? They were even taking over Hollywood movie studios and recording companies! The hype reached the point where if you took it seriously, you would have thought the United States was on the verge of being turned into a semicolony of Nippon.

With regard to German capitalism, the hype has had less of an openly racist and chauvinist edge, although the specter of the Hun, the kaiser, and the Third Reich has not been far beneath the surface in some bourgeois commentary—especially in the *New York Times* and in initially Thatcherite and now broadening ruling-class circles in Britain. If the propaganda never reached the point of predicting a German buyout of U.S. land and factories, at least the deutsche mark was allegedly destined to establish unbridled dominance over Europe, west and east.

As recently as the 1992 U.S. presidential elections, Clinton and some in his economic "brain trust" were still pointing to the postwar miracle of German and Japanese capitalism as a fount of practical lessons to help U.S. employers pull out of their malaise. This became a common theme among U.S. liberals in particular during the 1980s: emulate the German and Japanese capitalists, while bashing them with protectionist bludgeons to hold off their exports of commodities and capital.

Underneath these self-serving rationalizations for U.S. nationalism there is, of course, a partial truth—the relative decline of the domination of U.S. imperialism since the end of World War II. That is a glorious fact.

U.S. imperialism *is* the world's final empire; none will ever supplant it. The industrial monopoly position of U.S. capital coming out of World War II was substantially eroded in the 1960s and 1970s by the relative advance of its German and Japanese rivals. The U.S. rulers are less capable than anytime since their entry into the first imperialist world war some seventy-five years ago of using their massive economic and military might to impose their will on the peoples of the world. The rapid collapse of the promised New World Order into a deadly world disorder is the latest confirmation of this truth.

But ruling capitalist families in the United States have come out on top in the intensifying interimperialist competition of the past decade. What they have won, of course, puts them even more at the center of the deepening contradictions of the world market system. But the capitalist class in the United States, like those in Japan and Germany and everywhere else, doesn't deploy its capital on the basis of long-term time horizons. The employers compete to capture markets, drive down the price of labor power, and maximize profits.

THE U.S. CAPITALISTS have come back in industry after industry, dealing blows to the Japanese and German capitalists. GM, Chrysler, and Ford, far from being dinosaurs as they were portrayed just a few years ago, have taken back market share from Japanese capital. U.S. corporations like Hewlett-Packard, Motorola, Compaq, Intel, and now even IBM and others have maintained or reconquered dominant positions in the production of computers and computer parts. Caterpillar still outpaces Komatsu as the leading producer and exporter of heavy construction equipment, and John Deere remains on top in worldwide tractor production and sale. U.S. capital has made a comeback in steel production, with large integrated mills regaining an edge over both U.S.-owned minimills and foreign competitors. Wall Street in the 1980s took a decisive lead in mobilizing what it calls venture capital to finance the rise of initially small companies into dominant positions in various fields of technology: Microsoft in computer software, McCaw Cellular in wireless communications, Federal Express in delivery service, for example.

U.S. capitalists have so far been much more successful than their German or Japanese competitors in driving down the price of labor power. Reversing the trend over the previous several decades, unit labor costs in the United States were driven down by the employers in the 1980s, while they continued rising in Japan and most countries of capitalist Europe. Fewer than ten years ago, in 1985, hourly wage rates in the United States were higher than in any of its major imperialist rivals: Japan, Germany, France, Britain, Italy, or Canada. Of these countries, only in Britain today are hourly wages still lower than in the United States, and that gap has narrowed. U.S. exports have grown at three times the pace of those of Japan and Germany since the mid-1980s, and since 1991 U.S. capitalists for the first time are exporting a higher percentage of their domestic output than their Japanese competitors.

Only in New Zealand have the capitalists perhaps achieved more than in the United States, in relative terms, in pushing back the wages, conditions, and union rights of the working class. New Zealand took nearly a decade to pull out of the deep capitalist downturn of 1981-82. Under first a Labour Party and then the conservative National Party government, the bosses used these depression conditions to shift the relationship of forces between labor and capital to their advantage. Social security programs were slashed; union bargaining rights were undermined; and state-owned enterprises—from banks to steel mills, from Air New Zealand to the telephone company—were privatized. By the opening of the 1990s, the world business press was extolling New Zealand as one of world capitalism's major success stories of restructuring and union busting. New Zealand stocks were "overweighted," as they like to say, in the portfolios of the world's biggest brokerage houses.

The capitalists in Germany and a number of other countries in Europe suffer from the fact that they have not yet been able to smash the system of social insurance and related gains—health care, unemployment compensation, pensions, vacations—that the working class and labor movement won through struggles in the decades following World War II.

Workers in the United States can say to our sisters and brothers in Germany, France, Sweden, and elsewhere in capitalist Europe: "What has happened to us is now going to happen to you. And it's going to be rougher in some ways, because the capitalists have to chop more since the social conquests you won in struggles over the past half century were greater." As we approach the 150th anniversary of *The Conditions of the Working Class in England in 1844,* written by Engels to alert the democratic movement in Germany to what capitalism held in store for their future, communists in Europe today can point to the United States for similar lessons.

In fact, the employers and their governments from Bonn to Stockholm, from London to Rome have already begun to make headway in the past year or so in going after prior gains. But they need to take much, much more and are pressing to do so. As working-class resistance to these attacks develops, so too will the hunger of vanguard fighters to link up across national borders to engage in common discussion and action.

Japanese imperialism is paying a price for its relatively recent feudal past and the U.S. military occupation following World War II. This is part of the reason land prices are so astronomically high in Japan compared to other advanced capitalist countries. Among other effects, the monopolization of land ownership means the rent workers have to pay to keep a roof over the head of their families is also disproportionately high. The big majority of the value workers produce with our labor is taken by the employing class—that's what Marx called surplus value, out of which they derive their profits and their lavish personal wealth and incomes. But out of the value workers produce, the bosses also have to pay us enough to be able to live and work and to reproduce the next generation of workers. Marx called that the value of labor power, and it varies from one country to the next depending on a combination of historical factors, including the class struggle between labor and capital. So when housing rents are very high, as they are in Japan for historical reasons, that's not only bad for workers who have to pay those rents; it's also bad for the capitalists, who end up having to apportion a larger share of the value workers produce to making it possible for them to pay those rents. And that puts Japanese employers at a disadvantage to their rivals in other imperialist countries, where rents are relatively cheaper. Similar considerations apply to the very high food prices in Japan, which are another result of sky-high land prices, as well as of protectionist policies to benefit the big capitalist farming interests, landowners, and rice and meat traders in Japan.

What is on the agenda throughout capitalist Europe over the next several years will be a cost-cutting and downsizing offensive like we've seen in the United States for the past several years. We will see big rounds of layoffs; cuts in wages and the institution of two-tier scales; and the lengthening of the workweek and imposition of more shift work and weekend schedules. We'll see assaults on the wages, conditions, and union rights of workers launched by the employing classes under the banners of "privatization," "national pride," and anti-Americanism.

Since German imperialism's recovery from the devastating effects of World War II, for example, unions in the western part of Germany have never settled for wage rates less than inflation. But with the official jobless rate at 9 percent—and the real figure substantially higher, in the west let alone the east—unions both in manufacturing and white collar jobs are now accepting contracts with raises below the inflation rate. And they are agreeing to two-tier wage scales for the first time, too.

But there will be resistance by workers and the unions. We've already discussed what happened in France over the past year. Workers in Germany, east and west, have sought to hold off the mounting attacks by the employers and the government against their wages, hours, health care, jobless benefits, and other social rights. There have been strikes and union struggles in Spain, Belgium, and other countries.

RISING INTERIMPERIALIST CONFLICTS, combined with resistance by workers, working farmers, and youth, will further undermine the myth of a "common Europe." Even as the European Union—the new name of the European Community—grows in numbers, increased rivalry among these capitalist powers themselves will continually disrupt any steps toward a single currency or a common central bank, let alone toward a common foreign policy, armed forces, or "European government." That hope, which bubbled over decades and reached a crest verging on mania in the closing years of the 1980s, is now definitively behind us.

Instead, the European Union will be just that: a customs union, a common market within which capital, commodities, and labor will flow more freely across borders. For now, that setup advances a common interest of the national ruling classes in Europe in their competition against the U.S. capitalists, who enjoy a huge internal market and easier access to markets in Canada, Latin America, and the Pacific and much of Asia. Even these lowered trade and capital barriers within the European Union, however, are taking much longer than initially planned to implement, while those that have been put in place already have their rough edges. What's more, the freer flow of goods and capital exacerbates contradictions resulting from massive overproduction and redundancy of productive capacity throughout Europe—and throughout the world—in steel, auto, and other industries. This gives an added impulse to layoffs, plant shutdowns and restructuring, and employer demands for greater "labor flexibility."

The downsizing and cost-cutting process in Japan will be even more explosive, but it will also be more difficult and take longer to unfold. Nonetheless, over the past year the layoffs have been accelerating there too, notwithstanding the supposed "cultural tradition" of "lifetime jobs" we've all heard so much about. Toyota, Toshiba, Nissan, Komatsu, Nippon Steel, and other of the biggest Japanese companies have all begun carrying out extensive layoffs over the past year, as that country founders in its worst recession since World War II.

Stock market and real estate prices have plummeted in Japan since the opening of the 1990s. Its banking system, a big chunk of whose capital base is held in land and common stocks, is the most vulnerable of all the major imperialist powers. This Japanese bubble is yet to burst.

The deepening economic crisis is breaking up long-established capitalist parties and patterns of bourgeois politics in Japan. And there will be growing working-class resistance there too, although workers have more obstacles to overcome. Since the 1930s they have been subjected first to a semifascist imperial regime; then to Washington's antilabor occupation government under General MacArthur; then to the U.S.-organized Liberal Democratic Party's governments that succeeded in dealing blow after blow to the union movement in the fifties, sixties, and seventies. But as the pressures we've been describing build up, and layoffs and other assaults keep mounting, the myth of a permanent labor/management truce—punctuated by a ritual spring "labor offensive" at contract time—will come unstuck, sometimes explosively.

Cheap-labor "export platforms" in Asia can help slow falling profits rates for a time in Japan, but they don't resolve the fundamental conflict between capital and labor "at home," which will sharpen. Driven to export capital more deeply into Asia, moreover, the Japanese rulers will inevitably pursue an increasingly assertive foreign and military policy to protect their growing interests, bringing them into more frequent conflict with Washington and Wall Street and with governments throughout the region.

Protectionism and 'trade talks'

There is enormous overproduction in capitalist agriculture as well as industrial goods. There is world overproduction in rice, in wheat, in soybeans, in sugar. That doesn't mean an end to starvation and famine in Africa or elsewhere, of course. (Under capitalism, overproduction is not measured in relation to social needs, but what can be sold at a price high enough to realize a competitive profit.) Nor does it mean that the prices of particular farm commodities won't jump because of a flood or weather conditions or massive commercial convulsions.

But the general pressure on prices of agricultural goods is downward today. U.S. capital is determined to bash down barriers to exporting its rice, apples, and meat products to Japan, Taiwan, and Korea; it's determined to push up the price of grain sold by its competitors in France, Canada, Australia, and elsewhere. Over the past fifteen years, the capitalist rulers in Western Europe, especially France, have challenged their U.S. rivals' world market share in wheat and some other farm products, but agricultural productivity remains much lower than in the United States and European governments have had to bear much greater relative costs in subsidies to capitalist farmers.

The "trade talks" that go on around the GATT world tariff agreement and between Washington, Tokyo, Paris, Ottawa, and others—rough as these talks sometimes get, even publicly—are just polite cover for the real use of muscle to advance the interests of conflicting national ruling classes. U.S. military might stands behind its pressure on the capitalists in Europe, on its competitors in France, Japan, and elsewhere.

Think about what happened in February 1994, when President Clinton held a press conference in the White House with Saudi prince Bandar bin Sultan to announce that a $6 billion contract to supply commercial planes had just been awarded to Boeing and McDonnell Douglas, the two biggest U.S. aircraft companies. The purchase was financed by the Export-Import Bank, a government-sponsored consortium of U.S. banks. The French and other European capitalist governments had been calling on the Saudi government to give at least half the business to Airbus Industrie, the giant French-based aircraft manufacturer owned by capitalists from a number of countries in Europe.

Boeing must have done some hard bargaining, some real haggling! Of course, nobody ever doubted for a moment what was really involved. The Clinton administration simply told the Saudi Arabian rulers what to do.[14] The Saudi monarchy, another of the supposed victors in the Gulf War, emerged from that U.S. massacre more dependent than ever on Wall Street and Washington.

---

14. In May, the rulers of Saudi Arabia gave a $4 billion contract to rebuild its telephone system to AT&T, rejecting bids by big capitalist outfits in Canada, France, Germany, and Sweden (all of which insisted they had underbid AT&T).

The U.S. capitalists have declared open trade aggression against their Japanese rivals too. They are demanding that the Japanese government ensure annual quotas of U.S. agricultural and manufacturing imports. Of course, they insist they're not quotas, just "numerical targets"—but they're quotas. That's what Washington—the steadfast opponent of quotas when it comes to enforcing equal hiring or educational opportunities for Blacks or women, right?—is demanding from Japan. From hearing Clinton and his trade hit man, Mickey Kantor, talk, you'd think that Japan doesn't import much of anything from the United States. In fact, Japan imports more than 10 percent of all U.S. exports, and some 20 percent of U.S. agricultural exports, which are the crux of Washington's most demagogic and hypocritical grievance against Tokyo.

Every time we hear about one of these so-called trade deals on TV, or read about them in the papers, what we're watching unfold is the growing use of political and military clout to achieve economic ends. None of this has anything to do with advancing free trade, remedying unfair competition, or any of the other high-flown rationalizations emanating from the White House and bipartisan Congress. It's the use of power to drain surplus value from wherever it's produced by workers and toiling farmers into the pockets of capitalists in the United States.

Uneven and combined development sharpens

As 1994 opened, events in Mexico shone a spotlight on how the sharpening crisis of the world capitalist system exacerbates uneven development in those parts of the world in which the big majority of humanity live and work. These events showed how capitalism precipitates explosions arising out of the combination of forms of labor exploitation inherited from the past with the most modern production processes and marketing and financial methods of world capital.

The peasant-based rebellion in Chiapas is rooted in resistance to a form of peonage, of debt slavery, that has existed in that region of Mexico for generations and that has been superimposed onto and transformed by now-dominant capitalist social relations. The events in Mexico occurred almost simultaneously with workers uprisings in Santiago de Estero and other parts of Argentina late last year and early this year; those struggles signal something very important about the new generation of workers beginning to fight back in more economically advanced semicolonial countries such as Argentina, where the working class was brutally defeated by military dictatorships in the 1970s.[15]

CHIAPAS put the lie to the myth promoted in the big-business media of the homogeneous and non-class-differentiated march to modernization, industrialization, and progress in Mexico. If you want to get a feel for the still semifeudal overlay to the capitalist exploitation of many toilers in Chiapas, read the six jungle novels by a man named B. Traven. *The Rebellion of the Hanged, The General from the Jungle, Government,* and the others are all set in Chiapas in the early decades of the twentieth century.[16] Traven describes the bonded servitude that ties Indian peasants as debt slaves to the capitalist owners of the coffee and other cash crop plantations and mahogany logging camps in the region. Much remains largely unchanged seventy years later as the twenty-first century approaches.

The Chiapas events also help demystify what the so-called North American Free Trade Agreement—NAFTA—is really all about. It is not about free trade. It is not a plot by Yankee capi-

---

15. In the northern Argentine province of Santiago del Estero in December 1993, thousands of workers rose up in rebellion, taking over government buildings to protest the fact that public workers hadn't been paid since August. Other, smaller working-class explosions have hit the region, as well as the northern Argentine city of Tucumán, since then.

16. The novels are *Government, The Carreta, March to the Montería, Trozas, The Rebellion of the Hanged,* and *The General from the Jungle.* They are currently being reprinted in paperback by Ivan R. Dee publishers.

tal. Nor is it a road toward absorbing the majority of working people in Mexico into the middle class, as it is often presented. Instead, it is the codification of an agreement between capitalists in the United States, Canada, and Mexico, among other things, to carry through the wrenching, violent transformation of a still largely agricultural country into one that will serve as a platform for exporting manufactured goods. Capitalists on both sides of the border will profit. Mexico's bourgeoisie is catching up with a process begun earlier in the 1980s by the exploiting classes in Argentina, Chile, and a number of other relatively industrialized semicolonial countries.

This "national development strategy" for Mexico entails accelerating throughout the countryside what happened in Britain and across Europe leading up to and during the industrial revolution in the eighteenth and nineteenth centuries: driving peasants off the land and into the towns and cities where they have nothing to sell but their labor power in order to live. In the process, the living and working conditions are produced and reproduced to ensure they sell their labor power very cheaply.

"[G]reat masses of men are suddenly and forcibly torn from their means of subsistence, and hurled onto the labour-market as free, unprotected and rightless proletarians," Marx explained in *Capital*, describing what began happening in Europe more than three hundred years ago. "The expropriation of the agricultural producer, of the peasant, from the soil is the basis of the whole process. The history of this expropriation assumes different aspects in different countries," he wrote, "and runs through its various phases in different orders of succession, and at different historical epochs."[17]

To a substantial degree, of course, that process has been under way in Mexico for decades. But it will speed up in Chiapas and elsewhere during the closing years of the twentieth century

---

17. *Capital,* vol. 1, p. 876.

and opening years of the twenty-first. Throughout modern history, when foreign and domestic capital drive toward expanded manufacturing, they brutally destroy the toilers' ability to produce the means of life in the countryside. The consequences of this process are inhuman. Men, women, and children are pushed into expanding urban slums and are forced, under the most miserable conditions, to compete for jobs to survive. In England, this process was so violent in its initial stages in the last century that the very possibility of the working class reproducing itself was called into question.

That is what NAFTA is designed to further. It is intended to help capital—Mexican, Yankee, or otherwise—change the entire face of Mexican agriculture, driving millions more peasants off the land and increasing the hold of agribusiness throughout the countryside. It is intended to provide a huge reserve army of cheap labor power for the next stage of industrialization in Mexico. It will further shift the balance between countryside and the city in Mexico. In this sense, it is a model for much of the rest of the hemisphere, from Guatemala to substantial parts of South America.

But the Mexican and U.S. capitalists didn't count on one of NAFTA's first results being an outbreak of resistance in the countryside in Mexico. The toilers renewed the demand for what has been promised them since the Mexican revolution in the second decade of this century—the right to land for those who till it. That's what happened in Chiapas, virtually simultaneous to the NAFTA treaty officially taking effect on January 1, 1994. And Chiapas is much more the future of Latin America than Wall Street and Washington's promise of an increasingly stable, democratic, and economically developing continent.

This does not mean there was anything at all progressive about the anti-NAFTA campaign waged over the past few years by the union officialdom, a minority of business interests, and capitalist politicians of both liberal and ultraright stripes in the United States and Canada. Often shedding crocodile tears over the low wages and poor conditions of workers in Mexico, these

"America-" and "Canada-firsters" warned against the "flight of capital" abroad and in fact counterposed defense of "U.S." or "Canadian" jobs to the jobs of Mexican workers. On the part of the labor officialdom, this is nothing more than another rationalization for their class-collaborationist course of refusing to organize workers *anywhere*—on either side of the borders—to defend our living and working conditions against the capitalist rulers in all three countries and beyond.

Putting aside the demagogy of NAFTA's bourgeois proponents and opponents alike, however, the accelerated industrialization in Mexico, and elsewhere in the Americas is swelling the ranks of the industrial working class and generating even larger immigration flows into the United States. It is expanding and strengthening the battalions of capitalism's gravediggers on both sides of the Río Bravo.

We ARE SEEING similar developments halfway around the world in India, as well. I'm convinced that India will be one of the greatest arenas of the expansion of imperialist and domestic capital over the next decade.

The problem both for the imperialists and for the capitalists in India, however, is how to put together a unified national market in that giant country, with its legacy of colonial and semicolonial exploitation fastened onto centuries of precapitalist social relations. In a modern, unified country such as the United States—whether you live in Seattle or New Orleans or Buffalo—you know roughly what a Dodge Caravan costs, or a gallon of milk, or a pair of levis from the Gap, or jeans from Sears; the prices are all pretty much equivalent.

But in India you can go from one part of the country to another, even from one nearby valley to another if there is not good transportation, and the price of grain will be sharply different. The job of establishing a single national market, a mobile, countrywide labor pool, a uniform basis for wholesale and retail prices, is still incomplete, despite extensive capitalist industrial development there over the half century since gaining independence from Britain just after World War II.

That was the job that Bismarck galvanized the bourgeoisie to finally accomplish in Germany in the late nineteenth century. He got rid of the remaining feudal restrictions on trade and welded together dozens of duchies, baronies, and weak governments into a united German nation state. He pulled up the chain barriers in the Rhine, taking them out of the hands of arbitrary provincial princes and transferring them to centralized state toll takers (raising tax revenues in the process). These steps opened the door to a large home market and a system of more homogeneous prices. It fostered the expansion of a middle class with a rising average income capable of buying goods produced in capitalist-owned factories in Germany. That is what the capitalists did in Germany under Bismarck, a couple of decades after they had crushed prospects for a truly thoroughgoing democratic revolution at the end of the 1840s, a revolution under popular leadership of the working people and radicalized layers of the middle classes.

THE WORLD IMPERIALIST system needs dozens more aspiring Bismarcks throughout the semicolonial world today. They can be "socialist" and "populist" as well as "free-market" and "neoliberal." They are needed to marginalize remnants of precapitalist ruling classes, push aside the most outmoded and least productive capitalists, complete the formation of unified national markets, and increase the exploitation of labor and output of surplus value on that basis. But it is too late in history for a Bismarck to successfully transform a semicolonial country into an industrialized capitalist world power today, including countries with considerable industry and natural resources such as Argentina, Brazil, India, Mexico, South Korea, or Taiwan.

Capitalist development in these countries will inevitably deepen social unevennesses and heighten class conflict. The expansion of capitalism in India is creating a much bigger and better-off middle class and expanding a home market. At the same time, it is combining some of the most modern features of industrialized society with mounting social conflicts and violence over dowry prices and caste divisions that seem—and are, in their origins—prehistoric.

In a country where 70 percent of the population still lives in the countryside and some 15 million people are estimated to be held in debt bondage, conditions for rural toilers are becoming even more miserable, and struggles for land, cheap credit, and political dignity will grow. Class differentiation is increasing, as, side by side, the industrial working class grows and outright destitution multiplies among a vast army of the unemployed in the cities and countryside. Class tensions and political polarization are mounting, as rightist movements based among the middle classes and financed by layers of the bourgeoisie adopt the guise of national, religious, or caste-based movements.

Developments such as those occurring in India or in Mexico are being replicated elsewhere in Latin America, as well as elsewhere in East Asia—in Thailand, in Indonesia, and other countries. The class structures of these countries begins to change. A factory proletariat grows larger, and conflicts over unionization begin. City after city in Asia and Latin America is becoming more like St. Petersburg in Russia in the opening decades of this century, as peasants are drawn out of the countryside into a young and rapidly growing industrial working class. This will happen more and more in Africa too, which remains the most economically backward continent of the semicolonial world and where the process of industrialization is still in its infancy in most countries.

Further capitalist development in South Africa will accelerate the urbanization and proletarianization that has taken place there over the past half century as well. Further advances of the African National Congress–led democratic revolution and the beginning formation of a class-conscious proletarian vanguard, however, have the potential to prepare the toilers to resist the devastating economic and social consequences of what the domestic and foreign exploiters will try to inflict and open the door to deepening the revolutionary process. What happens in South Africa will greatly influence possibilities for the development of communist leadership elsewhere in Africa, especially south of the Sahara.

Overall, the bourgeoisie's privatization campaign and Washington's "free trade" offensive in large parts of the Third World will accelerate the inevitable and increase the social and political weight and leadership of the working class. Our class will emerge in a stronger position to take part in giant class battles between the urban and rural toilers and radicalizing youth, on one side of the barricades, and the exploiting and parasitic classes, on the other.

IV. CLASS POLARIZATION AND THE FORCES OF CAPITALIST RESTORATION IN CHINA, EASTERN EUROPE, AND THE FORMER USSR

THE DYNAMICS OF THE CLASS STRUGGLE set in motion by the brutalities of primitive capital accumulation in the semicolonial world will not escape the Chinese workers state either. For more than a decade, the Stalinist regime in Beijing has been on an accelerating course toward greater integration into the world capitalist market. There has been large-scale imperialist investment in manufacturing in the so-called new economic zones along China's southeastern coast in particular. Domestically owned capitalist enterprises have grown up in the countryside, in small towns, and, more and more now, in major cities across China.[18]

But the gains Chinese workers and poor peasants fought for

---

18. For a discussion of the concrete historical conditions and class relations underlying the developing crisis of the Stalinist regime in China, see "How U.S. Imperialism Lost the Cold War" and "Imperialism's Deadly World Disorder," forthcoming in *New International* no. 11.

and won in carrying through a deep-going anti-imperialist and then anticapitalist revolution in the late 1940s and early 1950s will continue to stamp the character of the resistance by new generations of working people in China. The Stalinists' misleadership, gross brutalities, and caste privileges horribly deformed and weakened the Chinese workers state from the outset. Despite these anti-working-class crimes by a regime parading as "communist," however, it is too late in history for capitalist social relations to be carried through and become dominant in China without massive struggles by workers and peasants to defend their living and working conditions, their desire for social security and equality.

Imperialist investors value the labor discipline, the no-strike pledges, and low wages enforced by the government in China. These anti-working-class policies are enforced not only by the Chinese government and its cops, but also by Communist Party representatives in the plants, by the functionaries of the state-controlled unions where they exist in foreign-owned enterprises, and by Red Army officers scrambling to get in on the take through the network of army-run factories and other businesses. This is one of the selling points that CEOs of major corporations report to shareholders in quarterly and annual reports. They put a premium on the Chinese government's guarantees of "stable labor relations" and a "manageable wage bill." They value the pledge that the government will step in to resolve any conflicts by arbitration.

To capitalists in the United States and other imperialist countries, China is not only Coca-Cola's dream of "a billion mouths." More importantly, it is an enormous reserve of very cheap labor power. Major U.S. companies such as Merrill Lynch, Eastman Kodak, and others have sent top corporate delegations to China to underline to their shareholders the profits to be made there and to solidify relations with the Stalinist regime. Motorola recently held its board of directors meeting in Shanghai! Can British Telecom, Ericson, Nokia, Siemens, Philips, and even Teléfonos de México be far behind?

World capitalism's dream is to exploit the labor of workers and peasants in China for as many hours a day as they can get away with and to sell consumer products to an expanding middle class, with no limitations. That's why the Clinton administration—with bipartisan support in Congress and overwhelming support from big business—will drop Washington's long-standing empty threat to tie renewal of Beijing's most-favored-nation trading status to alleged progress in respecting human rights.[19] The Tory government's campaign to "democratize" Hong Kong prior to its scheduled return to Chinese sovereignty in 1997 is also flagging, as capitalists in the United Kingdom seek to use the leverage of their soon-to-be former crown colony to compete for markets for capital and commodities in China.

But the capitalists' dreams leave out one thing—the response by the Chinese workers. The reports of strikes, slowdowns, peasant uprisings, and other forms of resistance by working people in China continue to mount. The attempt to restore capitalism in China will transform social struggles there. What we're learning about now is both partial and just the beginning.[20]

The working class in China is expanding at a rapid rate, drawing in young people from the countryside and small towns. These new layers of the working class have not been defeated. They have not been beaten down and demoralized. From their ranks, new working-class fighters will emerge and

---

19. In June 1994 the Clinton administration announced it was extending China's most-favored-nation status irrespective of State Department reports on human rights in China.

20. An article in the May 19, 1994, issue of the *Wall Street Journal*, just a few weeks after this talk was presented in Chicago, cautioned its "high net worth" readership with a sobering report that "strikes and labor unrest, though scattered and often disorganized, seem to be spreading" in China. In 1993, the article reported, "China's Labor ministry recorded more than 8,000 strikes—none legal. A report in the official Market News this month recorded 12,358 instances of labor arbitration last year—up from 8,150 a year earlier—many resulting from slowdowns or strikes."

the initial cadres of a new generation of communist workers will develop—genuine communists, not the counterfeit imposed by decades of Stalinist terror and miseducation.

Crisis in former USSR, Eastern Europe

An article featured on the front page of the *Financial Times* of London in February underlines the devastating impact of the evolution of the world capitalist order on workers and farmers in Eastern Europe and the former USSR. "Russia Faces Population Crisis as Death Rate Soars," was the headline. But it is not a "population crisis." It's a *social* crisis, a *class* crisis—of historic proportions, as the article reveals.

The article reported that average life expectancy for males in Russia has sunk to fifty-nine from sixty-two just over the past three years. The biggest cause was a sharp rise in heart disease and strokes; another was suicides and family violence. Short of major wars or raging epidemics (such as AIDS in several countries of Africa today), demographic shifts of that scope and suddenness are highly unusual in the modern world; it is compelling evidence of a deep-going social crisis. Average male life expectancy in Russia is today lower than it was in the mid-1960s, when it had reached 66; it began its slide as the crisis of the Stalinist regime deepened in the 1970s and 1980s. Infant mortality in Russia also jumped sharply, from 17.4 per 1,000 newborn babies in 1990 to 19.1 in 1993.

A related story a few weeks later in the *New York Times* reported that the birth rate in Russia had also fallen sharply in Russia over the past five years; the average number of children born dropped by 35 percent from 2.17 per woman of childbearing age at the close of the 1980s to 1.4 today. As a result of these rapid shifts in birth and death rates, the population of Russia dropped by nearly 800,000 in 1993.[21]

---

21. An article in the April 23, 1994, issue of the London weekly *Economist* reported comparable facts regarding eastern Germany. For example, the death

The promises by the imperialist bourgeoisie—and their imitators throughout Eastern Europe and in the former USSR—that capitalist market "reforms" would bring better living and working conditions have rapidly shown themselves to be lies. Production has fallen steeply since the opening of the nineties—by some 40 percent in Russia; 50 percent in Ukraine; almost 25 percent in Hungary; and more in several other countries. Real wages have fallen; pensions, medical benefits, education, and other social programs have been devastated. Unemployment has risen to double-digit levels, even by official figures, which are understated. Abortion rights and job and educational opportunities for women have come under assault.

Despite the horrors meted out to working people in the name of "socialism" by the former Stalinist regimes, workers were not so badly defeated by the bureaucratic castes in these countries that they have simply been ready to acquiesce to, let

---

rate for women between the ages of 25 and 45 rose by nearly 20 percent between 1989 and 1991; among men of the same age, the increase was 30 percent. There was a 70 percent increase in the death rate for girls aged 10-14. The birth rate fell 55 percent between 1989 and 1992.

The article also reported that "a steep rise in mortality has occurred" in other Central and Eastern European countries "in the past few years." It reported birth-rate declines of more than 20 percent in Poland, about 25 percent in Bulgaria, and 30 percent in Romania and Estonia.

The seriousness of this situation was confirmed by an October 1994 study by the United Nations Children's Fund of health and other social conditions in Albania, Bulgaria, the Czech Republic, Slovakia, Hungary, Poland, Romania, Russia, and Ukraine. In releasing the report, UNICEF director James P. Grant pointed to a "health crisis . . . unprecedented in the peacetime history of Europe in this century." The situation was worst in Russia, he said, where the mortality rate had risen 35 percent since 1989, according to the study.

These figures, which reflect social priorities and political and economic policies, can be contrasted to what has happened in Cuba since the opening of the 1990s, despite that country's prerevolution colonial legacy and the increasingly severe economic shortages it has faced over the past half decade, including in medicine and food. The Cuban government reported that infant mortality fell to 9.4 deaths per 1,000 live births in 1993 from 10.2 in 1992.

alone internalize, all the culture, values, and attitudes that are necessary to the expanded reproduction of capitalist social relations.

VIRTUALLY EVERY STEP by the U.S. rulers with regard to Russia over the past few years—whether advocated and guaranteed by the White House, by Congress, by university professors or Wall Street technocrats—has ended up setting back attempts by the regime there to win broader layers of working people to the glories of capitalism and has undercut Washington's chosen favorites. It's not that the U.S. rulers consciously set out to destabilize Russia. To the contrary! They aimed to collaborate with the aspiring bourgeoisie emerging out of the privileged caste in Russia to reimpose capitalism and zap the workers and other toilers. Given the decades of police-state repression by the Stalinist regimes in the USSR, the imperialist rulers assumed the working class in Russia would be an easy mark. They condescendingly told Yeltsin to use "shock therapy" against the workers, go along with U.S. foreign policy as Gorbachev had done during the Iraq war, and turn over Russia's nuclear weapons. The job would be even easier in the rest of Central and Eastern Europe, the U.S. rulers assumed.

But Washington and other imperialist powers and agencies delivered on only a small percentage of the billions of dollars in economic assistance they pledged to Moscow and the other regimes. The "shock therapy" urged by finance capital's academic wizards and other "advisers"—wholesale plant shutdowns; elimination of food, rent, and other price subsidies; the slashing of education, pension, health, and other hard-earned and desperately needed entitlements—magnified impoverishment and social instability. The new regimes have repeatedly been forced to back off these draconian policies in fear of setting social forces in motion that could spiral beyond their control.

The big majority of toilers in these countries reveled in getting the Stalinist boot off their necks. But they are resisting efforts to make them accept as normal the joblessness, social insecurity, and dog-eat-dog competition produced and reproduced by the workings of capitalism. They're defending the social conquests that have survived in the workers state, in however tattered condition, despite decades of police-state terror and massive corruption by the petty-bourgeois castes. It's a class question.

In the past couple of months I've noticed that even opinion polls in Russia and eastern Germany reinforce this assessment. One taken by the Russian Academy of Science at the end of 1993 found that support for "economic reforms" in Russia had dropped from about 40 percent of those surveyed in 1989 to less than 25 percent. The majority of those polled agreed with the statement that "privatization is legalized theft." And according to the German Economic Ministry itself, a survey in eastern Germany in December 1993 found that support for the "market economy" had dropped to 35 percent from 77 percent in February 1990.

Of course, this doesn't mean that the working class in any of these deformed workers states has a class-struggle leadership, let alone a communist vanguard. Communist continuity was broken by the Stalinist murder machine in these countries decades ago and is yet to be reknit. As a result of Stalinism's counterrevolutionary legacy, even the most rudimentary support for socialism versus capitalism as a conscious alternative exists only among small numbers of workers and youth.

But as events of the past half decade have demonstrated, it would be dead wrong to conclude that workers in these countries have been transformed into warm-blooded robots to produce surplus value for the world bourgeoisie. Neither Stalinist police terror nor the procapitalist course of the new regimes has been able to crush and atomize the working class.

Having gone through two presidents, Gorbachev and Yeltsin; too many prime ministers and cabinets to remember; and two botched coup attempts, the upshot of half a decade of U.S. imperialism's efforts to advance capitalist restoration in Russia is that the economy and society as a whole have been driven into deeper crisis and social dislocation. As Moscow seeks to reassert dominance over the now-independent countries that once made up the USSR, rival factions among the privileged layers in those lands divide over relations with Russia. The grab for territory and resources is draped in Yugoslavia-style nationalist demagogy on all sides. Parts of the former Soviet Union are intermittently engulfed in civil war.

But the workers in city and countryside in Russia and other former Soviet republics have not been won to the course of capitalist restoration, or to acquiescence to its consequences.

Washington publicly backed Yeltsin in October 1993 against the challenge to his government by opposition layers of the caste organized by leading figures in Russia's parliament. Working people in Russia, however, did not believe they had the kind of stake in the outcome of this intrabureaucratic struggle they had had in August 1991, when they mobilized to defeat a coup attempt.

In fact, the U.S. rulers' open intervention in Russia's affairs fueled resentment in Russia. It actually set Yeltsin up; it lent greater credibility to the attacks on him by the fascist current headed by Vladimir Zhirinovsky. Playing on the deep social crisis, Zhirinovsky uses Great Russian nationalism and populist demagogy to portray Yeltsin and other "reformers" as shills for the U.S. rulers' efforts to rob the country of its sovereignty and subject it to impoverishment and social polarization. He maintains tight control not only over his own apparatus, the Liberal Democratic Party of Russia, but has launched—at least as a trial balloon—"Zhirinovsky's Falcons," a cadre of young troopers outfitted with blue uniforms, black boots, and side arms.

Zhirinovsky is an effective demagogue. I watched him do an interview with a correspondent for a U.S. television network recently. A lot of U.S. corporations, Zhirinovsky said, are advertising their products in Russia these days. The ones that are the most galling to people in Russia aren't the ads for Cadillacs and other luxury items, he told the reporter. Russians are a sophisticated people. No, the ones that are intolerable are the ads for dog and cat food made by Purina. Because as they listen to the contents of the dog and cat food being described, most Russians know it has more nutrient value than what they themselves can now afford to eat. That's what Zhirinovsky tells the audiences he speaks to in Russia, too. And he gets not only a broad hearing, but broader support than "polite society" would like to admit.

T HE ZHIRINOVSKY PHENOMENON is not a development somehow peculiar to the breakdown of deformed and degenerated workers states. Nor is it the continuity of "age-old Russian autocracy" going back to Ivan the Terrible, as some bourgeois commentators claim for Zhirinovsky as well as the successive Stalinist regimes in the Soviet Union from the latter 1920s on. To the contrary, the Zhirinovsky phenomenon is a product of the crisis and failures of the capitalist system in the imperialist epoch. It is a product of the workings of capitalism. There could be no well-known fascist figure in Russia today if tens of millions there were not convinced by recent experience that the capitalist West—the "decadent" enemies of the "common person"—is responsible for the rapid deterioration in their conditions and the subjugation of their country.

Russia, the other remnants of the former Soviet Union, the countries of Eastern and Central Europe—none of these are heading toward stable democratic capitalism. They are tending, under different concrete pressures and at different speeds, toward becoming Bonapartist regimes. Washington will give the nod to the Bonapartist figure most compatible with U.S. capitalist interests and work with that regime against its opponents. That's what Yeltsin aspires to.

The end of the Cold War will bring neither nuclear disarmament nor common U.S. and Russian foreign policy interests and military objectives. When Gorbachev threw the Soviet government's support behind Washington's war against Iraq in 1990-91, communist leagues around the world, including the Socialist Workers Party, said that the U.S. government would never again put together such an international alliance to fight a war. The convergence of U.S. interests with those of all its imperialist rivals, numerous bourgeois regimes in the Arab East and other Third World countries, and the privileged caste in the Soviet Union as well as that in China was limited, momentary, and fraught with contradictions.

Today, as we see in major world events from the bloody slaughter unfolding in the former Yugoslavia to developments in the Korean peninsula, the foreign policies of Washington, Moscow, and Beijing diverge.

Moscow has a stake in ensuring the Serbian regime's dominance in the Balkans and uses what military and political leverage it has to block efforts by Washington and European capitalist powers to hold Serbia's territorial aggrandizement too tightly in check.

The breach between the U.S. and Russian governments is even clearer over U.S. imperialism's efforts to draw the armed forces of Poland, the Czech Republic, and other Eastern European regimes more tightly toward the NATO alliance. While Moscow recognizes it cannot simply block this course, it is doing its best to maintain its sphere of influence in the region. We should take it seriously when Yeltsin speaks of defense of Russia's strategic interest in the "near abroad" and of the Russian communities in the former Soviet republics.

The "Great Game"—the late nineteenth and early twentieth century rivalry between British imperialism and the tsarist regime over the lands stretching from Turkey through Iran to Afghanistan—is being played out once again, with Washington supplanting London as Russia's main adversary. But this time the regimes in China, India, and Pakistan also get in on the action as players, with Tehran too taking on a larger role than ever before.

Getting rid of its nuclear arsenal would greatly weaken the Russian government militarily and politically, which is why it will not accept doing so. To the contrary, despite Russia's deep economic and social crisis, it remains a strategic nuclear power. For similar reasons, it is far from settled that the governments of Ukraine, Belarus, or Kazakhstan will agree to dispense with their stocks of nuclear arms. Even if these governments succeed in putting a very lucrative price tag on their agreement to disarm, the follow-through on such an agreement could drag on for a very long time and never quite close. Nuclear arms are among the few weapons these fragments of the former Soviet regime have in standing up to the economic and military pressures of their old "comrades" in the former Soviet Union and their new "comrades" in the capitalist world.

This is why voices on the right wing of U.S. bourgeois politics—from Patrick Buchanan to Oliver North to various members of Congress—are calling on the U.S. government to recognize that there is no realistic possibility of a converging foreign and military policy on the part of Washington and Moscow. That's true. But right now the majority of U.S. rulers know they have no better way to try to keep a lid on the Russian masses than to continue supporting the Yeltsin regime.

That support, however, will not translate into delivery on the tens of billions of promised financial aid and capital investments from the United States and other imperialist countries.

V. FASCISM AND WAR

ZHIRINOVSKY strikes a chord among growing ultrarightist formations in Germany, Italy, Austria, France, and Britain. He has traveled to Western Europe and appeared publicly with leaders of fascist outfits in these countries. Most important, it is the same economic, social, and political conditions generated by the decaying capitalist system that give rise to all these fascist movements.

We should take seriously the political fact that for the first time since 1945, a fascist party is today serving in the government of a major capitalist power in Europe—Italy. The National Alliance (formerly the Italian Social Movement—the MSI) is sometimes called "neofascist" by the big-business press. As a general rule, when you see the word "n-e-o" in the big-business dailies, you can safely drop it. They mean "we're a little embarrassed." But "neo" simply means "new," and the fascists of today are born of the same kinds of political and economic conditions as those of yesterday.

The MSI is a *fascist* party, and it now has ministers in the government of a member of NATO and the European Union. Its leaders openly laud Mussolini and call for restoring the greatness that was once Italy's—against America, against Germany, against Slovenia and Croatia, against the immigrants, against the homosexuals and the Jews, against the unions and the communists, against all the "filth" that, under the banner of democracy and tolerance, has permeated the land of Romulus and Remus.

What we've pointed out about Patrick Buchanan and other spokespeople for incipient fascist movements within the United States holds true for similar movements in other imperialist countries. As capitalist instability heightens, as sharp alternations between good times and bad bring growing insecurity to the daily lives of millions, social tensions mount, political polarization increases, and class bias becomes more naked. The radical right, not the revolutionary workers movement, will be the first to grow, because it has a foot firmly planted inside bourgeois politics and its existing institutions. The far right grows out of bourgeois politics, but working-class politics requires a radical break from the political tutelage of the bourgeoisie—the only kind of politics known to the petty-bourgeois misleaderships within the labor movement.

Rightist forces will win a hearing among the panicky middle

classes. They will mislead some disoriented or better-off layers of the working class, wrapping their nationalist and other irrationalist and reactionary notions in packaging that sounds popular and even anticapitalist. Wings of fascist movements will operate inside traditional bourgeois parties or form coalitions, even as they begin to send their shock troops into the streets to terrorize immigrants, to break up strike pickets, to attack meetings and demonstrations of workers organizations and social protest movements (and to put fear into "legitimate" bourgeois rightist politicians). Fascist terror will start with small rightist actions, like those we're already seeing in Germany and elsewhere, and will increasingly be aimed against selected targets within the unions. But larger battles will start taking place as sections of the workers movement begin forging their own alliances to defend labor and its allies.

Contrary to the claims of all the bourgeois propagandists, capitalism and democracy are not identical; they don't go hand in hand. The truth is the opposite. Under the depression conditions spreading across the capitalist world, the bourgeois democracies in Europe, North America, and Asia and the Pacific are moving not toward greater democracy, but toward growing pressures on democratic rights, toward Bonapartism, and toward the growth of fascist movements. In times of crisis Bonapartism remains, as Marx and Engels described it more than a century ago, the "religion of the modern bourgeoisie."[22]

---

22. Engels, letter to Marx, April 13, 1866, in *Collected Works*, vol. 42, p. 266.

Originating in a period of social crisis, a Bonapartist regime tends to concentrate power in a strong executive branch that balances between two contending class forces, neither of which is secure from challenge by the other. This centralization of executive power is often presided over by a "strong man" who presents himself as standing above the conflicting classes and exerts a certain independence of action, in order to maintain the power of the dominant social layer. Karl Marx and Frederick Engels coined the term during the rise of the industrial bourgeoisie, basing it on the experience with the regime of Louis-Napoleon Bonaparte in France from 1852 to 1870, in the wake of the capitalist reaction against the revolutions of 1848-49. They sub-

It may be too late in the history of capitalism for there to be successful new Bismarcks in the semicolonial world, but there will be new Hitlers, new Mussolinis in the imperialist world. They will arise at the head of fascist movements in North America, in Europe, in Japan, in New Zealand, in Australia; that is inevitable. What is not inevitable is that they will triumph. While the class-conscious working-class movement will not be the first to grow, its ranks too will swell, as vanguard workers begin organizing our class to fight back against the devastating toll we are made to pay for the deepening crisis of capitalism. The future of humanity will be decided in the contest between these contending class forces, in the United States and on a world scale.

Of course, communist workers know that bourgeois political democracy is not and never has been fully democratic. But the concrete evolution of capitalism that we must come to grips with today is not just a timeless truism. With the prolonged capitalist expansion coming out of World War II, broad democratic rights and institutions of bourgeois democracy were maintained, within which the labor movement and movements of social protest have been able to function and make gains. Working people and youth have had to fight repression, politi-

---

sequently applied the term to the regime of Otto von Bismarck in Germany from 1871 to 1890.

During the period of capitalism's historical decline in the post–World War I twentieth century, Bonapartist regimes in Italy and Germany paved the way for victories by the fascist movements led by Benito Mussolini and Adolf Hitler. Following the fascist triumphs, these regimes beheaded the mass petty-bourgeois movements that brought them to power and were transformed over time into Bonapartist-type military-police dictatorships like those that have exercised power in many other capitalist countries in this century, both in the imperialist countries and in many colonial and semicolonial countries. In the 1930s the communist movement also used the term Bonapartism to refer by analogy to the Stalinist regime in the Soviet Union, which brutally usurped political power from the working class on behalf of a large, materially privileged social caste in the state and party bureaucracy.

cal and union frame-ups, racist assaults, and other government attempts to roll back rights, but for several decades these rights on balance have been extended in struggle rather than pushed back.

The Bonapartist regime of Gen. Charles de Gaulle, established in France in the late 1950s; the military-police regime of Gen. Francisco Franco, consolidated through a fascist victory at the end of the 1930s; and the military dictatorship in Portugal that survived from the early 1930s in Franco's shadow—all went down to defeat in the late 1960s and early 1970s under the impact of rising anticolonial struggles and the political radicalization of workers and youth in the imperialist countries. (The pattern has been much more mixed in the weaker capitalist countries of the Third World since World War II, but we're looking at the class tensions and political polarization in the imperialist countries right now.)

While bourgeois democracy expanded during the postwar decades, at the same time the growing power of the executive branch in the United States and other imperialist countries strengthened the Bonapartist tendencies of the state and posed a threat to political freedoms that has increased slowly and unevenly, but surely.[23]

What we see happening in the imperialist countries today, however, marks a shift from what most working people, including ourselves, have experienced so far in our lives. There is a rise in political polarization and ultraright demagogy and activity in the imperialist countries.

As working-class resistance to the capitalist offensive grows, more fascist outfits will take to the streets to assault strikers, union meetings, and social protest demonstrations. Ultrarightist forces will more often gain strength in bourgeois governments,

---

23. See "Washington's Fifty-Year Domestic Contra Operation" by Larry Seigle, in *New International* no. 6, and *FBI on Trial: The Victory in the Socialist Workers Party Suit against Government Spying* edited by Margaret Jayko (New York: Pathfinder, 1988).

as we see previewed in Italy today. The pace of history, that is, the pace of class conflict, will quicken.

Pornographication of politics

The workers movement can and must fight to defend and extend democratic rights when they come under attack by rightist movements and by the capitalist government. Doing so, and drawing broad layers of the population into the fight, is part of the process of mobilizing opposition to rising fascist currents and building a communist vanguard of the working class.

During periods like we live in today—when a capitalist social crisis is deepening but a communist leadership is not yet growing out of rising mass workers struggles—demagogues get a hearing not only in the middle class but also in the labor movement. If no solutions are being advanced on any mass level to the burning problems created by the decline of capitalism and liberal democracy, then growing numbers reach out for radical, "decisive," and "popular" answers, regardless of their scientific value and ultimate class implications. Growing numbers become susceptible to crank ideas, conspiracy theories, and a variety of reactionary explanations of why society is gripped in a deepening crisis and what can be done to "restore order."

It is from this vantage point that communist workers must judge how we respond to and politically explain the interlaced sexual and financial scandals involving ruling-class figures in many of the imperialist countries. Headlines are being grabbed by exposés involving President Clinton and Hillary Clinton in the United States, Prince Charles and members of Parliament and cabinet ministers in the United Kingdom, prominent bourgeois politicians in Germany, Italy, Spain, and other countries.

The reason that political figures seem more vulnerable to scandals today is not that such conduct is something new in ruling circles over the history of capitalism or class society. Whatever the facts about Clinton's libido, lechery, and all-around offensive behavior, he is certainly not unique among U.S. presidents—including hallowed liberal icons like Franklin

Roosevelt, let alone John Kennedy. Nothing that comes out about the current royal family in the United Kingdom can approach King Henry VIII more than four hundred years ago and many of both sexes who followed him. The greater *vulnerability* to scandals today is a reflection of the instability of the world imperialist order and the growing lack of confidence in this system and its leading personnel expressed both by its beneficiaries and by millions of others.

Of course, most workers justly despise the hypocrisy, the pretenses, the sanctimonious sermonizing of bourgeois politicians in both parties. We despise the "humane" excuses they give for degrading social brutality and racist abuse. We detest the way hired scribblers of the parasitic classes write off entire layers of our class as lazy or self-indulgent. We're sickened by their gall in demagogically railing against "the greed of the eighties," while they themselves have actively engaged in and profited handily from the same greed-inspired conduct.

B UT THE WORKING-CLASS VANGUARD must not fall into the trap of thinking that simply "exposing" the dissoluteness and corruption of bourgeois politicians helps the workers movement. It's barking up the wrong tree. The problem with the capitalists and their political representatives is not that they are immoral, hypocritical people as individuals. The scandalmongering is an effort—organized from within bourgeois politics, largely by its ultraright wing—to exacerbate and profit from middle-class panic and to drag workers along with the declining class itself down into the pit of resentment and salacious envy.

This "pornographication of politics," as we might call it, is part of the politics of resentment that benefits the ultraright, not the working class. It is demagogues like the Buchanans who raise the banner of "the culture war" and "the religious war" and rail against the degeneracy of "the elite" who set a bad example for the working class. This became a stock-in-trade of the Nazis in the 1920s and early 1930s as they decried the "filth" and "degeneracy" of the Weimar Republic and its dominant bourgeois parties, politicians, and moneyed beneficiaries. This was how the Nazis explained Germany's increasingly desperate economic and social conditions to small shopkeepers and other petty-bourgeois sectors, to housewives and women in the countryside, and to layers of workers as well.

From the standpoint of the working class, it's much better when every worker could care less about the sex life of Clinton, or Kennedy, or Prince Charles—or of any other public figure. It's an enervating diversion, one that gets swept aside in times of ascending class battles.

What the working class needs is not exposés of bourgeois politicians and their personal weaknesses. We need to be able to explain politically why the working class has no common interests with the class these bourgeois politicians speak for. We need to spotlight every form of abuse of power by them, individual or corporate, including the so-called "Whitewater" revelations of how Bill and Hillary Clinton used the Arkansas state house to enrich themselves and promote big-business interests at the expense of working people and the unions—and then used the White House to cover up those earlier abuses. We need to advance a class understanding of politics and help our class forge an independent proletarian political organization that can lead a fight for a social and political program to advance the interests of the oppressed and exploited.

Until resistance grows to the point that workers begin generalizing lessons stimulated by sharp struggles and swelling the ranks of a communist party, the ideology of the ruling class—including its unctuous and hypocritical official moralism—will continue to shape the ideas and values of all but a small vanguard of the working class. But communists and other thinking workers must always fight for our class and its organizations to take the moral high ground and chart our own course independent of the bourgeoisie, its opinion makers, and the middle-class layers they set into motion. The workers movement strives to develop our *own* values, *collectively*, out of working-class *political practice*.

Deepening political polarization is inevitable in today's world. This does not mean, however, that the gains our class has won through decades of struggle are destined to be reversed. The workers movement must take the lead in defending every inch of ground our class and its allies have conquered.

Vanguard workers, for example, welcome the historic fact that anti-Semitism in the United States has declined and continues to decline among workers, of all skin colors. At the same time, we recognize that growing rightist movements, in the course of broader class confrontations, can initiate relatively sudden surges of anti-Semitic activity that have an impact on bourgeois public opinion and reinforce Jew-hatred in sections of a more and more resentful middle class and in the broader population. That underlines the importance of communist workers explaining to co-workers why anti-Semitism is a deadly trap for the working class. We must explain that anti-Semitism is based on gross and unjust falsehoods and why the labor movement must not only oppose it but also take the lead in mobilizing opposition to every manifestation of such bigotry, whatever its source.

The workers movement must stand at the head of the fight to defend affirmative action gains, abortion rights and other advances for women's equality, school desegregation, and a broad range of democratic rights and freedoms. The liberals and middle-class radicals, of all political stripes and all nationalities, shrink in fear from the reality of what growing fascist movements will do. Despite their democratic pretensions, they are utterly incapable of defending democratic rights. But none of the assaults by the right need succeed if the working-class movement resists effectively and strengthens a communist leadership in the process.

Fascism, Bonapartism, and imperialist war

The rapid emergence over the past several years of serious fascist and Bonapartist currents in bourgeois politics in the advanced capitalist countries creates the conditions in which the possibility of a war between imperialist powers in North America, Europe, and Asia—fighting on different sides, in some combination of shifting alliances—is once again beginning to be posed. Such a development, with the threat it represents to humanity, is something several generations of thinking workers have virtually ruled out. For half a century it has not been on the horizon.

The communist movement began pointing to this historic logic inherent in the world capitalist system in late 1990 and early 1991 during Washington's war against Iraq, which revealed growing conflicts among the imperialist powers that made up the U.S.-led military alliance. Since then we have seen the Patrick Buchanan and Ross Perot presidential election bids in 1992, the inclusion of a fascist party in the new Italian government, and the growth of anti-immigrant violence by fascist gangs in Germany. These and related developments in the imperialist countries can help us understand more concretely the road toward World War III, the "opening guns" of which could begin to be detected during the Gulf War.[24]

Right now the first European war since the end of World War II is being fought; it has been under way for three years in what used to be Yugoslavia. It is a war in which modern weaponry is being used not just, or even primarily, in military engagements but to bombard and slaughter civilian populations—an extension of the terror bombing that during World War II became an established part of capitalist warfare on all sides, including the assaults by the "democratic Allies" on cities such as Dresden, Tokyo, Hiroshima, and Nagasaki. The war in the former Yugoslavia threatens not only to become an arena of expanded imperialist intervention, carried out by the U.S.-dominated NATO military alliance under United Nations cover; the conflict, as long as it lasts, also holds the potential to spread

---

24. See "The Opening Guns of World War III" by Jack Barnes, in *New International* no. 7.

into a broader Balkan war.

The social democratic government of Greece has imposed a blockade against the landlocked former Yugoslav republic of Macedonia, where Washington has stationed a contingent of some 300 troops.[25] The Greek government is preventing ships in the harbor at Thessaloníki, including ships of other members of the European Union and NATO, from unloading oil and other imports; it is barring trucks from crossing the border from Greece into Macedonia. Greece currently occupies the revolving presidency of the European Union, but other EU members have sharply condemned the embargo and demanded that Athens end it. The Greek bourgeoisie and its political representatives across a spectrum of parties are whipping up nationalist sentiment to justify its steps to establish Greece as the dominant imperialist power in the Balkans, in competition with its more powerful rivals elsewhere in Europe and in North America. In the course of this conflict, Athens has also intensified its military pressure against Albania.

We're not predicting that events in the Balkans will head in the direction of a military conflict between the imperialist powers in NATO in the coming months. But we should be aware of the fact that even the prospect of such a conflict would have been unthinkable just a few years ago.[26]

It's not military conflicts such as this possible one in the Balkans that we're talking about primarily, however, in raising the prospect of a renewed march toward interimperialist war. We're not talking about a world war between imperialist countries

---

25. In May 1994 Washington upped its troop strength to some 520, as part of the overall imperialist deployment in Macedonia of more than 1,000 soldiers.
26. There have been military conflicts between the Greek and the Turkish governments over the past two decades. The government of Turkey, one of the militarily strongest semicolonial countries, was admitted to NATO in the early 1950s due to its particular place in the imperialist-organized military alliances in both the First and Second World Wars and its strategic position vis-à-vis the Soviet Union and the oil-rich Middle East.

with relatively stable bourgeois-democratic regimes; that remains unlikely. We're talking about the logic of the deepening economic, social, and political crises *within* the imperialist powers.

T HE EVENTS THAT BY 1939 made the second imperialist slaughter inevitable were inextricably bound up with the deep world economic, social, and political crises that had led to the defeat of the working class, the triumph of fascist movements, and the momentum these fascist victories gave to military-police regimes in Italy, Germany, and Spain. The consolidation of the imperial regime in Japan and the rise of fascist movements in the United States and other imperialist democracies in the 1930s were rooted in the same crises. Earlier in this century, World War I had involved governments on both sides still marked by the crisis-ridden remnants of precapitalist forerunners of Bonapartism and fascism—the monarchist, imperial, landlord-capitalist regimes of the kaiser in Germany, the Hapsburgs in Austria, the tsar in Russia, and the Ottoman rulers in Turkey.

Under the impact of growing social conflicts, the Bonapartist tendencies toward stronger executive power in the imperialist countries will be further accelerated. Regimes that are more aggressively nationalistic, jingoist, and racist will come to power first in one country, then in another. Rightist and openly fascist movements will carve out growing space in bourgeois politics. And if the workers movement in the imperialist countries is not capable of forging a communist vanguard in time to lead successful anticapitalist revolutions, then wars among the declining imperialist bourgeoisies will be launched, as they have been twice before in the past eighty years.

The point is not that imperialist democracies don't initiate war moves against their imperialist rivals; the most powerful bourgeois democracies in this century bear decisive responsibility for the onset of both World War I and World War II. The U.S. rulers, for example, were determined in the 1930s not only to defend but to extend their sphere of exploitation in the Pacific against their rising competitor in Japan. Washington's tightening squeeze on Tokyo's oil supplies in the late 1930s made war with Japan virtually inevitable. But the consolidation of the semifascist Japanese imperial regime in the 1930s, and the smashing of the labor movement that had gained strength there in the wake of the Russian revolution of October 1917, were preconditions for Tokyo to carry out its expansionist course in Asia and launch the assault on Pearl Harbor.

Similarly, in the aftermath of World War I, U.S., British, and French imperialism pursued a brutally rapacious course toward Germany that resulted in extreme deprivation and resentment and fostered the growth of a mass fascist movement there, sparking the tinder that exploded in a second imperialist slaughter by the end of the 1930s.

World War II was far from inevitable, however. To the contrary, during the 1930s the working class had its chance to take political power out of the hands of the war makers in at least Germany, France, and Spain and to build a powerful, independent political movement of labor and its allies in other imperialist countries, including the United States. The inevitability of a second imperialist world slaughter was not settled until the closing years of the 1930s, when the workers movement had proven incapable, under Stalinist and social democratic domination, to lead the working class in a successful socialist revolution anywhere in Europe. Only such a victory could have stemmed the spread of fascism.

Thinking workers don't believe that Washington, Bonn, London, and Paris are going to go to war against each other today over their conflicting stakes in the former Yugoslavia and the Balkans. We should never say anything that implies that, because serious workers and youth won't listen to us if they think we're exaggerating. It doesn't ring true to them that the Washington of George Bush or William Clinton will go to war tomorrow against the Germany of Helmut Kohl or the France of François Mitterrand and Edouard Balladur. Thinking workers don't believe that sharp trade conflicts between Washington and Tokyo, or Washington and Ottawa, will escalate in some linear way until they get out of control and erupt in a war.

And these workers are right. Trade wars do lead to shooting wars, as they did in the 1930s, but not without the kind of social upheavals and devastating defeats of the working class that increasingly marked that decade and provided the context for those trade wars. The direct result of mounting trade wars is not military conflict and never has been. First there are growing tensions and conflicts between rival powers; the intensification of economic and social crises and antagonisms within these countries; and the strengthening of rightist, ultranationalist groups that agitate to defeat the "foreign powers" that are pressuring "our country," "stealing our jobs," and "trampling on our national honor."

WASHINGTON'S CURRENT sharpening trade conflicts with Tokyo, for example, will not lead directly to war with Japan. But if the U.S. capitalists push too hard in the ups and downs of their campaign, these pressures can unleash unanticipated political forces in class relations and politics in Japan. The deep recession there could be exacerbated; a number of banks could collapse and set off a financial crisis; a fragile new government could fall; wind could be put in the sails of new rightist, anti-American movements. Such developments could begin changing the character of economic, political, and military relations between Washington, Tokyo, and other governments in Asia and the Pacific.

It seems crazy to think about the German government going to war against the French government today, or the U.S. government against the governments of Japan or Canada. But then think about the world we've been describing, and what the German government, or the French government, or the U.S. government may look like a few years from now. Think about a Buchanan-type government in the United States—not necessarily Buchanan himself, but someone else who picks up that rightist thread in bourgeois politics. Think about a government in Germany that incorporates elements of the growing fascist organizations there. Think about a further shift to the right in Italian bourgeois politics. Think about ultranationalist currents emerging as part of a government in Japan. Think about a Bonapartist government coming to power in France, with its nuclear-armed *force de frappe* [strike force]. Add to this, as possible catalysts, a Zhirinovsky regime in Russia, an out-of-control first strike by a government in Israel, or a sharp conflict between ultranationalist regimes in Pakistan and India. Then the slowly but surely mounting dangers of a new world war come more sharply into focus.

When you listen to Patrick Buchanan today, he often poses (as do others in the right wing of the Republican and Democratic parties) as the great, America First isolationist—don't get "our boys" involved. But workers shouldn't be fooled by that for a minute. Buchanan's entire political course is part of the preparations for imperialist military intervention and war. His message to others in U.S. bourgeois politics is simple: No more defeats like Vietnam. No more fiascoes like the Gulf War. When we go to war, we go to war to win. And, by God, we'll have the support of *all* the American people with the exception of a few fifth-columnists.

Looked at from this vantage point, it is much easier to explain the increasingly dangerous logic of the reemergence after half a century of the conflict between the U.S. rulers and the imperialist powers they defeated in World War II. We can explain the relationship between the growing trade conflicts with these powers and the increased efforts by Tokyo and Bonn to get out from under their dependence on the strategic nuclear power of Washington. We can explain why the German and Japanese governments are seeking to strengthen their respective land, air, and naval armed forces. We can explain why they will push to overcome domestic and international political obstacles—above all, the deep opposition among workers and farmers at home—to intervening with their armed forces to advance their class interests abroad, and to becoming strategic nuclear powers in their own right.

This course becomes more and more inevitable, as the capitalist rulers in Germany and Japan become more and more convinced they must be prepared to fight their U.S. rivals sooner or later. Sharp rightward shifts in the governments of any or all of these countries will accelerate this combined political and military trajectory.

We should add one final element to this picture. How will the Japanese, German, and other imperialist governments build up the kind of armed forces that in some combination can challenge the military might of U.S. imperialism? To a great degree, it will happen in the same way that these governments armed themselves leading up to World War II. Capitalists in the United States, as well as in Britain and France, will push and compete to sell the weapons, the advanced technologies, and the factories that lesser-armed governments will use to swell their arsenals of mass destruction.

Intervention and war in semicolonial world
So, the threat of imperialist war today comes from two intertwined directions:

The first, and more fundamental, is the one we've just been discussing: the mounting social tensions and growing potential for the rise of Bonapartist, ultrarightist, and fascist forces in capitalist regimes in the imperialist countries. Right now, in 1994, the kind of explosive social conflicts that lead directly to a major interimperialist war of this kind are still in their incipient stages. But for the first time in half a century, we are seeing the emergence of the kinds of class forces and pressures that bring closer the day when the fight to stop the drive toward a third world war will be a pressing, immediate task of the workers movement in one country after another.

The second source of the war threat is conjunctural military interventions by U.S. imperialism, as well as by other imperialist powers, to protect capitalist interests wherever they are threatened in the semicolonial world (or, today, in some parts of the territory of the former Soviet bloc). Finance capital will defend its continued oppression of nations and nationalities in pursuit of the superprofits it obtains from the exploitation of the toilers in these countries. We've seen wars of this kind throughout the post–World War II period, and they will continue to occur under the increasingly unstable conditions that mark the world imperialist system today. Such interventions always put uncontrolled forces in motion.

THE U.S.-ORGANIZED ASSAULT against Iraq in 1990-91 was the most recent example of the types of wars we can anticipate in the years ahead. The imperialist intervention in Somalia a year and a half ago never developed, nor could it have, into a war of that scope. As they are doing with regard to Bosnia and Haiti today, numerous petty-bourgeois radicals and pacifists adapted to liberal rationalizations for the invasion of Somalia, arguing that imperialist intervention—especially if carried out behind a United Nations facade—was a "lesser evil." Communist workers, of course, denounced the brutal aggression that Washington organized under the banners of a UN Security Council "peacekeeping force," and we sought to mobilize opposition to it. But we recognized that the U.S. rulers had no pressing class interests in allowing that intervention to develop into a protracted war.

The Iraq war was the fruit of processes U.S. imperialism had set in motion over the previous decade—only to face consequences that later began to harm its class interests in unexpected ways. The Israeli regime is especially bitter toward Washington over this war and the course that inevitably led to it. Tel Aviv knows that U.S. enterprises along with their rivals in Britain, Germany, and France helped build up the Iraqi regime militarily and economically throughout the 1980s—with the complicity of all the imperialist governments involved. Washington saw the Iraqi regime and the war Baghdad launched against Iran in 1980 as a necessary counterweight against the impact of the Iranian revolution and its spread elsewhere in the region to the detriment of U.S. interests. Capitalists in the imperialist centers made big money off "secret" arms deals throughout these years. Meanwhile, it was left to the Israeli government to take the heat from these same imperialist "friends" for bombing alleged nuclear weapons research facilities in Baghdad in 1981.

Then, when Washington concluded from the Iraqi regime's invasion of Kuwait in 1990 that U.S. imperialism needed a more reliable client state in power there, Tel Aviv paid the price for the U.S. rulers' entire prior course. The Scud missiles that came down on Israeli territory during the 1991 war had been produced with equipment and technical know-how sold by U.S., European, and Japanese capitalist firms.

What has been the upshot of the so-called Iraq-gate scandal and investigations? They revealed that Washington and all of its imperialist allies, especially London and Paris, made big profits off business with Baghdad—just as Washington will rearm the capitalist rivals it will eventually seek to defeat in an interimperialist war. In fact, in Britain members of the Tory cabinet were still involved in selling war matériel to the Iraqi regime right up to the eve of the war drive against Iraq in late 1990. This has become an even bigger scandal in Britain than similar revelations in the United States.

This is how the imperialist ruling classes have always operated. They will do so more and more as the crisis of their system deepens. That's the main lesson of the final report on the earlier Iran-Contra scandal that was released at the beginning of this year. The bipartisan U.S. rulers increasingly need to conduct their business behind a veil of secrecy. They need a stronger and stronger executive power to defend their class interests both against their imperialist rivals and against resistance by workers and farmers in the United States and around the world.

I've read only excerpts from the concluding portion of special prosecutor Lawrence Walsh's 2,500-page report on Iran-

Contra, but I've also read a couple of detailed summaries of it.[27] What I found most moderately stated in the account in the *New York Review of Books* by Theodore Draper—the liberal historian who has closely followed the affair and written extensively about it—is his conviction that such covert military activities abroad have become a permanent part of U.S. government functioning. "Can something on the order of the Iran-contra affairs happen again in the United States?" he asks in the conclusion of his long article. "I am not sanguine that we have been inoculated against some sort of repetition. . . . Iran-contra events may be more important as a warning of what can go wrong in the American system than as a bar to its going wrong again."

Sad, for a liberal, but true. "The American system," in fact, can't operate without such secrecy, and it will "go wrong" again, and again, and again.

VI. EMPLOYERS' OFFENSIVE AND WORKING-CLASS RESISTANCE

DOMESTIC POLICY in the United States has become increasingly more bipartisan since the mid-1970s, when the twin bourgeois parties began coming to terms with the social and political consequences of the fact that capitalist profit rates had turned downward. The joint banner has been "equality of sacrifice" to defend the dollar, improve the competitiveness of "our" industries, and restore "our" unchallenged manufacturing and export dominance in the world capitalist market.

Through nearly two decades of a grinding offensive against

27. For more on the conclusions of the report by Reagan-appointed special prosecutor Lawrence Walsh on the Iran-Contra, or Contragate, affair, see "In This Issue" by Steve Clark, in *New International* no. 9 on "The Rise and Fall of the Nicaraguan Revolution," pp. 22-25.

workers' wages and conditions and accelerated cost-cutting and downsizing moves since the late 1980s, U.S. big business has regained an edge against its major imperialist rivals. Success in driving down not only the price of workers' labor power, but even its value, has reinforced the conviction of the capitalists and their political representatives that they are on the only possible road to maintain and widen U.S. imperialism's leading position. They are determined to take further steps to lengthen the workday, intensify speedup, and reduce spending on wages and social benefits.

This year both parties are trying to convince working people and the middle class that the rulers have a plan—many different ones have been floated in Washington—to meet "the nation's" medical needs. All of the plans with substantial ruling-class support, including the program proposed by the Clinton administration, are designed to socialize the risks and losses of the big insurance companies, medical-related businesses, and drug companies. All of them are part of the rulers' assault on the social wage of the working class, not an extension of social security for all. None of these programs has anything to do with establishing universal, equal, government-funded health care as a right, as an entitlement. But since none yet promises enough budget cuts to satisfy the "bond community," none will be easy to pass.

One of the most important social questions that the labor movement should be campaigning around today is the fight for the shorter workweek. Despite the current upturn in the business cycle and increased hiring, the official unemployment rate remains over 6 percent. In fact, many Democratic and Republican politicians alike now talk of this as the "natural rate" of unemployment! And the real figure is roughly double that, including workers who have involuntarily had to take part-time or temporary jobs or who have been pushed out of the workforce for now.

At the same time, the employers are increasing absolute surplus value by lengthening the workweek to the highest levels in half a century. Average weekly overtime has increased by a full hour just since mid-1991. A fifty-hour workweek in auto is standard right now, and the situation is comparable in some other industries.

The situation is even worse in Western Europe (let alone in the Third World, where unemployment levels of 50 percent or more are not uncommon). In the countries that make up the European Union, official unemployment rates average nearly 11 percent, with the real figures well over 20 percent. In Spain the official jobless rate is almost 25 percent; in France, Belgium, and Denmark, more than 12 percent. In Britain, where the government has changed the way of measuring unemployment thirty times over the past decade in order to pretty up the truth, the official rate is nonetheless still over 9 percent. The official rate in Sweden has shot up to more than 7 percent from only 2 percent a few years ago.[28] Government figures in Canada have put joblessness over 10 percent for most years since the early 1980s.

T HIS IS A DEEPENING CRISIS for the working class worldwide. As we explain in *An Action Program to Confront the Coming Economic Crisis*,[29] the deepest economic division in our class is between those who have a job and those who don't. Growing joblessness saps the strength, the morale, and the fighting capacity of the working class and labor movement. If the workers movement doesn't lead the fight for a shorter workweek *with no cut in pay*, then the bosses will exploit the growing pressures and demoralization of joblessness—as they have done in Germany,

---

28. At an August 1994 international conference of top government officials and central bankers sponsored by the Federal Reserve Bank of Kansas City, a professor from the London School of Economics pontificated that the "natural rate" of unemployment in Europe has now reached 10 percent!
29. *An Action Program to Confront the Coming Economic Crisis* (New York: Pathfinder, 1989).

in France, in Canada, and I imagine elsewhere—to start writing into occasional contracts a shorter workweek *with a proportional pay cut*. And behind that formula, temporary and part-time work—at lower pay and with fewer benefits—will increase.

We must continue to link the fight for the sliding scale of *hours* to a sliding scale of *wages* to protect the working class against the effects of inflation. Workers must not let the deflationary pressures we've been discussing be used by the employers as a rationalization to deny cost-of-living protection to workers' wages and social entitlements. Even if we are correct and inflation continues to moderate for the immediate future, we should keep several considerations in mind.

First, even with today's deflationary pressures real wages fell once again by 1 percent over the past year in the United States. Buying power declined both because the employers succeeded in pushing down actual wage rates—of union and nonunion workers alike—and because there continues to be inflation even if at a low level of around 3 percent officially. The cost-of-living adjustments—COLA clauses—that a lot of unions fought to include in contracts in the sixties and seventies fell short of keeping up with rising prices. But the number of workers covered by even this partial protection has fallen to its lowest level in a quarter century, as the officialdom in one union after the next has succumbed to the bosses' concession demands.

Second, there have been explosions of currency inflation in the midst of depression conditions in this century and there will be again. This is the situation in many semicolonial countries right now, as well as in the USSR and Eastern Europe. We should never have the illusion that the kind of hyperinflation that ravaged workers, farmers, and the middle classes in Weimar Germany in the aftermath of World War I is no longer possible in the imperialist countries. Working people had to carry money in wheelbarrows and suitcases just to buy a loaf of bread; what your money would buy slid hour by hour. That can and will happen again. And long before prices reach runaway levels, inflation has a devastating impact on workers' wages and living conditions.

The threat of sudden inflationary explosions is built right into deflationary depression conditions. Because in the face of plummeting profit rates, increasing unemployment, and a rise in working-class resistance, the bourgeoisie will divide over how to attempt to weather the crisis. Sooner or later, some capitalist governments will panic and simply begin pumping out money in hopes of buffering the shocks. When that happens, workers and working farmers get slammed with the worst of both worlds—high levels of unemployment and explosive inflation. Employed workers will see real wages plunge; working people living on pensions will be devastated; and farmers will be hit with a new wave of foreclosures. This is what the working-class movement must prepare for.

This has happened before in the history of capitalism. It happened during the long depression in the closing decades of the last century. And it happened during the so-called Great Depression of the 1930s. After more than half a decade of deflation, monetary inflation reappeared in the United States in 1936-37, accelerated at the end of the decade, and then shot up even more sharply during the wartime expansion after 1941.

Despite their names, *inflation* and *deflation* are not opposite, mutually exclusive phenomena under capitalism. *Inflation* is a monetary phenomenon that arises when the purchasing power of a national currency declines. Governments and banks crank out money in various paper forms, eventually far outstripping the output of commodities that could be purchased with that money. Under such conditions, competing capitalist commercial interests bid prices up and up and up and up, in an ultimately self-defeating effort to reap surplus profits. *Deflation* is something quite different. It is not primarily a currency phenomenon. It is the product of the long-term tendency of capitalist profit rates to fall, heightening price competition among rival capitals and putting enormous downward pressures on capacity-increasing investment and expanded production—the conditions we've been discussing.

So the question for the workers movement in a depression is not an "either . . . or": *either* to prepare for deflation *or* to prepare for inflation. There will be unanticipated currency inflation superimposed on the deflation endemic to depression conditions. A sudden disastrous collapse of productive employment can soon be accompanied by a terrible price explosion.

That is why the labor movement must be ready to unite working people nationally and internationally around the fight for a program to advance workers' common interests, including measures to protect our class and its toiling allies against the ravages of both capitalist-caused joblessness and inflation.

Working-class fightback picks up

Over the past year there has been a substantial pickup in the United States in working-class resistance to the bosses' takeback drive.

In 1993 a nationwide coal miners strike pushed back the coal operators' efforts to expand nonunion mines, and there has been a small round of successful United Mine Workers organizing drives. Flight attendants put up a solid front and forced American Airlines to back off its union-busting plans in November 1993. Caterpillar workers have continued their resistance, with ongoing protests and guerrilla warfare in the plants against the company's refusal to negotiate a contract and brief strikes against management victimization of union militants.

Steelworkers in four states employed by Allegheny Ludlum are fighting the company's new "flex-time" policy that imposes mandatory overtime and a brutal extension of the workweek. Workers at the A.E. Staley plant in central Illinois are waging a hard-fought battle against a management lockout and concession demands, linking up with Caterpillar workers and other unionists in the area and around the country.[30]

---

30. The pattern of worker resistance noted in this talk continued and by June

An indication of the changing climate was the success earlier this year of the one-day walkout by Teamsters-organized United Parcel Service workers. The UPS bosses evidently figured that since drivers make very good money, that's all they cared about. So management suddenly more than doubled the maximum weight drivers and warehouse workers were required to handle. The last thing the employers expected was that the majority of workers would say "no," but that's what happened. And the UPS bosses had to back off.

I was struck by this example, because it tells us something about the human solidarity that resides in the working class as a pledge for the future. In saying "no," these workers didn't do what the employers count on workers to do. The employers expected the youngest and the strongest workers to say "yes" in their majority. They expected a lot of male workers to say "yes," including as a way of erecting more barriers to women being hired as drivers. "To hell with those who can't handle 150 pounds. I can. This is a good job. I'm making good money." That's what the employers counted on a lot of the younger, stronger workers to say. But that's not what happened. More than 12,000 workers said "no" together and staged the first-ever nationwide strike against UPS.

U.S. employers will keep pushing. But they will make the same mistake that UPS management did, and to their surprise, workers will pull together and fight.

The current issue of *Business Week* features an article headlined, "Why Steel Is Looking Sexy." That headline alone in a major U.S. business weekly says something about the employ-

---

1994 had developed into a small but real strike wave in the United States, for the first time in years. The round of local walkouts and actions by UAW-organized Caterpillar workers in Illinois and Pennsylvania became a nationwide strike in July, in face of the company's ongoing victimization of union militants and other unfair labor practices (all designed to further management's refusal to negotiate a contract). The Allegheny Ludlum strike concluded in June, after ten weeks, with the union making advances.

ers' mood and tone right now. The article describes how both the traditional big U.S. steel companies and some of the newer and smaller "minimills" have driven down costs over the past decade and taken back a growing share of the world market from companies in Japan, France, Britain, and Germany. Among other things, it confirms that hiring is going on in steel all over the country.

One of the heroes of industry interviewed in the *Business Week* article is the chairman of Birmingham Steel. Relatively smaller companies like that, the article says, "are creating a new manufacturing culture." (Yes, he said "culture"!) At Birmingham's rebar plant in Kankakee, Illinois, it says, "the parking lot is full of Toyotas and Nissans. Inside, the workers are young and disdainful of unions. 'I think if minimills are going to move on, they're going to have to stay nonunion,' says Tim Metcalf, 31, son of a Ford Motor Co. production worker."

Then *Business Week* quotes the chairman of the company, James A. Todd, Jr. "We don't make any bones about it," he says. "We run sweatshops. But we don't pay sweatshop wages." (Now we see the "culture" he's so proud of producing—the sweatshop culture!)

Think about that article for a minute. First of all, they're not going to be paying those wages forever. Workers at Birmingham will discover that sooner than they would like to.

Second, and more important, that statement by Birmingham's chairman is false. The history of workers struggles teaches us that as hiring picks up, conditions that were once acceptable to workers—often as a tradeoff for what they thought was their only chance to get a job at all—start becoming unacceptable to growing numbers.

Wꜰ nHEN BOSSES START BOASTING publicly that they "run sweatshops," they're not ready for things to go differently. They may not know it yet, but what they are doing is picking a fight. That's what they are seldom capable of seeing until it is too late. They say they are practicing "scientific management." They think they can fine-tune everything—what they can get away with, how much the workers will take.

But the employers always make the same crucial error. They can't think of workers as acting, thinking social beings. They think of workers as a special kind of tool. They don't understand scientifically what it is that's special about workers, but whatever it is enables the employers to produce more and make more profits. Just cutting costs, spinning off divisions, or adding new computers cannot accomplish that. To expand production and, over time, increase profits, more of this special tool has to be hired. That's how the capitalists look at workers.

The employers think that if they just pay this special tool a little bit more than is being paid at some factory down the road, then management can use and manipulate that tool just like any other piece of equipment. The bosses don't even care as much about the workers in the plant as they do about their computers. They're more worried about a virus getting into their computer network than they are about the lives, limbs, and futures of the people who work for them. Isn't that right? Because they can just go out and hire another worker, another one of these tools, at no extra cost! But they've invested capital in those computers, and they're expensive to replace. Talk about the social consequences of the commodity fetish!

The employer says: "OK. You get your paycheck every week. If you don't like it here, or if we don't like you, then we'll hire somebody else. There's a lot of unemployment. There are a lot of people who would be grateful to work this job."

But it's not so simple. Especially as younger workers get hired, the bosses make what may initially seem to be isolated misjudgments. They overstep the line, and some younger workers say "no." Some older, more experienced workers get picked up by the experience, and some of them say "no" the next time too. And before long, conditions that had been accepted for quite a while begin sparking struggles. Some unexpected walkouts and strikes take place. Fights that have been going on for a long time, like the one at Caterpillar, begin to take on new life as workers keep resisting management abuse. Suddenly, running a sweatshop isn't so easy, even if you don't pay sweatshop wages (once again demonstrating that some "cultural" changes are less stable than others!).

This is what we've been seeing more of recently. Without promising some major shift in the class struggle, we can say that we will see more resistance, on various levels, as long as there is hiring going on. New generations of workers will be coming into the plants. Workers' confidence will be buoyed. Old patterns and old ways of doing things won't be acceptable to many of the younger workers. And there will be greater resistance. We don't need to say anything more than that.

Even some of the cost-cutting innovations of the employers end up backfiring on them when resistance begins. Business is all slim and trim. Unnecessary storage costs are a thing of the past; inventory is just in time. Right? They brag about that. But everything employers do to set up production assuming there will never be any hitches makes them more vulnerable when there *are* hitches. And that gives the working class and labor movement more leverage against the bosses.

A convergence of resistance

These modest but important shifts I've been describing in the labor movement might well be one of the last things youth who aren't currently workers would point to as a reason why they are becoming socialists. This is true even if they come from a working-class family. Most young socialists today are more likely to point to one or another of the evils of capitalist society they became aware of and began fighting against: assaults on a woman's right to abortion, the U.S. economic embargo against Cuba, a racist cop, attempts to dehumanize immigrant workers, destruction of the environment. From there, they began looking for answers to what causes such things. They began reading, going to public meetings, looking for a socialist organization.

But if we dig a little deeper, we'll find that the developing fights by workers and the politicization of layers of youth accelerate together in reaction to the world economic and political situation we've been describing. The two phenomena both reflect resistance to the inhumanity of capitalism, to its negation of human solidarity. Above all, a rise in workers resistance offers radicalizing youth their first glimpse of the potential vulnerability of the hated system as a whole, and this is a precondition to winning young people and integrating them into a proletarian communist organization.

OF ALL CAPITALISM'S EVILS, the most fundamental one is how that system of exploitation reproduces its social relations as a condition of producing its profits. How its workings, its blind methods of functioning, keep grinding toiling humanity into the ground. How this operates in a differential way on various layers of working people, reaping superprofits for the capitalists on the basis of forms of oppression and prejudice inherited from precapitalist modes of social organization. That's what workers and young fighters alike discover when they become part of the socialist movement.

Just follow the papers carefully every week and you'll see how this works. A recent government study, for example, reports that the paychecks *25 percent of employed workers* in the United States are bringing home consign them to a standard of living that falls below the official poverty level; the figure has risen 50 percent since 1980. That fact is another refutation of the lie by the bipartisan capitalist politicians that working people won't work if they can sit around collecting welfare payments. Well, here's more proof that millions and millions of workers who do have jobs and who are fighting to keep them are nonetheless falling further and further into poverty. At the same time, a growing percentage of the millions of unemployed are no longer receiving jobless benefits.

Class differentiation and inequality are accelerating. Those with incomes in the top 1 percent, the top 5 percent, even the top 20 percent are doing better and better. The bourgeoisie, the professionals, others in the upper middle class—they are doing better.

As social differentiation widens within the working class itself, the rulers try to pit working people against each other to rationalize the austerity measures they are carrying out to augment their own wealth and incomes. They tell us they have to cut back payments for Social Security, Medicare, unemployment insurance, workers compensation, and education because otherwise America just can't compete against other countries where workers get by on a lot less. Plus, they say, all the money being paid out on food stamps, Aid to Families with Dependent Children, Medicaid, and other welfare programs is bankrupting the government. Children of workers who are undocumented immigrants are draining the education system and "taking advantage" of hospital emergency rooms. Employed workers can't be paid as much because the boss is being taxed to pay for all those people "living off the state."

The bourgeoisie and their "experts" keep coming up with new, self-justifying explanations for the impoverishment of working people: There's an exploding "culture of poverty" among a Black urban "underclass," we're told. Affirmative action gains for women are making it harder and harder for men to get jobs. Immigrants are willing to work for less. Blacks are the problem. Women are the problem. People who can't speak English are the problem. The bourgeois politicians, columnists, and academics have all varieties and combinations of rationalizations.

All these "explanations" have one thing in common: the problem for them has nothing to do with *capitalism,* only with its "excesses." Impoverishment, unemployment, racism, women's oppression, ecological destruction, fascism, and war have nothing necessarily to do with the fact that one class comprising a tiny percentage of the population grows wealthy off the labor of working people in city and countryside who make up the overwhelming majority.

And, of course, their solutions have nothing to do with workers organizing themselves politically to transform their self-defense organizations, the unions, into the vanguard of a social movement of all the oppressed and exploited. Their solution has nothing to do with working people forging a revolutionary movement to fight for a workers and farmers government, open the road to socialism, and begin transforming themselves into more truly human beings as they do so. These are the conclusions the capitalist rulers *do not* want workers and youth to begin drawing.

Bourgeois public opinion over the past decade has been saturated by an advertising campaign telling youth to "just say no" to drugs. "Just say no!" The revolutionary movement more than any other in bourgeois society knows how much human potential is wasted and destroyed by drugs. But what's wrong with the bourgeoisie's "Just say no" campaign?

The problem—and this is what the capitalist spokespeople don't dare say—is that their society doesn't offer the vast majority of youth and working people anything to say "yes" to. (Leave aside that drug trafficking is a big-time capitalist business targeting working people, with cops and politicians massively on the take.) Millions of people won't start saying "no" to things that are damaging to them—whether drugs or anything else—until they have something to say "yes" to.

And the "yes" must be to something bigger than ourselves. It must be an affirmation that we, along with millions of others like us, are actors in history. We can change society. We can do something about the evils we see all around us. We can do what they can't!

Once we can say "yes" to that kind of active life with a purpose, to that kind of organized political life that leads to a future, then no one has to exhort us to say "no" to a million things. Instead, we will begin organizing together with others to say "yes." We will begin using our time and energy to become the kind of person the schools, the media, the churches, and other institutions of capitalist society try to teach us we can never become.

All of bourgeois society teaches and preaches to most youth, as it does to workers, to say no to our own worth, to our own potential to transform ourselves and the world in which we live, to the revolutionary potential of the working class. We're made to think of ourselves as the objects of history, not the makers of history. We're made to feel we're the dependents of the rulers' largesse. We're lied to, praised, cajoled, and shamed into accepting that we are treated like tools, like pieces of equipment to crank out profits for the employers. We're told that it's our fault if we end up without a job, without a living income, without an affordable place to live. It's our fault if we don't say "no" to drugs and other manifestations of human demoralization and degradation. Young people are to blame. Workers are to blame.

This is the lie that workers and youth reject when, and only when, they start organizing with others to resist what capitalism has to offer. Beginning to resist the dehumanizing social relations endemic to capitalism opens the way for a layer of these fighters to begin acting against this system on a broader plane. Some are attracted politically to socialism, to the working class.

VII. BUILDING THE COMMUNIST MOVEMENT

UP UNTIL MID-1992 the Young Socialist Alliance (YSA) had functioned in this country for almost thirty-five years as an independent revolutionary socialist youth organization in political solidarity with the Socialist Workers Party. As we discussed at the opening of this talk, by the early nineties the communist movement had been declining in numbers and rising in average age for several years under the cumulative effects of the retreat of the labor movement and the defeats of workers and farmers governments in Nicaragua and Grenada. The age and level of political experience of the big majority of those who had earned the leadership of the YSA was such that a gap was widening between them and the small numbers of young people who were joining the organization.

Given this situation, the YSA leadership, in consultation with the SWP National Committee, concluded in March 1992 that the YSA should dissolve. At the time, nothing occurring in politics indicated any reason to expect substantial renewal in the short term. Most important, as developments opened down the road that would draw a new levy of youth toward the communist movement, the YSA—given the rising average age of its cadres—could not be an effective vehicle to draw this new generation into organized political activity and leadership responsibility. In the meantime, the SWP needed the political capacities and energies of experienced YSA members to help strengthen the union fractions, branches, and propaganda institutions that would be a working-class pole of attraction to young people as new opportunities arose to work alongside them and win them to the communist movement.

We were convinced that sooner rather than later, fighters from a new generation would create an organizational form, on a younger and thus more solid footing, to take up the political continuity of communist youth work that the YSA had been part of in the United States. That continuity reached back to those who drafted the Communist Manifesto, who helped lead the October 1917 revolution in Russia, and who launched the world communist movement to build on and emulate what the Bolsheviks had done.

Many YSA members at the time the organization dissolved joined the Socialist Workers Party if they had not already done so. Along with other SWP members, they continued working with young people in activities in solidarity with the Cuban revolution and in protests and demonstrations around a wide variety of political questions.

Relaunching nationwide socialist youth group
Less than two years later, here at this conference, we are seeing the

results of the course we've charted—some 100 young people get-ting together from all over the United States to form an organiz-ing committee aimed at building toward a conference to relaunch a nationwide socialist youth organization.

This development has been, if anything, more rapid than we might have anticipated two years ago. And what explains it, I am convinced, is imperialism's continuing march toward fas-cism and war that we've been discussing.

The unrelenting character of this evolution, even with ups and downs, is sensed by those young workers and students most interested in politics and drawn to the potential power of the organized working-class movement. They sense that a titanic showdown is coming in the history of humanity and they want to be part of preparing to fight—and win.

Revitalizing the party's turn to industry
This initiative to build a socialist youth organization coincides today with efforts by members of the Socialist Workers Party to organize—and this sometimes, to our surprise, may involve a wrenching reorientation—to take full advantage of the hiring during the current upturn in the business cycle.[31]

Since the mid-1970s, the SWP has organized to take full ad-vantage of the opportunities that opened for the big majority of its members and leaders to get industrial jobs and carry out communist political activity as members of the industrial un-ions. But the experience of the communist movement from the 1930s to today confirms that it's not enough to establish frac-tions of socialist workers in these unions and carry out organ-ized political and union work alongside other workers. Com-munist workers must also stay alert to—and move with—shifts in hiring patterns and other changes in industry that can allow our fractions to remain integrated with new generations of

---

31. See the introduction to *The Changing Face of U.S. Politics: Working-Class Poli-tics and the Trade Unions* by Jack Barnes (New York: Pathfinder, 1994).

workers, learning from and growing with their experiences.

This is especially important during periods, such as today, when the communist movement is not undergoing the kind of net growth that tends to promote such renewal in the normal course of things. The cadres of a communist party always have a bigger margin for error when we're experiencing substantial growth, since the momentum makes it possible for many sins to be bypassed and largely forgotten in the trail of progress.

For these reasons, the SWP has given top priority to turning toward the new hiring. It is a continuation of what the party cadres who initiated the turn to industry set out to do in the late 1970s and early 1980s. These worker-bolsheviks, along with others who have gotten into industry over the subsequent fifteen years, are now leading this effort to revitalize the turn to the industrial unions. Many of those who are already experienced, capable unionists in party fractions are volunteering to pick up stakes and look for new jobs, often in bigger plants, where substantial numbers of young workers are being hired. They are encouraging other party members not currently working industrial jobs to join them in this effort. Some young socialists are now getting their first experience working in industry and carrying out politics collectively as members of the party's union fractions.

THIS RENEWAL takes conscious political work. It involves restructuring the precise mix and balance of our union fractions in cities where branches of the communist movement exist. But that is what is necessary so that communist workers can be *part of* the generations being drawn into the mines, mills and factories and go through experiences *with them*. In the process, all our trade union work will begin to be transformed and rejuvenated as well.

A week or so after this conference, Pathfinder Press will be bringing out an expanded edition of *The Changing Face of U.S. Politics: Working-Class Politics and the Trade Unions*. In many ways it's a brand new book. It is entirely reorganized, and it incorporates substantial additional material from the party's turn to industry up through the working-class campaign against imperialism and war that we organized through our union fractions and party branches during Washington's assault on Iraq in 1990-91. Given the openings we're discussing, this book will be an even more important political weapon for communist workers and youth to read, study, and circulate as widely as possible. The book's new introduction, moreover, will present the current, and improved, perspectives for strengthening the communist movement in the unions.

Organizing to respond to the hiring that's under way is the most important new step in the party's turn to industry since the launching of the Iowa District and the beginning of a national meatpacking fraction in the United Food and Commercial Workers union in 1986, and perhaps even since our decision in February 1978 to get the big majority of party leaders and members into the industrial unions. It is the road not only to the revitalization of the party's industrial union fractions but also of the propaganda institutions of rounded political branches of a communist workers party.

This renewal of the turn is the single most important thing that members of the Socialist Workers Party can do to move along the same lines as those who are working to rebuild a nationwide young socialists organization in the United States. The larger the numbers of experienced party cadres who directly take part in rebuilding, restructuring, and rejuvenating our fractions, the more successful the communist movement will be in winning the young fighters who are being attracted to socialism today. And similar opportunities and responsibilities confront communist leagues in other countries where the cyclical upturn in the capitalist business cycle is leading to new hiring in industry.

We're not doing this because it's our assessment that a generalized upsurge of labor struggles is on the agenda, like the mass CIO-led social movement that built the industrial unions in the 1930s. Those battles will come. But we can't say how or when, and it's not the reason to take this step.

What we can and do say, however, is that the modest increase in union resistance we've pointed to is already creating better political conditions to make this centralized effort a success. More resistance along these lines will take place as young workers keep coming into the factories and as the bosses keep pressing on wages, hours, and conditions. These younger workers haven't been through the one, two, or three rounds of givebacks that many of their more experienced co-workers have taken at the hands of the bosses over the past two decades. Younger workers have fewer wounds and bruises from these past stalemates and defeats. Even as they are laid off, younger workers are more confident about being rehired and are ready to take up the fight again. This renewal affects other workers as well, who will be a little readier themselves to "just say no" in ways the bosses never intended.

Forging a world communist movement

The workers of the world have paid an enormous price for the fact that no socialist revolution has succeeded in any industrially advanced capitalist country. Anyone who reads the speeches and writings of communist leaders such as V.I. Lenin and Leon Trotsky will find out what it would have meant to the workers and peasants of the young Soviet republic if the revolution had triumphed in even a single highly industrialized country such as Germany, as the Bolsheviks hoped for, considered possible, and worked very hard to help advance. That would have lifted enormous pressures off the toilers in the Soviet Union and shifted the balance of forces to their favor in resisting the counterrevolution by the parasitic caste that Joseph Stalin came to speak for.

Successful proletarian revolutions in the industrialized countries, however, were blocked by the weight of the class-collaborationist social democratic and later Stalinist misleaderships of the workers movement. With the qualitative weakening of the Stalinist movement in recent years, and the continued strengthening of the working class as a percentage of the producing population on a world scale, there is no reason to assume that the pattern of failed revolutions in the imperialist countries will be repeated in the decades ahead. That fact underlines the enormous responsibilities of the working-class movement in the imperialist countries, including the small political vanguard gathered in communist leagues such as the Socialist Workers Party and our co-thinkers in other countries.

We've explained many times before that any meaningful communist continuity was broken in the Soviet Union and Eastern European workers states several decades ago. In all of these deformed and degenerated workers states, the Stalinists—the embodiment of a bloody counterrevolution against Bolshevism and against communists in the workers movement—systematically murdered any revolutionists whom they failed to corrupt or to demoralize and hound out of active political life.

For now, the police-state terror and repression that blocked off workers and youth in the imperialist countries from our sisters and brothers in the former Soviet Union and Eastern Europe are things of the past. The working class in these countries and, as we've seen, the rapidly expanding working class in China, can no longer be driven out of political life as they have been for half a century or more. They count very much in the equation as the class struggle unfolds on a world scale.

What's more, for most of this century, the best of each new generation of revolutionary-minded workers and youth in the imperialist countries and the Third World were won in their overwhelming majority to what they thought was communism but was in fact the Stalinist movement—and then corrupted and destroyed over time as revolutionists. That's how it's been since the end of the 1920s. But that enormous political obstacle, too, has been qualitatively weakened.

Throughout the previous half century and more, communists were prevented from becoming a current with meaningful social weight inside the labor movement except in Cuba. At certain times we here were in the leadership of important class battles that showed what would have been possible under other circumstances, but never more than that. The best example, and the one we know the most about, is the leadership communist workers were a decisive part of in the Teamsters union in Minneapolis and the Upper Midwest in the 1930s. The four volumes by Farrell Dobbs, published by Pathfinder, recount that experience and its lessons.[32]

Even in this case, we should remember what Farrell explains: that communist workers never became part of the leadership of a class-struggle left wing of the union movement. They were the organizers of a leadership nucleus that could have shouldered such responsibility had the class struggle continued to advance. But that possibility was cut off by the weight of the Stalinists' misleadership in the broader union movement, by Washington's escalating preparations to enter World War II, and by the consequent frame-up and imprisonment of eighteen Teamsters and SWP leaders in the lead-up to U.S. entry and during the war itself.

If we understand why communists since the 1920s were blocked from becoming a powerful pole in the international workers movement, then we can appreciate what the emergence of the communist leadership of the Cuban revolution meant to us. The leadership of the July 26 Movement around Fidel Castro, Ernesto Che Guevara, and others was the first revolutionary current to bypass the Stalinists and lead the workers and peasants in a victorious anticapitalist revolution that was not grotesquely deformed from birth. It opened the socialist revolution in the Americas.

I N CUBA a radical petty-bourgeois leadership, several of whose central leaders had educated themselves in Marxism early in their political lives, organized and tempered a revolutionary

---

32. See *Teamster Rebellion, Teamster Power, Teamster Politics,* and *Teamster Bureaucracy* by Farrell Dobbs.

movement able to lead the workers and farmers to carry through an anti-imperialist revolution to its necessary anticapitalist conclusions. As they did so, these leaders pushed aside those who pretended to speak in the name of communism and built a genuine communist party based among the working people of Cuba.

Nearly thirty-five years later, however, that pattern has never been repeated. Promising developments in Grenada and Nicaragua advanced a certain distance in that direction before being reversed and finally defeated, with Stalinism bearing decisive responsibility for the first setback and substantial responsibility for the second.[33] In South Africa, greater space to forge a communist leadership of the working class from among the most self-sacrificing cadres of the African National Congress–led revolutionary movement has been opened by the advance of the national, democratic revolution there.

But nowhere in the world has a petty-bourgeois Stalinist misleadership ever been transformed into a proletarian communist leadership. Not even in the post–World War II revolutions in China, Yugoslavia, and Vietnam where—for reasons specific to that historical conjuncture—Stalinist parties went farther than we had previously considered possible and stood at the head of powerful worker and peasant revolutions that overturned capitalist property relations.[34] But the Stalinist leaderships in China, Yugoslavia, and Vietnam never were, and never became, proletarian communist leaderships. They in fact

33. See "The Rise and Fall of the Nicaraguan Revolution" in *New International* no. 9. The documents in this special issue explain in detail what the July 1979 triumph in Nicaragua opened up, the impetus it gave to advancing revolutionary leadership not just in the Americas but worldwide. It also presents the lessons that workers and youth everywhere can and must learn from the revolution's rise and decline over the decade that followed.

34. For a discussion of these exceptional circumstances, see *The Workers and Farmers Government* by Joseph Hansen, as well as *For a Workers and Farmers Government in the United States* and "Their Trotsky and Ours: Communist Continuity Today" by Jack Barnes (in *New International* no. 1). All these publications are available from Pathfinder.

hounded, jailed, and, when that didn't work, in a number of cases slaughtered revolutionary proletarian leaderships that fought to act along the line of march of the working class. The historical balance sheet on that score should be clear by now.

This historical record is a striking confirmation of the reasons why the communist movement—from its origins with Marx and Engels and the revolutionary workers of the Communist League, through Lenin and the Bolsheviks, to the communist opposition led by Trotsky, right down to today—has always sought to steel itself and the workers movement, first and foremost, against the influence of and illusions in middle-class misleaderships, with their inevitable adaptations to capitalism.

The crisis of proletarian leadership remains the biggest obstacle to the advance of the socialist revolution, as it has been throughout most of this century. Without resolving the crisis of the leadership of *our* class, the workers will never be able to take on the bourgeoisie and win.

In resolving that political crisis, the workers' most important problem is not the bourgeoisie. As bigger and more violent class conflicts develop, above all in the imperialist and most industrially advanced semicolonial countries, the working class will not look to the bourgeoisie or its parties for leadership in battle. When workers in their hundreds of thousands and in their millions go into action in rising class struggles—which is when true revolutionary politics begins—they don't follow the bourgeoisie. In fact, they are impelled by their struggles to oppose capitalism and begin breaking from subordination to the capitalists and their political institutions. Workers more and more reject bourgeois leadership.

At such turning points in history, the best fighters in the workers vanguard are not directly fooled and misled by bourgeois political forces. If they become disoriented, it is almost always by looking to petty-bourgeois forces inside the workers movement proclaiming themselves to be a proletarian socialist leadership. That's what happened in the opening years of this century, when the leaderships of the vast majority of parties of the social democratic Socialist International led the workers of their respective countries into the slaughter of the first interimperialist world war. And that's what happened in the late 1920s and 1930s, as Stalinist misleaderships around the world carried out the dictates of the international murder machine centered in Moscow and led the workers into one defeat after another—from China, to Germany, to Spain and France—finally making it impossible for the workers movement to turn back the capitalists' march toward World War II.

Of course, communists know from prior history that as the working class demonstrates its social leadership in powerful class battles, not only toilers who are not proletarians but also large numbers of the middle classes will be won toward the workers movement. Many of these individuals will become loyal communists. Entire layers of the lower middle class can and will be won away from attraction to fascist demagogues and join with communist workers in the fight for a workers and farmers government. But this will happen only if the workers vanguard charts a consistent political course along the strategic line of march of the working class, not by adapting to middle-class hesitations, wavering, attitudes, values, or concerns, or by addressing our program to them.

Building a proletarian party in time

Earlier this year, in January, several SWP leaders represented the party at the Fourth Latin American and Caribbean Conference for Solidarity, Sovereignty, and Self-Determination held in Havana, Cuba. The article in the *Militant* newspaper reporting on that gathering quoted from the closing speech by Cuban president Fidel Castro.

"On New Year's Day, when we reach the year 2000," he told the 1,200 delegates and observers from throughout the Americas, "we won't be able to greet each other with best wishes for a 'happy new century,' not in Latin America or many other parts of the world. The reality that awaits us—which is manifest now before the turn of the century—is a reality of much effort and struggle."

Castro is right about the unstable conditions and social conflicts that will mark the end of this century and beyond—and not only in the semicolonial world but in the imperialist countries as well. But something else needs to be added: The most important lesson the working class has learned so far in the twentieth century is that if the work of building a communist party hasn't been done beforehand, it will be too late to do so when a revolutionary situation does develop.

Our class from its infancy has had repeated experience with radicalized middle-class leaderships, going back to the revolutions of 1848 and the Paris Commune in the last century, through the experiences in this century that we've already referred to.[35] History shows that other political currents, whatever accomplishments some may have to their credit, will crack and capitulate under the pressures of the mighty, titanic class struggles that capitalism inevitably brings. If the working class does not have a leadership from its own ranks—one that is experienced in politics and tempered in class battles, that will not panic, will not collapse, when a revolutionary situation opens —then it will be defeated.

But the only time revolutionary workers can *prove* why it is worth building a communist party is when it's already too late if we haven't done a substantial part of the work. It's when the most difficult, the most important tests in human history are being posed that every class-conscious fighter will know—at that moment—that the party that can lead and act confidently and decisively, regardless of this or that individual, was truly worth building.

Revolutionists must learn to see the present as history and to live and act accordingly. Theory is not dogma, nor an IOU. It is

---

35. See "Communism and the Fight for a Popular Revolutionary Government: 1848 to Today" by Mary-Alice Waters, in *New International* no. 3.

the living generalization of the line of march of a class, of the strategic political lessons our class has learned through bloody sacrifice and struggle. These lessons are the most valuable asset of the communist movement, our most valuable weapons. It is the absorption of these lessons into the day-by-day, week-by-week political practice of an organized world communist movement that makes it possible, when the crunch comes, for millions of individual communists to think and act in a disciplined way to do the necessary.

At moments like that, the politics, the strategy, and the discipline have either been internalized by millions of individuals who simply act on the basis of what their entire political and class experience has prepared them to do—or the struggle will go down in defeat. Either communist workers will react and guide others in ways that are the opposite of everyone else who has pretended to leadership of the oppressed or exploited—or the capitalists and their petty-bourgeois labor lieutenants will drown the revolutionary movement in blood. That is why a communist party must be built.

EVERYTHING COMMUNISTS DO today is designed with that single goal in mind: the preparation of a party capable of confronting such challenges in the revolutionary struggle for power. Everything we do is to prepare a party of worker-bolsheviks capable of leading our class and its allies in the conquest of a workers and farmers government that can prevent the catastrophe into which the capitalists are leading humanity. As the veteran communist leader Joseph Hansen explained:

"Seemingly remote theoretical questions have a way of suddenly imposing themselves in the political arena and demanding answers that can decisively determine the fate of groups and currents bidding for leadership of the working class. Thus problems related to the struggle for power cannot be placed in deep freeze to be brought out 'when the time comes.' They are with us now, both in the sense of internationally important events on which stands must be taken (the Cuban victory, for instance), and in the sense of gaining a more concrete appreciation of the possibilities in coming struggles.

"Moreover, the struggle for power, along with the accompanying problems and tasks, must be kept constantly in mind. As the goal, that culminating phase dominates our decisions in selecting the means required for its realization."[36]

There is always a gap between what appears to be the evidence in front of us, on the one hand, and, on the other hand, the conviction of communists that it is necessary to carry out a revolutionary course. It is not true that the conduct of communists in and of itself, and its seeming results in the short run, are sufficient to convince fighting workers, and youth who are attracted to the workers movement, of the need for a communist organization.

Only to the degree that communists succeed in presenting history as part of the present, in making theory part of the practical weapons that fighters need, will we succeed in forging a communist party and world movement. Fighting workers and youth must learn discipline, must learn how to study, must learn how to think for ourselves. We must learn to treasure the lessons that previous generations of our class have conquered in sweat and blood. Nothing in the political traditions of the workers movement is of value for sentimental or ceremonial reasons. They are part of our revolutionary political arsenal or we don't need them.

If instead we try to justify a communist course on the basis of day-to-day results, we will appear to be—and we will become—simply the chanting members of a sect. We will be misunderstood as people who want to stand aside from struggles for immediate, partial, and democratic demands and who don't want to work with others in a broad, united way. Communists

---

36. "Introductory Note" by Joseph Hansen to *Workers and Farmers Governments since the Second World War* by Robert Chester, available from Pathfinder.

who have absorbed this understanding to the marrow of their bones are by far the best at mass work. Because they are comfortable that everything they are doing today is a necessary part of preparing themselves and others in their class for bigger struggles to come. There is no conflict between these limited fights and our strategic line of march, even if there is also no direct link from success or failure on any single front and achievement of workers' ultimate goals.

This is important, because there is a lot of clock time between today's preparatory struggles by sections of our class and the development of prerevolutionary situations. Bolsheviks make maximum use of that clock time to test whether space is opening up for revolutionary political work in our class, for expanding the circulation of revolutionary newspapers, books, and pamphlets, and for building a communist youth organization, other auxiliary organizations of the communist movement, and a communist workers party.

Nobody ever becomes a communist before joining a communist party. But neither is there any guarantee that by joining a communist party any single individual will become a communist. That takes both collective political work and individual effort and discipline. Real discipline in a communist party can never be external; it must come from within each individual. And it is voluntary in the deepest sense. It is the product of the political experience, understanding, and commitment of the human beings who make up the party, contribute to its discussions and decision-making, and then act in politics and the class struggle collectively on the basis of that understanding as well as those decisions.

MOST OF THE TIME and under most conditions, activists we work with cannot tell the difference between communists and many centrists, pacifists, and other petty-bourgeois radicals. Measured by activism or hard work, there's often little to differentiate. Most activists draw initial political conclusions on the basis of tactics and their immediate results. As individuals or groups of individuals, communists have no better or worse batting average than others on many tactical matters. These factors will never clarify who we are or what we stand for to anybody. If we try to make our participation in politics with others bear that kind of freight, then we'll end up being abstentionist. If we don't bring our politics with us into every struggle we are part of, however, then we will not produce any communists. And willy-nilly, regardless of our intentions, we will start adapting to those we would be horrified to become.

Being alone politically, which communists are and will be until there are some fundamental breaks in the class struggle, is not the same as abstaining from politics. The way to keep turning out into organized political activity with others is not through political adaptation to petty-bourgeois currents. That's the road to absolute political ineffectiveness.

The world we have been describing, the world Fidel Castro foresees as we approach the millennium, is one in which the economic, social, and political evils created by the workings of capitalism will have multiplied. It is one in which a showdown between the working class and capitalist reaction—in its most virulent form, fascism—will be on the agenda for resolution before anything can be settled. Communist workers must never lend credence to the idea that there's "no way out for the capitalist class." There is a way out, always, if they can destroy enough capital and inflict severe enough defeats on the working class. Under those conditions, certain groups of capitalists will come out on top and find a way to turn profit rates upward for a sustained period—before they begin falling once again.

Humanity will pay a terrible price for such a "solution," however. We will pay the price of fascism and world war. But well before that happens the working class, too, will have its chance. That's what we are preparing for. That alone justifies the wrenching effort worker-bolsheviks are making to become part of the new generations entering the industrial workforce right now. That alone justifies the unconditional support of worker-bolsheviks to the determined efforts by revolutionary-minded youth to move toward relaunching a nationwide young social-ists organization before this year is out.

That is the perspective that communist workers, farmers, and young people in Cuba can look to as the way forward—out of the difficult conditions and necessary retreats that have been imposed on them by defeats of revolutionary struggles in the Americas over the past decade. It is the course that working people and youth can be won to from Toronto to Tokyo, from Shanghai to Soweto to Stockholm, from Moscow to Seoul to Mexico City.

Communist workers don't need any IOUs from history. We don't need any guaranteed timetables. We don't claim to know what the exact ups and downs of coming business cycles will bring, or when the next stock market crash or a major banking collapse will occur. We don't know when a particular sequence of confrontations on the Korean peninsula, or once again some-where in the Middle East, or somewhere in the Balkans might ex-plode into a war of unanticipated proportions.

We *do* know that the speed of some of these developments, their unexpected character, and their even more explosive po-tential should be taken seriously by every revolutionary-minded worker. Because we know that the social crisis and class antago-nisms will grow, that Washington's bipartisan course toward war will sharpen, and that the manifestations of these underlying pressures will not only continue but will accelerate.

There are no simple promises to make, but we are confident in the capacities of our class to become the kind of people we are capable of being—leaders of the battle for human solidarity, not the self-centered, family-absorbed money-grubbers the capital-ists project us as. And that makes the work to build an interna-tional communist movement worth the effort in and of itself.

The Frame-Up of Mark Curtis

A Packinghouse Worker's Fight for Justice

Margaret Jayko

The story of the frame-up of unionist and political activist Mark Curtis on rape and burglary charges. His real crime, in the authorities' eyes, is that he is part of a layer of young workers active in supporting the rights of immigrants, strengthening the unions, and campaigning against U.S. government intervention from Cuba to the Mideast. Booklet. $5.00

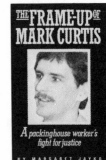

FBI on Trial

The Victory in the Socialist Workers Party Suit against Federal Police Spying

Edited by Margaret Jayko

The victory in the case, fought from 1973 to 1987 "increases the space for politics, expands the de facto use of the Bill of Rights, and increases the confidence of working people that you can be political and hold the deepest convictions against the government and it's your right to do so and act upon them." — from the introduction. $17.95

An Action Program to Confront the Coming Economic Crisis

A Program for International Working-Class Struggle Today

Cancel the Third World debt!

Shorten the workweek!

Enforce affirmative action!

Edited by Doug Jenness

How a program to fight for jobs and affirmative action, and to combat imperialism's pillage of the Third World, is crucial to uniting working people internationally. Also available in Spanish, Icelandic, French, Swedish. Booklet. $3.00

Available from Pathfinder. See page 2 for addresses.

Join the fight for freedom for Mark Curtis

MARK CURTIS, a union and political activist, has served more than six years in Iowa prisons, framed up on charges of rape and burglary.

Curtis's real "crime," however, is being part of a generation of workers and youth active in union struggles, in fights against racism and for women's rights, and in protests against U.S. government intervention from Cuba to Haiti to the Middle East. Just prior to his arrest, Curtis had taken part in a fight to win freedom for seventeen co-workers at the Monfort meatpacking company rounded up in an immigration raid.

Upon his arrest, Curtis was brutally beaten by the Des Moines cops. Sentenced to twenty-five years in prison, Curtis—a leader of the Socialist Workers Party—has repeatedly been denied parole.

Join unionists and supporters of democratic rights around the world in the fight for freedom for Mark Curtis.

Find out more about the frame-up, the campaign to vindicate Curtis, and his fight for parole. Contact the Mark Curtis Defense Committee, Box 1048, Des Moines, IA 50311 Tel. (515) 246-1695.

✂ —

❑ Add my name as an endorser of the Mark Curtis Defense Committee

Signature_____

❑ Please send me more information ❑ Enclosed is my contribution _____

NAME

ADDRESS

CITY/STATE/ZIP

COUNTRY

UNION/ORGANIZATION

Revolutionary Leaders Speak

The Communist Manifesto

Karl Marx and Frederick Engels

Founding document of the modern working-class movement published in 1848. Explains how capitalism arose as a specific stage in the economic development of class society and how it will be superseded by socialism through worldwide revolutionary action by the working class. Booklet. $2.50

Speeches at Congresses of the Communist International

V.I. Lenin

In discussion and polemics at the first four congresses of the Communist International, its central leader discusses prospects for world revolution; the relationship of national liberation and socialism; the New Economic Policy and worker-farmer alliance; and much more. $12.95

Leon Trotsky Speaks

The major political questions of the 20th century, discussed by an outstanding communist leader. Includes a defense of the right to revolution, made in 1906 in the prisoner's dock of the tsarist courts; speeches as a leader of the revolutionary government following the Bolshevik-led revolution; and "I Stake My Life," Trotsky's 1937 defense of his twenty-year Bolshevik course and challenge to the organizers of Joseph Stalin's frame-up trials. $23.95

Rosa Luxemburg Speaks

Edited by Mary-Alice Waters

From her political awakening as a schoolgirl in tsarist-occupied Poland until her murder by thugs in 1919 during the German revolution, Rosa Luxemburg acted and wrote as a proletarian revolutionist. *Rosa Luxemburg Speaks* takes us inside the political battles between revolution and class collaboration that still shape the modern workers movement. $22.95

Che Guevara Speaks
Selected Speeches and Writings

"A faithful reflection of Che as he was, or, better, as he developed"—from the preface by Joseph Hansen. Includes works by Che not available elsewhere in English. $12.95

Maurice Bishop Speaks
The Grenada Revolution and Its Overthrow, 1979-83

Speeches and interviews by the leader of the workers and farmers government in the Caribbean island of Grenada. With an introduction by Steve Clark. $20.95

Nelson Mandela Speaks
Forging a Democratic, Nonracial South Africa

Mandela's speeches from 1990 through 1993 recount the course of struggle that put an end to apartheid and opened the fight for a deep-going political, economic, and social transformation in South Africa. $18.95

Thomas Sankara Speaks
The Burkina Faso Revolution, 1983-87

The leader of the Burkina Faso revolution recounts how peasants and workers in this West African country began confronting hunger, illiteracy, and economic backwardness prior to the 1987 coup in which Sankara was murdered. $18.95

Eugene V. Debs Speaks

Speeches by the pioneer U.S. socialist agitator and labor leader, jailed for opposing Washington's imperialist aims in World War I, Debs speaks out on capitalism and socialism, anti-immigrant chauvinism, how anti-Black racism weakens the labor movement, Rockefeller's massacre of striking miners at Ludlow, Colorado, and more. $19.95

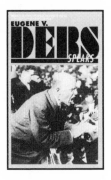

Available from Pathfinder. See front of magazine for addresses.

The struggle for a proletarian party

LEON TROTSKY

JAMES P. CANNON

In Defense of Marxism

THE SOCIAL AND POLITICAL CONTRADICTIONS OF THE SOVIET UNION

by Leon Trotsky

Why only a party that fights to bring growing numbers of workers into its ranks and leadership can chart a revolutionary course. In response to rising pressures of bourgeois public opinion on the middle classes in the buildup toward World War II, Trotsky explains why workers must oppose imperialist assaults on the degenerated Soviet workers state, and defends the materialist foundations of scientific socialism. 280 pp., $18.95

The Struggle for a Proletarian Party

by James P. Cannon

The political and organizational principles of Marxism, presented in a debate that unfolded as Washington prepared to drag U.S. working people into the slaughter of World War II. A companion volume to *In Defense of Marxism*. 302 pp., $19.95

Background to 'The Struggle for a Proletarian Party'

by Leon Trotsky and James P. Cannon   45 pp, 8½ x 11, $6.00

The Structure and Organizational Principles of the Party

by Farrell Dobbs   37 pp., 8½ x 11 format, $6.00

DYNAMICS OF THE CUBAN REVOLUTION

by Joseph Hansen

How did the Cuban revolution come about? Why does it represent, as Joseph Hansen put it, an "unbearable challenge" to U.S. imperialism? What political challenges has it confronted? This compilation, written with polemical clarity as the revolution advanced, is irreplaceable in understanding the Cuban revolution today. $19.95

New International

A MAGAZINE OF MARXIST POLITICS AND THEORY

NO. 7

Opening Guns of World War III

Washington's Assault on Iraq

BY JACK BARNES

- **1945: WHEN U.S. TROOPS SAID 'NO!'** by Mary-Alice Waters
- **LESSONS FROM THE IRAN-IRAQ WAR** by Samad Sharif

$12.00

NO. 4

The Fight for a Workers and Farmers Government in the United States

BY JACK BARNES

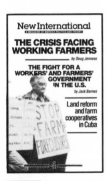

- **THE CRISIS FACING WORKING FARMERS** by Doug Jenness • **LAND REFORM AND FARM COOPERATIVES IN CUBA** two speeches by Fidel Castro $9.00

NO. 3

Communism and the Fight for a Popular Revolutionary Government: 1848 to Today

BY MARY-ALICE WATERS

- **'A NOSE FOR POWER': PREPARING THE NICARAGUAN REVOLUTION** by Tomás Borge • **NATIONAL LIBERATION AND SOCIALISM IN THE AMERICAS** by Manuel Piñeiro $8.00

Nueva Internacional

UNA REVISTA DE POLITICA Y TEORIA MARXISTAS

Número 4. El número 4 incluirá los artículos que aparecen en este número (no. 10) de *New International.*

Número 3. **El ascenso y el ocaso de la revolución nicaragüense** $15.00

Número 2. **Che Guevara, Cuba y el camino al socialismo** Artículos por Ernesto Che Guevara, Carlos Rafael Rodríguez, Carlos Tablada, Mary-Alice Waters, Steve Clark y Jack Barnes $12.00

Número 1. **Los cañonazos iniciales de la tercera guerra mundial** por Jack Barnes $13.00

Nouvelle Internationale

UNE REVUE DE POLITIQUE ET DE THÉORIE MARXISTES

N° 5. Le cinquième numéro va comprende les articles parus dans ce numéro (no 10) de *New International.*

N° 4. **Les premières salves de la troisième guerre mondiale** par Jack Barnes $13.00

N° 3. **Le deuxième assassinat de Maurice Bishop** par Steve Clark $11.00

N° 2. **La révolution à venir en Afrique du Sud** par Jack Barnes $11.00

N° 1. **Le communisme et la lutte pour un gouvernement révolutionnnaire populaire** articles de Mary-Alice Waters et Joseph Hansen. • **Leur Trotsky et le nôtre** par Jack Barnes $11.00

Ny International

TIDSKRIFT FÖR MARXISTISK POLITICH OCH TEORI

No. 2. Artiklarna i detta nummer (nr 10) av *New International* kommer att publiceras i nr 2 av *Ny International.*

No. 1. **De första skotten i tredje världskriget** av Jack Barnes • **Kommunistisk politik i krig och fred** av Mary-Alice Waters $19.00